To March or to Marry

To March or to Marry

Violet Snow

To Thurman /
In thanks
Violet

Epigraph Books

Rhinebeck, New York

To March or to Marry © 2021 by Violet Snow (Ellen Carter)

ISBN 978-1-954744-23-3

Library of Congress Control Number 2021908023

Book layout by Violet Snow
Cover design by Colin Rolfe

Epigraph Books
22 East Market Street, Suite 304
Rhinebeck, NY 12572
(845) 876-4861
epigraphps.com

To

Mary Davies Wingebach,

Helen Wingebach Keller,

and

Barbara Keller Carter,

my foremothers

Table of Contents

First, Facts

On May 28, 1916, an estimated 27,000 women descended upon New York City from all parts of the United States. Solid, sensible matrons posed for photographs that covered the front page of the Sunday graphics section of the *New York Tribune*. These women had not gathered to march for the vote, as had a like number of suffragists the previous fall, protesting New York State's continued failure to pass legislation for woman suffrage.

The 27,000 who arrived in 1916 were clubwomen attending the thirteenth biennial convention of the General Federation of Women's Clubs of the United States. These mostly white, mostly middle-class women represented over 1.5 million members of clubs, large and small, that met in thousands of cities, towns, and villages.

In 1912, when this story opens, American women could vote in only six states, all of them in the far West. Some clubs were involved in the suffrage movement, but the majority of clubwomen favored a more genteel kind of feminism, rooted in home and family.

I learned of the clubs through the letters of my great-grandmother, Mary Wingebach, who lived in the Bronx, a few blocks from the northern edge of New York City. She referred so often to her club that I suspect it helped maintain her sanity as a young wife and mother.

Chapter 1

LOUISE

On a sunny April day, twelve weeks into her marriage, Louise Blake was looking forward to an afternoon's respite from the servitude of housework, regardless of her husband's wishes. After a silent lunch, Charles kissed Louise on the cheek and returned to work at the building site with his father. Half an hour later, she put on a shiny sateen afternoon dress, pinned on her hat, and slipped her essay about *The Odyssey* into a linen bag with her purse. Downstairs, she put on a gray wool cape and a pair of white kid gloves. Before unlocking the front door, she hesitated. Charles may have remembered her women's club meeting. What if he had posted one of his employees outside to keep an eye on her? No, he wasn't that tyrannical, even if he did have old-fashioned ideas about women.

When Louise stepped through the front door, there on the stoop was her husband, leaning against the railing, his black dog at his side. Charles snatched her bag and looked inside it. Then he seized Louise's arm and dragged her into the house.

"Let go! You're hurting me!" Her shout drew her mother from the parlor to the hallway. Charles's mother appeared at the top of the staircase.

Sportie barked and jumped around his master's feet. Louise's mother began wheezing asthmatically. Charles slammed the door and released his wife, then stood against the door with his arms folded. The two older women looked on disapprovingly, and Louise knew it was not Charles's behavior they disapproved of. She thought of the back door.

"You said I should mail my paper last night, but I forgot. I was going to look for a neighbor boy to take it over to the club for me."

"Dressed like that?" he said.

"I wanted to do a bit of shopping. I haven't been out of the house in two days."

"You're not going anywhere. I've been patient with your cooking and your lazy housekeeping, but lying to me?" Long ago she had learned to lie to evade her father's temper, and Charles was beginning to resemble him.

She looked down at the bag in his hand. There was no way to get it back. Better to go to the meeting without the paper than not to go at all. "All right," she said. "You win." On her stately walk to the kitchen, she brushed past her mother, who was gasping for breath. Charles's mother clumped down the steps, muttering in disgust. Louise went into the kitchen and closed the door behind her, then darted through to the mud room and the back door. As she tried to turn the bolt, it stuck, and she cursed in a whisper. The kitchen door opened just as the bolt clicked. She had one foot on the back porch when Charles's fist struck her cheekbone. Pain burst across the side of her face

She fell out onto the porch, hearing a scream from one of the mothers. Charles grabbed Louise by the arm and tossed her back inside. She scrambled up from her knees and ran for the front door, hoping he hadn't locked it. Charles stumbled over the barking and leaping Sportie, giving her a few extra moments. Once outside, she figured she would be safe. He wouldn't assault her in front of passersby. Intent on escape, she barely noticed the throbbing around her eye as she flew down the front steps.

On the sidewalk, several people looked at her with concern, but she strode past them, trying to catch her breath and pat her hat and disheveled hair into place. She didn't look back to see if Charles was watching from the front stoop. By the time she reached the streetcar stop, the mix of fear and rage had turned entirely to rage. She remembered she had no money for the car, since Charles had taken her bag. Without bloomers to cover her legs, there was no point in going back for her bicycle.

Louise turned down the avenue. It would take an hour to walk to the club meeting, but she'd only be half an hour late. And then what would happen when she went back home? She decided not to think about it yet. Instead, she berated herself for making such a terrible mistake by marrying this man.

He wanted to make her a prisoner in her own home, and she had given up a tiny but perfectly good apartment to live with him. At least when Louise was an unmarried seamstress, she could make her own decisions. She'd believed Charles to be different from her own father, who had abandoned his family after smacking his wife around and having an affair. But her friend Abbie had been right.

Six months earlier, when Charles had proposed, Louise had spent the following afternoon at Abbie's house for their weekly sewing session. Usually she sewed piecework at home for a living, but she didn't mind traveling twelve blocks for a chance to chat with her dearest friend while working, and Abbie was happy to lend Louise her sewing machine. Since their first encounter at the Athenaeum Club, they had bonded over their shared love of learning.

"You'll make a handsome couple, both of you so tall and good-looking," Abbie said. "But three months is such a short engagement. Why the rush?"

Louise finished hemming a hankie and bound it into a bundle of ten before placing the next white square of cambric on the sewing machine. "We could wait for a year, until we've saved enough money to build our own house, but we want to marry right away. Mama and I will move in with the Blakes, and I won't have to sew piecework anymore. You know how I hate this job. And Charles just can't wait to be with me every day."

Abbie was mending a quilt, her slender fingers propelling the needle swiftly through the fabric. The needle paused, and she pushed her curly blonde hair back from her temples as she considered how polite she was obliged to be with Louise. It seemed honesty was called for. "Forgive me for saying this, but I suspect what he can't wait for is to have you in his bed."

The sewing machine treadle ceased its rumble. Louise shrugged. "And how do you know I'm not curious to bed him as well?" Abbie's blush reminded her they had never discussed the topic of sex. But why shouldn't they? Looking sidewise at her friend, Louise dared to go even farther. "So many men don't expect women to have that kind of pleasure, but I'll bet Walter is not one of them."

The blush intensified. "I . . . well, he . . . I suppose."

"I'm sorry, I don't mean to embarrass you. But you brought up the subject."

Abbie's concern for her friend overcame her reticence. "But . . . how do you know Charles has that sense of . . . Have you discussed it?"

"Of course not." Louise's feet returned to pumping the treadle.

"I'm just saying, you only met him a few months ago. How well do you know him?"

"I'm a good judge of character. How long did you know Walter before you married?"

"Almost two years. Not so very long, but certainly longer than—"

"I'm not worried. Charles is kind to me, and he's so romantic, and he makes a good living."

"You know that instead of doing piecework, you'll be doing housework."

"My mother and Charles's mother will help out. Mrs. Blake has a washwoman come in every week. Their house is lovely. It's in Mount Vernon, just a few blocks over the border from the city. I hope you'll come and visit us."

Abbie gave up. "Of course I will."

But it turned out that, just as Louise was happy about giving up her job, Mrs. Blake was happy about turning over the bulk of the housekeeping to her daughter-in-law. Because she had Louise on hand, she decided to save money by letting the washwoman go. Louise's mother, already frail, was immediately exempted from work when she came down with asthma, possibly an allergy to the dog, but there was no question of Charles getting rid of his darling Sportie.

Meanwhile, the gallantry of courtship evaporated. Charles ignored his wife except to give orders around the house and take her under the covers. Their initial awkward fumblings gradually developed into a moderate ability to satisfy each other's desires, although his pleasure inevitably took precedence. Elsewhere, she found him as withdrawn as his father.

During the first two months of her marriage, Louise sometimes thought longingly of returning to the Athenaeum Club, but she had so much to learn at home, such as the quirks of operating the big coal stove and where to find warm spots in the big drafty house when she had a moment to rest. She fell into the routine of cooking and cleaning. Then in April came the strenuous week of replacing the winter curtains with lighter chintz, followed by washing the heavy drapes and quilts before storage. As Louise labored alone, climbing on stools, hauling, washing, folding, and hanging, she decided she had earned the right to go back to the club.

She wrote to Mrs. Fulton, the club president, who replied that Mrs. Hoag, who was supposed to read the following week, had been ill. Would Louise be able to take her place? This year's theme was German culture, but any literary topic would do in a pinch.

Louise had been reading Homer's *Odyssey* during breaks from housework. At first, she'd settle in the parlor to read, but her mother-in-law's comments about indolence sent her to hide in the bedroom, where she could pretend to be resting from a headache. After receiving Mrs. Fulton's letter, she wrote the paper in hiding as well, neglecting to dust the parlor several days in a row.

In retrospect, Louise realized she had been foolish not to tell her husband immediately about the club meeting. She had an intuition that he might not respond favorably to the disruption in their routine, so she decided to postpone the possible conflict. Anyway, the club was no one's business but her own. But the day before the meeting, when she'd casually mentioned her plan to attend, Charles had forbidden her to go.

"What do you mean? I have to go. I'm delivering a paper on classical Greek poetry." Louise immediately regretted mentioning the topic of her paper. Her husband had no respect for poetry and even less for ancient Greece.

"But you're married now. You have a family. Why do you need to sit around with a bunch of biddies talking about dead writers?" Charles had come home for his Monday lunch and was gnawing on the leftover lamb from last night's dinner.

"But the clubwomen study together," Louise said. "No one reads books in this house but me."

"If you're going to study something, it should be cooking. This stuff is like boot leather." Her father-in-law grunted. Mrs. Blake and Mrs. Kelley had already left the table to take their afternoon rest.

Charles was six feet tall and well-muscled, and it took a lot of lamb and potatoes to fill his belly. Louise had the urge to stuff the whole plate down his throat.

Fifty years ago, a dictate like his would have been commonplace, but by 1912, most middle-class husbands had come to accept that their wives might want to spend a few hours a week with a local women's club. Especially in a New York City suburb like Mount Vernon, his attitude was out of place. "I told you about the club when we were going together," Louise said. "Why didn't you tell me then that you didn't want me to belong to it?"

He shrugged and sawed theatrically at the lamb with his knife. "We weren't married then. It was different."

"You knew I would get upset. You were afraid I wouldn't marry you." The elder Mr. Blake coughed, dropped his fork and knife onto his plate with a clatter, and left the table.

"I had no reason to think the club was more important to you than your husband would be."

"It's not more important. It's just something else I need. The club is nourishing to me."

"The club is 'nourishing'? Who is feeding you? Who pays for the food you have made into boot leather?"

"I'm sorry about the lamb. My mother always did the cooking. I just never learned."

"So you'll stay home and learn. If I say so, Mother will give you lessons." Charles spat a mouthful of gristle onto his plate. Sportie whined from beneath the table, and Charles slipped him the gristle.

"I'm going mad here, Charles. I have to get out of the house for something besides shopping. All I do is clean and cook and wash, and your mother treats me like her maid."

"I warned you, didn't I?"

He held up this statement every time she complained about her mother-in-law, who was relentless in her criticism of Louise, declaring carpets, dishes, and clothes were never clean enough. Charles was right, of course. He had told her not to accept his proposal of marriage if she wasn't prepared to live with his mother for the first year. Louise stabbed her fork into the chunk of meat on her plate. He was right about the roast, too, unfortunately.

"Intellectual labor isn't womanly," Charles said as he handed down a second glob of gristle to Sportie. "Women are meant to put their efforts into home and family. That's what they're good at."

"But when we have a son, don't you think I can be a better mother if I know about the sorts of subjects he has to study in school?"

"I'll be in charge of his education. You won't have to worry about it." She considered pointing out that she had been to almost two years of college, while Charles had not even finished high school before going to work for his father, but surely the injury to his pride would not help her cause.

Exasperated, Louise stalked off to the parlor. There she found her mother lying on the sofa, smoking one of her asthma cigarettes. The heady smell of menthol, mixed with dried mullein and coltsfoot, filled the room. "You heard?" Louise asked, flopping into an armchair. Mrs. Kelley nodded. "What do you suppose I should do, Mama?"

"He's your husband. He has authority. In the Bible it says, 'As the church is subject to Christ, so let wives also be subject in everything to their husbands.'"

Louise groaned. "Incredible. After the way Papa treated you, that's what you still believe."

"Someone has to be in charge. Charles is a good man, not a drunk like your papa."

"But he doesn't understand how important the club is to me. He's wrong about this, Mama. He's thoroughly and completely wrong."

Chapter 2

ABBIE

A YEAR EARLIER

Clouds of steam sent sweat dribbling down Abbie's cheeks as she stood over the vat in her kitchen and decided washday was a corner of hell reserved for women. And she hadn't had to die to get there. All she'd had to do was marry.

After ten years of employment as a secretary at Dodd, Mead Publishing in Manhattan, mingling with poets, authors, and editors, working with words—the editors' elegant words that leapt from her fingers as she tapped the keys of a typewriting machine—now here she was, laboring to wrangle a wooden paddle through boiling water, agitating the soapy clothing while her shoulders ached and scalding water splashed her forearms.

Worse was yet to come.

Abbie was only five foot two, so she had to stand on a footstool to lever the whites from the vat to the first of the tin basins for rinsing. Then she ran the cloth through the mangle. The crank needed oiling, so it shrieked at each turn, as the rollers squeezed water out of the clothes. On the last rinse, she dipped the bluing bag in with Walter's white shirts to brighten them. When the first shirt came out of the mangle, she held it up and saw brilliant blue splotches along the sleeves. She wilted onto the footstool and began to cry.

Her own stern mind objected. "Don't be a baby, Abigail Bergholtz. You're a married woman, and a strong one. You will solve this problem. Just set it aside and move on." She threw out the bluing bag and went back to rinse the bedsheets and pillowcases. No one but she and Walter would see them, so what did it matter if they weren't sparkling white? Her own shirtwaists and petticoats were mostly covered when she was out and about. She'd blue them next time.

When she lugged the basketful of wrung-out whites up the steps to the roof, the sun was shining in a half-hearted way, and the wind was blustering. Gray clouds on the western horizon made Abbie hesitate for a moment. Her stomach, which had been deprived of lunch due to the washing, growled. The wind would dry the clothes in a snap, she decided. The whites flapped in her face as she pinned them to the clotheslines, the damp cloth soothing her raw arms. When she had finished, she admired the long rows of white billowing in the breeze.

She picked up the basket and returned to the apartment. In the kitchen, she smeared mustard on a slice of bread and cut herself a slab of last night's ham, just a snack before tackling supper. Her volume of Tennyson's poetry lay on the sideboard, and she settled down with it as she ate at the oilcloth-covered dining-room table.

"The Brook" began:

I come from haunts of coot and hern,
I make a sudden sally
And sparkle out among the fern,
To bicker down a valley.

She read the thirteen stanzas slowly, relishing the words and scribbling down ones she didn't know, so she could look them up later in the dictionary. What, for instance, was a "hern"? As she read the last line and reached for the second half of her sandwich, a peal of thunder announced her doom.

An unladylike word sprang from her lips. She grabbed the basket and pounded up the steps to stumble out under a gun-metal sky and escalating rain. Clothes pegs popped off as she tore the sheets from the line. Under the pelting drops, she threw the already sodden whites into the basket, grumbling to herself. Why had she ignored the clouds in the west? Why hadn't she waited for a sunnier day to do the washing? Because she was out of clean waists, that's why, and they couldn't afford to buy extras on a violinist's earnings. Should she be urging Walter to find more work? Why did every problem fall on her to solve? And now she would have to store her wet laundry and pray it wouldn't turn moldy before the sun came back out. Otherwise, she'd have an extra washday this week.

By the time she reached the kitchen with her soggy laundry, the tears had surged again. She stood there, shivering in her wet dress, hair escaped from its pins and falling around her shoulders, which shook with sobs.

She heard the front door click open. "Abbie, my love! Guess who I ran into on the way home!" Walter appeared in the kitchen doorway. "My darling! What's the matter?" Two people peeked over his shoulder: his older brother Joseph, a schoolteacher, and Joe's wife, Nell, a solidly built mother of two.

Nell stepped into the room and sized up the situation. "Did the rain catch you?" Tugging on a blue-spotted sleeve, she drew a shirt from the basket. "I did just the same the first time I washed Joe's things. I forgot to check for holes in the bluing bag. We had to buy all new shirts."

"But we don't have the money," Abbie lamented.

Walter examined the marred shirt. "There are no stains on the front. I shall simply have to keep my jacket buttoned. Not a soul will notice."

"You fellows go have a smoke," Nell said, "and I'll help Abbie sort out these wet things."

"Oh no, you'll get all damp," Abbie said, sinking onto the stool. "Just sit and talk to me, please."

As the men departed, Nell pulled up a chair and took her hand. "Washing is awful. Joseph finally let me hire a washwoman."

"It's not just the washing, or even the sweeping and polishing and cooking. It's . . . I miss my job. It's only three weeks since we got back from our honeymoon, and I'm bored to death. Once I have a child, I know it will be different. But right now . . . all the neighbor women talk about is their dyspeptic stomachs and the price of beef. I'm longing for an intelligent conversation."

"Don't you and Walter talk?"

"Yes, but he's so busy giving lessons, and each time he finishes, I expect we'll have time together, but instead he has to go walking up to Mount Vernon because he has so much restless energy. And I can't go because the roast is in the oven or the floor is half-washed. I just can't bear it. I'm so lonesome."

"I know what you need." Nell gave Abbie's hand a squeeze. "You must come with me to the Phalo Club."

"The Fallow Club? As in, nothing growing?"

"It's spelled P-H-A-L-O. The letters stand for Philosophy, History, Art, Literature, and Oratory. It's a woman's club that meets every Monday for study and discussion. This year our theme is the art and philosophy of India. We have such a lively group, and the members have become my dearest friends."

"Where do you meet?"

"At a home on Riverside Drive, with gorgeous views over the Hudson."

"That's too far for me to go every week."

"There are other clubs, all over the city."

"You like going to yours?"

"I adore it. And it's important for us to educate ourselves if we're going to get the vote."

"The vote? Are you a suffragist, Nell?"

"I don't go parading about with a sign, but I'm sure we'll get the vote eventually. And why shouldn't we?"

"I didn't need the vote to learn typewriting and shorthand and find work in publishing. I don't see what's so important about voting. It's not going to help with my washing or make me less lonesome."

"Joining a club won't help with the washing either, but it *will* make you less lonesome."

"All right, if you vouch for your club, I'm willing to try one. Do you know of any up here in the Bronx?"

"My friend Mrs. Fulton is president of the Athenae-um Club, right in Wakefield. I'll tell her to get in touch with you."

"Thank you, Nell."

"Don't worry, we'll get you out of these doldrums."

Chapter 3

THE ATHENAEUM CLUB

Abbie, who insisted on punctuality, was the first to arrive at Mrs. Flint's for the club meeting, precisely at two-thirty. "Oh, you're one of the new prospective members. There are two of you, you know," said the slender, gray-haired hostess. "I'm told Miss Kelley is quite a firecracker." Abbie wondered what she meant. Surely the clubwomen wanted sober, serious members. Did Mrs. Flint simply mean Miss Kelley was expressive? She couldn't possibly be wild.

Mrs. Flint led Abbie into the parlor, which was crammed with twelve chairs, some wooden ladderback and some wicker. At the far end of the room a table was laid for tea, alongside tall windows draped in filmy voile. Abbie, groping for a way to begin a conversation, chose to praise the glass-fronted cherrywood cabinet that dominated one wall of the room.

"It was made by my late husband, a cabinetmaker," said Mrs. Flint. "I moved to this apartment after his death because the house was so empty with the children grown and gone, and me all alone. The cabinet is really too large for the room, but it's a handsome piece, and I just couldn't part with it." The doorbell rang, and she excused herself.

Abbie walked around the room, looking at the pictures on the walls, including a seascape with a wave-tossed skiff and a Currier and Ives print of two high-stepping horses pulling a carriage. Four new arrivals came into the room, including Mrs. Fulton, a woman in her late forties, wearing a huge, plumed hat that resembled the prow of a ship. A green brocade coat was pulled tight over her substantial bosom, and she wore ugly brown shoes. A pale young woman clung to her left arm. After pumping Abbie's hand, Mrs. Fulton introduced her daughter. "Jessie started coming to the club last year, when she turned eighteen."

"Are you a student?" Abbie asked the girl.

"Oh no, I keep house for Mama. She's busy with her cake-baking business."

"Your sister-in-law tells me you have been a working woman as well," boomed Mrs. Fulton.

"Yes, I used to be, but not since I married."

"My husband died of yellow fever in Cuba in the Spanish-American War. I've had to support myself since Jessie was a child."

They were interrupted by a plump woman with hair in dark ringlets that bounced when she nodded her head. "I'm Betsy Lappe. I hear you're fond of sewing, Mrs. Bergholtz, and so am I. We'll have to exchange patterns."

"Why, you're such a little thing," said Mrs. Lowitz, a tall woman with spectacles. The doorbell rang again. "Isn't she darling, Mrs. Lappe?"

In came two pregnant ladies, both cupping their bellies protectively, as Mrs. Everett told Mrs. Caterson,

"My first just popped out, which isn't the usual way, but it does happen. It was the second that took a day and a half. But you have nice wide hips, so I bet you'll have a quick delivery. I'm just so narrow."

Abbie was trying to memorize all the names. Mrs. Crump, a stick-thin woman in ruffled lavender, was introduced as a lover of art who even painted her own landscapes. Mrs. Hoag and Mrs. Varian were pointed out to Abbie but sat down without meeting her, immersed as they were in a discussion of the relative merits of the two butcher shops on 233rd Street, one run by a German, the other by a Ukrainian.

The last to arrive was Miss Kelley, who was fifteen minutes late, Abbie noted. However, she had to admire the woman's simple pearl-gray tunic and matching skirt, with white bloomers peeking out from under the hem. She must have cycled over, Abbie thought with a flicker of envy. Miss Kelley did not appear in the least flustered by her tardiness but greeted the room with a cheerful wave.

Mrs. Fulton urged everyone to sit. The secretary, Mrs. Flint, took the roll call and reported the receipt of a thank-you letter from Mrs. Everett's mother for the flowers the club had sent while she was in the hospital. The treasurer, Mrs. Crump, announced that everyone had paid this year's dues except Mrs. Lappe, who blushed and said her husband's payroll had been late last month.

The committee chairs made their reports, starting with Mrs. Hoag of the Program Committee, which had determined the year's topics, drawn from French art, literature, and history. Mrs. Hoag read off the names of members who would be reading papers this month.

"Then we need people to write on the following topics for next month," she said. "Édouard Manet, Guy de Maupassant, Victor Hugo, and Napoleon III."

Hands sprang up to volunteer for the first three subjects, but no one seemed inclined to tackle Napoleon III. "I'll do it," Abbie said. "That is, if I'm admitted. I love history."

Several women tittered. "You young women are so forthright," Mrs. Hoag nodded. "That's just why we need more of you. Mrs. Bergholtz, I'll put you down tentatively for Napoleon III. Tentatively until the vote, I mean." Abbie saw a look of admiration on the plain, wan face of Miss Fulton, seated at her mother's side.

Mrs. Lappe said the Reception Committee was just beginning to plan the annual event. They had determined that the gathering would be held in the parish hall of the Presbyterian church, of which Mrs. Crump was a member. The supper would be spread at Mrs. Varian's, and the decorating would be in pink, the club's color.

The Library Committee, on the other hand, had plenty of news. Thanks to a donation from a Manhattan bookstore, said Mrs. Flint, twelve new books had been added to the shelves housed in the basement of the Presbyterian church, bringing the library's total to 162 volumes. "And I hear Mrs. Bergholtz used to work at a publishing house," Mrs. Flint added. "We're hoping she might be able to obtain another donation for us."

Mrs. Lowitz leaned over and whispered to Abbie, "You're in, I'm sure."

Speaking as head of the Membership Committee, Mrs. Fulton announced, "We are fortunate to have two young ladies applying for membership this month. If accepted, they will quite fill us to capacity, but as we have two ladies retiring temporarily to have their babies, I believe it's a timely moment to add to our membership. I will allow them to introduce themselves and explain why they wish to join. First, I present Miss Louise Kelley."

"I had the shining good fortune to attend Barnard College for two years," began Miss Kelley.

Abbie's sense of inferiority flared. She batted it down by reminding herself that, despite not having gone past the eighth grade, she had worked for a publisher and met famous writers. And it didn't matter if Miss Kelley had long limbs and a delicate nose and abundant chestnut hair, which made Abbie feel mousy, with her blunt features and unruly curls always escaping from their bun. Attractiveness to the opposite sex didn't count in this league of female minds.

"I studied biology at first, intending to become a nurse," Miss Kelley was saying. "It chanced that I was required to take English literature my second semester, and I found the study of glorious words the most rewarding of all. I thought I might become a teacher, maybe even—oh my!—a professor. And then, six months ago, my father died." Abbie studied Miss Kelley's eyes, expecting to see sadness, but instead, the corners creased in a flash of anger that was instantly extinguished. Abbie was puzzled. Why would the woman be angry at her father for dying? Or was she not being entirely honest?

After a ripple of sympathy from her audience, Miss Kelley resumed. "I was forced to quit college and support my mother and myself by working as a seamstress. There is nothing I miss nearly as much as I miss those English literature classes. I have come to you brilliant ladies to ask if I might mingle with you and share your knowledge of elegant writing and profound human insight. I long to re-open the windows of my suffocated mind. You can't imagine how tedious my work is!"

Is that considered firecracking talk? Abbie wondered. The use of pretentious adjectives and inappropriate metaphors?

"My dear," said Mrs. Caterson, "you've come to the right place. I only regret that I'll be leaving next month to have my baby. But I'll be back in a few months."

"Excuse me," Mrs. Lowitz said, "but don't the Irish women have their own club over in Woodlawn Heights?"

Miss Kelley looked taken aback for a moment, then replied. "Yes, but it's only a social club. I'm interested in literary subjects."

"Oh, Mrs. Lowitz," said Mrs. Varian, turning on the questioner, "why didn't you join a Jewish club?"

Blushing, the lady answered, "Because the only one around here is Orthodox, and my husband is Reform."

"Then hold your tongue."

Other ladies began to speak but were silenced by Mrs. Fulton. "Come, come, you know the rule—no discussion of religion, politics, or suffrage. Let's keep harmony. We'll hear now from Mrs. Walter Bergholtz."

Abbie stood, smoothed down the front of her skirt, and began. "My grandparents came from old English stock, and they moved out from Connecticut to a farm near Columbus, Ohio, when it was just a frontier town." She felt it important to mention her English pedigree, but she chose not to mention that her father had been a Welsh immigrant. "My father died when I was fourteen, and I also had to work to support my family, just like Miss Kelley." A murmur came from Miss Fulton. Abbie glanced over to see how Miss Kelley was reacting, but the handsome face was frozen except for the blue eyes darting around the room. Abbie felt a flash of sympathy. Her suspicion was growing that they were similar in more ways than one.

"I taught myself typewriting and stenography and found a job with a publisher. Later my sister moved to New York with her husband, and my mother and I came East as well. I was secretary to the publisher of *The Bookman* literary magazine for ten years, until I married Mr. Bergholtz, who is a violinist. Now that I am no longer working, I am, like you, Miss Kelley, starved for words."

This time their eyes met, and Miss Kelley smiled, ever so faintly.

"Thank you, Mrs. Bergholtz," said Mrs. Fulton. "Before we move on, do you ladies have any questions for the club members?"

"Yes, I do," Miss Kelley said. "Would you kindly explain the club's philosophy?"

Mrs. Fulton smiled and launched into a lecture she clearly enjoyed delivering. "We find women to be morally superior to men, thanks to our focus on child-rearing and making a home for our families. But in order to educate our children properly, we need the company of other mothers who can share with us what they've learned, and we need the uplifting influence of the arts. Men are so busy pursuing their ambitions and earning money, they have no time for appreciation of literature. It's our job to keep the study of literary culture alive. We are naturally suited to be the conveyors of beauty to the next generation."

Abbie said, "I never thought of it that way, I suppose because my husband is a musician. But I do love culture, and I am pining for the company of intelligent women."

"Excellent. Any other questions? No? Now we will have our paper for the afternoon."

Mrs. Crump stood to read aloud her paper on the French artist François Millet, whose first name she pronounced "Francis." She stumbled over many of the words, but the information was concisely presented and reasonably interesting. When she had finished, it was time for tea, and the women clustered in pairs and threes to chat. When all the teacups were taken, Abbie went to Miss Kelley and maneuvered her into a corner.

"How exciting to study literature in college!" Abbie began.

"And you, working for a publisher. But you had to start so young."

"Yes, it was difficult. I wish now I could have stayed in school."

"I was lucky even to go to high school, but college was so much better."

"Tell me," asked Abbie, "what did your father die of?"

"He . . . tuberculosis. And yours?"

"Oh . . . he was kicked by a horse."

They both sipped their tea, an aura of falsehood hanging in the air between them. Miss Kelley examined the pattern in the lace curtains at her side. Abbie debated whether to tell her the truth. After all, it had happened more than a decade ago. No, she shouldn't.

"A terrible disease, TB. You're lucky you didn't catch it from him."

"Yes."

"Were you and your father close?"

"No."

Miss Kelley looked bitter. Abbie burned to know if her guess was correct, and the only way was to tell her own secret. If it was a comfort to Miss Kelley, Mama wouldn't mind. Abbie cleared her throat. "Actually, my father didn't die until 1905. When I was young, he beat my mother, and they divorced."

"I see." Miss Kelley sounded cool, but Abbie heard a tremor in her voice. "So your father went away after your parents split?"

"My father stayed on the farm, and we moved to Columbus and made up the story of the horse kick. My mother couldn't have had a social life as a divorcée."

Miss Kelley's voice went down to a whisper. "That's what my mother fears. I'm not supposed to tell."

Abbie warmed to her, especially now that the pretentious diction had faded away. Perhaps Miss Kelley was not as self-confident as she appeared. "I'm sorry. I know what a burden it is. It's terrible how many divorces there have been since the war. The men came home changed forever. My father was captured by the Confederates and spent three months in a horrid prison."

"How awful!"

"Still, it's no excuse for taking a horsewhip to my mother."

"My father's moved away to Boston, where he's from. They aren't actually divorced because we're Catholic, but they may as well be. You won't tell the ladies, will you?"

"Of course not. Was your father in the war too?"

"No. He's just an ordinary drunk."

"But he earned enough to send you to college."

"He's a tool-and-die worker."

"What's that?"

"He designs molds for making metal tools. It's highly skilled work, and he's very talented when he's not drinking. He worked in a factory, but he wanted me to be educated and rise up in the world. That's one of the few things I miss about him."

"My father drank too."

"The curse on mankind. I hope someday we'll outlaw alcohol."

"Really, Miss Kelley? Do you think it's possible?"

"Why not? I'm completely in favor of temperance. And please call me Louise, at least when it's just the two of us."

"All right then. I'm Abbie."

"Agreed." They shook hands, just as Mrs. Hoag came over to say, "Now you must let the rest of us get to know you two. It's no fair to hole up in the corner."

The Hoags, it turned out, were classical music lovers. At least Mr. Hoag was, and his wife was coming around to an appreciation of the form. "We go from time to time to hear the Philharmonic. Such a shame about Herr Mahler. He was a superb conductor. And to die so young. It started with a sore throat, you know. But he had a defective heart valve, which makes one susceptible to pneumonia."

"Well, I shall have to invite you next time Mr. Bergholtz gives a concert."

"He suffered from anti-semitism, you know," Mrs. Lowitz said. "Herr Mahler, I mean. Even though he converted to Catholicism to take the job."

"What about Mr. Bergholtz? Is he an immigrant?" Miss Flint asked. A knot of ladies was beginning to form. Abbie felt excited, as if she were successfully campaigning for her seat at the club.

"No, his parents came over from Germany before he was born. His father works as a tailor, but the whole family is musical." She felt compelled to add, "We're not Jewish."

"Perhaps your husband could play for the club. We have musical interludes from time to time." Abbie overhead Louise telling another small group, "Yes, I have a beau. He works in his father's construction business."

"By the way, every member must be on at least one committee," Mrs. Flint pointed out, drawing the two conversations together. "I do hope you'll join us on Library, Mrs. Bergholtz."

"I should like to be on the Program Committee," Abbie replied. "I love the idea of picking topics." Mrs. Flint looked offended. "But if I can be on more than one," Abbie hastened to add, "I should like to be on Library too."

"Can we start new committees?" asked Louise.

"Well," said Mrs. Varian. "We don't, generally. What did you have in mind?"

"Perhaps a temperance committee."

"Oh no, we stay away from controversy. Our goals are self-improvement and sisterhood. If you're looking for politics, you'd better find another club."

"No, I was just curious. I'm really here because I love literature."

"I think," said Mrs. Fulton, "it's time to vote on our prospective members. We're going to shoo the two of you into the dining-room for a few minutes."

Mrs. Flint led Abbie and Louise into the next room. "We won't be long," she said, closing the door behind her.

"I believe we'll both get in," Louise said. "Unless they hold it against me for being Catholic. Or for bringing up temperance."

"I think you made a good impression," Abbie replied. "And I hear your beau is in construction. My father worked as a carpenter at times."

"We have much in common, don't we? Divorce, literature, hammers and nails." For a moment Abbie worried she was being sarcastic, but Louise smiled at her.

"I hope you'll come visit me," Abbie said. "If you're sewing piecework, you could bring it along, and we could sew together."

"All right, then. I'll come tomorrow if that's all right."

"Oh yes, please do."

The door opened, and Mrs. Flint called them back to the parlor. "I am delighted to announce," said Mrs. Fulton, "that you are both now members of the Athenaeum Club."

Abbie felt exultant. Looking around at the applauding women, her new compatriots, she felt sure her life was going to improve.

Chapter 4

SUFFRAGETTES

On the day Louise defied her husband and ran from the house, only rage kept her from falling into despair. Still slightly out of breath, she was pounding her feet against the sidewalk, wondering what her mother thought of Charles now that he'd turned his fists on his wife, when she saw a group of women on the street corner up ahead. They were handing out yellow bills to people who passed, few of whom took the slips of paper. As she approached, she heard one of the women call out, "Votes for women! March with us!"

Her first impulse was to ignore them. She knew suffragettes were rude, loud women. Their cause may have been just, but their methods were unpleasant and would surely never succeed. A young woman detached from the group and came toward her with a bill outstretched. "Votes for women!" she enthused. "March with . . . Oh dear, what happened to you?" She turned and shouted, "Emily!"

Two others came over, as Louise reached up to her hat, thinking it must have come askew again. When she lowered her arm, she saw blood on the cuff. No won-

33

der people had been looking at her. "Does someone have a mirror?" she asked the three women.

One of them took a small mirror from her handbag. Another gave her a handkerchief, saying, "It's clean."

"Oh, dear." Louise daubed at the blood on her cheekbone and peered at the bruise rising beneath her eye. "I hate that man!" Later she reflected that she would not have had the courage to make such a bald statement in front of strangers if she hadn't known they were passionate about the rights of women. At the time, she was simply touched to know these ladies were trying to take care of her. Fury gave way to tears. The whole group of seven gathered around. "My husband. I thought he was so gentle, and it turns out he's a fiend. Just because I wanted to go to my club."

"You should join us," said Emily. "We're having a parade for the vote on May the fourth. We need the power to make our own decisions, and the right to vote is the first step. Men shouldn't be allowed to do what your husband has done."

"But how is voting going to help?"

"What would happen if you called a policeman after your husband hit you?"

"Nothing, I expect. It's between him and me."

"Well, if there was a law against a man hitting his wife, then the policeman would have to do something. Do you think men are going to make that law? Not unless we have a say in the matter."

Louise looked around at their outraged faces and felt comforted. "You've been very kind to me. I have to get to my club meeting."

"Our headquarters is right down the street," said Emily. "Bring your clubwomen, and we'll all hand out bills, and next weekend we'll parade together on Fifth Avenue. We suffs are going to change the world."

Buoyed by their support, Louise hiked onward to Mrs. Lowitz's house, arriving near the end of the meeting, when the ladies were chatting over tea and cakes. She told her story, this time in more detail, ending with, "I don't know what to do. I have to go back there tonight, but I don't know how I can stay with Charles after what happened." To her surprise, the clubwomen's reaction was nothing like the suffragettes'.

"Well, he may have knocked you about a bit, but he's a good provider, isn't he?" asked Mrs. Fulton.

Louise glared at her. "Are you serious?"

"Well for goodness' sake, look at Mrs. Bergholtz. Her husband's a lamb, even sweeps the parlor for her, but he barely supports the family. She has to scrimp every month just to buy coal. We all have a cross heavy on our shoulders, do we not?"

For the second time in an hour, Louise assessed the faces of a group of women. Some were nodding in agreement, others looking doubtful. Abbie's eyes were aflame. "Why Mrs. Fulton, I would never trade Mr. Bergholtz for a man who beat me, no matter how much he earned!"

"You say that now," said Mrs. Fulton, "but wait until you have three children wearing you to the bone day in and day out, and the cupboard is bare half the week. I tell you, a woman in those circumstances would prefer a slap on the face now and again to a man who can't earn the family's bread." Abbie gasped.

Louise was riled. "Is that what happened to you?" she asked Mrs. Fulton. "Did your husband knock you about after your third was born?"

Color flew up the woman's cheeks, but she parried with dignity. "If he won't let you go to the club, rebellion is not the proper path. When a wife wants something, she must make the man think it's his idea."

"Oh, and how would I go about that delicate procedure?" scoffed Louise. "Hire a hypnotist?"

"Remind me what business Mr. Blake is in?"

"He's a carpenter."

"You find other carpenters whose wives are in clubs, and you cozy up to them. Get them to tell their husbands why you aren't in a club and how much our group needs smart women like you. To keep the peace, the husbands will put pressure on Mr. Blake, and you will have your way. Although we are the weaker sex, we are smarter than men, and we must make use of our feminine wiles."

"That's disgusting," Louise said. "We shouldn't have to connive to get what we want."

"Shouldn't?" repeated Mrs. Fulton. "This is not an ideal world, my dear, and we must adapt."

"Don't I know it?" Mrs. Varian agreed. "It's a lot of work to get my way, and my husband has no idea. But I almost always win out."

"That's not what the suffragettes are saying," Louise retorted. "They say women should have rights. They want to change the world."

"Oh, really? You think if we get the vote, men will be pliant and respectful? More likely they'll be resentful and make life even harder for us. You, my dear, are extremely naïve."

Louise shook her head. "I can't believe you women. Maybe I don't want to come back here after all." She stomped to the door and slammed it on the way out.

Abbie caught up with her on the sidewalk. "What will you do?"

Louise stood gazing at an ice wagon across the street, its skinny horse standing with drooping head. "I guess I'll go home."

"Mrs. Fulton and Mrs. Varian are rather conservative, but I don't think everyone agreed with them."

"Well, you were the only one who stood up for me the slightest bit."

Louise was thinking that even Abbie had barely defended her. Of course, Mrs. Fulton was fierce, and everything had happened so fast. "I'm sorry they weren't kinder to you," Abbie said.

"At least Charles and I agree about one thing now. I'm not coming back to the club."

"I don't blame you for saying that, but I hope you give the club another chance. I'm going to speak to them. He shouldn't hit you. It's wrong."

"Of course it's wrong."

"You'll tell me if I can help somehow, won't you?"

"Yes." Louise hugged her and kissed her cheek. "Thank you, Abbie."

Once again, Louise was almost to the streetcar when she remembered she had no carfare. Rather than go back and face the clubwomen again, she started the long walk home to her husband.

Charles's mother had been forced to cook dinner because his wife was still out of the house at five o'clock. Nevertheless, Mrs. Blake was in as cheerful a mood as she was capable of. She had told her son this Irish girl was too headstrong to make a good wife, and Louise's outrageous behavior had proved her right.

When Charles returned from work to find his wife still absent, his already foul mood worsened. He and his father ate their dinner without commenting on the gossip Mrs. Kelley reported from her trip to the bakery. Then both men went up to their respective marital chambers, the father to prepare for sleep, the son to brood over the actions of his wife. Mrs. Blake also retired for the night, after noisily cleaning up the kitchen with a martyred air.

Louise arrived at eight o'clock and ate the leftover beef stew from the icebox while her mother sat with her, repeating the gossip about the baker's wife and her thieving brother. "Are you all right, dear?" Mrs. Kelley asked when she had finished her tale, and Louise stood up under the lamplight. "You have a bruise."

"I'll be all right, Mama. Don't worry about me."

When Louise went upstairs, Charles was in bed, reading the newspaper by the light of the gas lamp. Or at least he appeared to be reading. She did not hear pages turning.

Neither of them spoke while she took off her dress, corset, and stockings, changed into her white cotton nightgown, and brushed out her hair. Sitting at the mirror, she wove a thick braid. She pinned it around her head and slipped on a cotton night cap to keep the braid from unraveling. She brushed her teeth with tooth powder over the water basin, then slid under the quilt, turning her back to Charles. The newspaper rustled at last as he folded it and placed it on the bedside table. "See here, Louise," he said. "I'm sorry I hit you. It's . . . it wasn't kind."

The grandfather clock's tick drifted up the stairs. A wagon rattled past in the street. "No," she said, "it certainly wasn't kind."

"But you weren't kind either. Lying to me and running out."

"You injured me. You tried to stop me from getting what I need."

"I'm the head of the household. If I think your . . . what you're trying to do isn't good for the family, it's my job to stop you."

"Well, you're wrong. Striking me is what's not good for the family. For me to spend time with other women, thinking women, is healthy."

Charles turned off the lamp beside the bed, and the flame guttered out with a hiss. Louise lay still in the darkness. "If it means that much to you," Charles said, "I'll let you go to the club."

Louise had to bite her fist to keep from shouting at him. The man's arrogance was beyond belief. As if she needed permission to take care of her own needs. Despite her exhaustion, she lay awake late into the night, thinking.

Louise had a tendency toward impulsiveness, but if she were going to leave her husband, she had to make sure it was the right step, and she needed a plan of action. For the next two days, she behaved like a model wife, while behind her expressionless façade, thought moved incessantly. She was polite to Mrs. Blake, gentle with Mama, and attentive to Charles's needs. Even when he turned over in bed to demand her body, she acquiesced, separating her mind from the movements of her hands and hips, noting he had become, over recent weeks, even more selfish as a lover.

Because of the black eye, she asked her mother-in-law to do the marketing. Mrs. Blake agreed with a dramatic sigh, implying Louise had hopefully learned her lesson and wouldn't have to make such a request ever again. While she was gone, Louise slipped out for a ride on her wheel, since no one could see the bruise as she zipped past with her hat brim pulled low. For half an hour, she forgot the decisions she had to make, reveling in the breezy freedom and the vigor of her pumping legs. It occurred to her that riding a bicycle gave her considerably more pleasure that coupling in bed with Charles. As she weighed the reasons to leave, she thought of one possible advantage to staying that she had never discussed with him.

That night, when they were settled in bed and Charles was reaching to turn out the lamp, she said, "I was thinking. I know I blamed you for not telling me before we married that you didn't want me going to the club. But I kept something from you too. And now I think we'd better get it cleared up."

He pulled his hand back, leaving the light on. "Go ahead. What is it?"

"You know that I attended college for two years before my . . ." She realized she hadn't told him her father was really alive. One revelation at a time, she decided. ". . . before my father died. And then I had to quit so I could work. But I loved my studies. Once we've saved enough for a house of our own and can pay for a housekeeper, I want to go back to college."

He reached out again and turned off the lamp, then lay back on his pillow. Louise could hear the grinding of his teeth. "No," he said, "I don't think that's a good idea. Anyway, we'll probably have a baby by then."

"Mama will help with the baby. She loves babies."

"It's not right. Women's brains are too delicate for study. It's one thing to dabble in before marriage, but it would not be healthy for you as a mother, or for our child."

"That's absurd. Our brains are just as strong as yours. You're mixing up brains and bodies."

"Oh, I suppose you know as much as we do. I suppose being able to sew a dress proves that you could design a house if we let you. You could measure everything, calculate the loads and forces, and then . . . I can just see that house falling down around the woman who made it." He chuckled as if he'd made a joke. "You stick to keeping house and trying to make a baby. I'll take care of the rest."

Charles leaned over to kiss her, and she jerked her head away. The acid comments that came to mind seemed too dangerous to express.

"At our wedding," Charles said, "you promised to love, cherish, and obey. I take that promise seriously. Don't you?"

"You promised to love me, but you don't even know me, and I don't know you."

"We're getting to know each other. I want to know you better."

"No, you don't. You want me to be your idea of a perfect wife. I can't be the woman you want."

"You'll change. You just have to get accustomed to being married."

She sat up. "I don't want to change. I want to read literature. I want to study, not do housework. I hate cleaning and cooking."

"You make me feel lonesome when you talk like that." His voice turned petulant.

"Charles, you have no idea how lonesome I've been feeling. Every day, stuck here in this house." Tears smarted behind her eyes, but she wasn't going to show weakness.

"You're not alone. You've got me and Mother and your own mama."

"Are you blind? Your mother is mean to me, and my mother is . . . she doesn't even count."

"You must learn to get along better with other women, Louise. You need more humility."

The urge to strike out was so strong, she had a moment of sympathy with him, thinking of how angry he must have felt when he hit her. She lay back down, agitation coursing through her breast. The conversation was only making her feel worse, so she wished him a good night, even though she knew sleep would again be a long time coming.

After breakfast, Louise changed into her bloomers and split skirt. Charles had already left for work, and the two mothers were sitting over cups of tea in the parlor. As Louise descended the stairs, she heard Mama saying, "Oh yes, it was an agony losing the two boys. One at birth, and the other was taken by the cholera when he was nine. At least I was left with a girl to look after me in my old age."

Louise paused to hear the reply. "Well, isn't that a coincidence! I lost two also, both from scarlet fever.

And here we are, brought together by our only remaining ones."

It pained her that her mother was so chummy with the enemy, but their friendship also made it easier to take the next steps, diminishing her guilt over leaving Mama with the Blakes. Anyway, she barely ate anything and never complained about sleeping in a room the size of a closet. They certainly wouldn't throw her out. And Louise was not going to stay in a loveless marriage as her mother had done. She was getting out before there were children to complicate the leaving.

She clattered down the stairs and called, "I'm going out," pulling open the front door before they had time to respond. Let them wonder where she was going and fume over the piles of laundry she was supposed to attack today. In that moment, she felt, the die was cast.

The wheel carried Louise through the sunny spring morning, along a circuitous route of asphalt streets and a couple of sidewalk stretches to avoid cobblestones. She found the corner where she had met the suffragettes and walked her bicycle along 242nd Street to the plain brick building with the words "Women's Political Union" printed on a signboard in the window. A young woman sat at a desk in the dingy lobby, tapping at a typewriting machine, surrounded by piles of handbills and posters. She asked, "May I help you?"

"Yes, I . . . oh, you're Emily."

The woman smiled. "Mrs. Blake! You're looking much better today. I do hope you've been all right."

"Well . . . not exactly."

"What can we do for you?"

"I need a job. I thought you might know of one."

"Well, all of us here are volunteers, but there are always people needed at the office in Manhattan while we're organizing for the parade. The pay is little, but you have the satisfaction of helping us all get the vote."

"Where is the office, and whom should I ask for?"

Emily scribbled on the back of a yellow bill. Louise thanked her and went back to her wheel.

Abbie answered the door in a clean but faded housedress, hair tied up in a scarf. "Thank goodness it's you. I wouldn't want anyone else but a tradesman to see me like this." She dropped her dusting rag on the hall table and led Louise into the parlor. "I'm working on the bedroom, but the parlor is all done."

"I'm sorry to call on you unannounced, but I need to talk to you."

They had barely sat down when Abbie jumped up, holding a hand to her mouth. "Excuse me," she said and rushed down the hall to the water closet. Louise heard the sound of retching. When Abbie returned, her brow was damp with perspiration, and her face was flushed.

"Are you ill?" Louise asked. "I don't have to stay—"

"Oh, no. I'm . . . it seems . . . I believe I'm with child." A smile fit for an angel lit her face.

"Oh, my. You seem quite happy about it."

"Yes. I've been yearning for a baby."

"Then I'm happy for you, dear. Congratulations!" Louise embraced her. "Does Walter know?"

"Yes, I told him last night. But aside from Walter, you're the first."

"What a privilege! You'll have to tell this child Auntie Louise has looked over her almost as long as her mama has."

"I'm so glad you're the first to know." Abbie squeezed Louise's hand. "But why have you come? Is everything all right?"

"No. Everything is awful."

"Oh, dear. What happened?"

"I tried to speak to Charles about going to college someday, and he treated me like . . . like . . . He thinks more of his dog than he thinks of me. We nearly came to blows, and this time I was the one who wanted to do the hitting."

"Most couples have trouble at times. Walter and I have had our differences, especially in the first months of living together. We had to adapt to each other."

"He's not going to adapt. He only wants *me* to adapt, and I don't want to."

"Compromise is often difficult. Of course, he shouldn't hit you, but maybe if—"

"I decided last night. I'm leaving him." Saying the words aloud both thrilled and frightened her.

"Oh no! Are you sure that's the right thing to do?"

"Yes. We'll never be happy together."

"But . . . but it's so . . . sudden."

"What do you mean? Do you think I should wait until he breaks my arm?" Louise found her voice turning shrill. Abbie, the one person she'd thought would understand and support her, was turning against her in this momentous decision. She felt the ground falling out from underfoot. "I can't believe you're saying this, when your own mother left a violent man."

"Yes, but we had a house in the city to live in, and uncles who had a bit of money to help us out. Of course, you must do what you think is right, but where will you go? How will you live?"

"I'll have to get a job, of course."

"Piecework again?"

"No. I can't face sewing. I'm told there's work at the Women's Political Union office in Manhattan. I'm going over there tomorrow to inquire."

"What? The suffragists?" Abbie looked horrified.

"Yes. What's wrong with them?"

"Well, they're so . . . unfeminine."

"You think parading down Fifth Avenue is unfeminine? You know what's unfeminine? Mrs. Fulton telling me to accept that my husband strikes me. That's not something a woman should do to her friend."

"But the suffs are . . . all they want is the vote. They don't care about . . . about families or babies or anything like that."

"You know what the suffs said when they saw my black eye? They said Charles shouldn't have done it, and they wanted to help me. That's how women are supposed to behave with each other. That's feminine!"

Abbie looked down at the floor. "You're shouting at me."

"I'm sorry for not being more feminine, Mrs. Bergholtz. Good luck with your baby."

And Louise stormed out.

On the way home, doubts overcame her. She shouldn't have shouted at her friend. How had she become so volatile? She'd planned to ask to stay at Abbie's house till she sorted out her life, but now she had to find another place, and she still had moments of guilt about leaving her mother at the Blakes' for the meantime. Furthermore, she had told Abbie she was definitely leaving Charles, but in her heart, she wasn't so sure. What if Abbie was right, and it was natural to argue during a period of adjustment to marriage? Louise had said Charles would never change, but he had actually changed his mind about the club, although his manner had been so infuriatingly imperious.

She pedaled slowly, taking a detour through the cemetery, where she and Charles used to walk when they were courting, occasionally indulging in a kiss in the shadow of a mausoleum. The day was warm, and the sun shone cheerily over the gravestones. She stopped at one of her favorites, a monument with a long, flat surface that met an upright stone with a carving of an angel on top. She read the names of the husband and wife inscribed below the angel. She wondered if they'd been happy together, or if they'd fought like wildcats. Legs stretched out, she leaned back against the upright stone and closed her eyes, letting the sun spread a reddish cast across her eyelids.

The clang of shovels woke her. Across the way, two men were digging a grave, and the sun was sloping towards the western horizon. She had missed lunch. She rode home with apprehension, preparing herself for reproach.

When she opened the front door, Mrs. Blake practically leaped from the parlor. "Where have you been? Charles has been looking everywhere for you."

"I . . . I went cycling. I fell asleep in the cemetery."

"I had to make lunch for the men, and now Charles is beside himself with worry. What kind of a wife are you? No wonder he gets angry when—"

"I'm not speaking to you." Louise spun around and ran upstairs, just as Mama came out of her bedroom.

"Oh, Louise, I'm so glad you're back. We've all been awfully upset."

"Can't I do anything on my own? Must everyone fall to pieces just because I go off for a few hours?"

Louise went into her bedroom and slammed the door. She sat on the bed, shaking with a potent blend of guilt and anger. She heard the front door open and close, then the rise and fall of voices. Footsteps sounded on the stairs, and the door opened. "Where have you been?" Charles demanded.

"Cycling. I needed air."

"Where did you go?"

"To visit Abbie."

"Really? Father saw you riding your wheel down 242nd Street."

"So you've got him spying on me?"

"I can't have this, Louise. You must behave like a wife."

"Or what will you do? Strike me again?" She stood up and took off her cape. "Do you suppose it will make me love you?"

"Are you saying you don't love me?"

Arrested by the question, she looked him over, groping within herself for some semblance of affection. His scowling face looked ugly, and the meaty hands, clenched at his side, filled her with aversion when she thought of them stroking her body. She hung up her cape in the wardrobe.

"Answer me," he said.

"I can't."

"You're a cold woman."

"Just because I don't enjoy being struck and being told I don't deserve to read and study, that makes me cold? Oh, the stupidity of men."

He slammed her up against the wardrobe. She cried out. Mama knocked on the door, calling, "Are you all right?" Charles threw his wife on the bed and strode out of the room. Louise lay there, her back bruised and her heartbeat stuttering. Mama came in and stroked her brow. "My poor girl. Why must you keep making him angry?"

"Why must *he* keep making *me* angry? That's the question." Louise stood up, pulled a suitcase from the back of the closet, and began throwing clothes into it.

"Where are you going?"

"I don't know."

When she went downstairs with the packed grip, Charles and his mother were talking in the doorway to the kitchen. "What are you doing?" he asked Louise, and she didn't answer, just headed for the front door. He followed, yanked her arm, and slid between her and the door. "You're not going out. Mother, stand by the back door."

"What am I, a wild beast to be caged up?"

"Yes, you're being wild, and you must calm down."

Anger was exhausting, Louise realized, and she hadn't eaten since breakfast. It was no use trying to leave now. She closed her eyes and willed her heartbeat to slow. "I'm sorry. I lost my head. I need something to eat."

Charles took the grip and steered her into the kitchen. "Mother, heat up some soup." As Louise slid into a chair, she took note of where Charles set down the suitcase, against the wall near the door. She prayed he would forget it.

He sat down at the table. His mother served Louise lukewarm chicken soup and bread, then left the kitchen. Mama sat next to Charles and told him, "She gets this way with her menses at times. They're probably about to start."

"Mama!"

Charles looked embarrassed. He nodded. "I have much to learn about women, Mother Kelley."

Mama gave her a look that said, "See how kind and humble he is." But Louise kept thinking it was only a few minutes ago that he had slammed her up against the wardrobe.

The clock in the hall struck three. Louise hadn't slept at all since her nap in the cemetery. She crept out of the double bed, took the frock, corset, and petticoat she had left hanging on the back of the door, and tiptoed downstairs. She dressed in the kitchen, where she discovered merciful God had answered her prayer for the suitcase. Her spring coat was hanging on a hook in the front hall. She unlocked the door, moving like a thief, and stepped into the night.

Chapter 5

TO ESCAPE

A sharp but sensuous breeze swayed the tree branches with their baby leaves. It lifted the panels of Louise's coat as she slipped her arms into the sleeves on the front stoop. She pulled on a pair of black cotton gloves, picked up the grip, and turned south. There was no one about to observe her passage but raccoons, possums, and rats, which trundled away at her approach. In the trees over Gramatan Avenue, an owl hooted twice, and from a side street came the snarl and scream of battling alley-cats.

She had never traveled late at night, so she didn't know if the streetcars were running. At the nearest car stop, she stood for twenty minutes, until clapping her arms no longer stopped her from shivering. The northernmost station of the elevated train was at West Farms, down near Bronx Park. She wasn't sure what time the trains started up. She set off down West First Street, past the sleeping shops. A half-moon peered between buildings, giving off little light to compete with the streetlamps.

West First turned into White Plains Road, and the buildings grew larger as suburb melted into city.

Louise heard a low and distant stammer, as if the city were muttering in its sleep. She willed her feet to make as little sound as possible on the sidewalk slabs, despite her rapid steps.

At the corner of 235th Street, she stopped and set down her grip, raising both hands to adjust her slipping hat. From a doorway, a shadow stepped forward, nearly the same shade as the surrounding dark except for a pale face and a pale square of cleavage. "Beat it," the woman said in a raspy whisper.

Louise grabbed her suitcase and fled. She hiked even faster, afraid to look around, wondering if every doorway held a similar shadow. Behind her, hooves clopped, and wheels rumbled on cobblestones. As a wagon passed, piled with cabbages, the driver made a strange sound, not unlike the hooting of the owl.

Perspiration coated her face, then cooled in the night air, setting her to shiver in the flimsy coat. If only she could have a cup of tea. In response to her thought, a white light materialized over the sidewalk in the distance. As she approached, she made out a tea stall, made of a few planks set on blocks, with a brazier glowing orange under a tripod, a brass teakettle, and stacks of cups. By the light of a hissing gas lantern, a hawk-faced man was talking to the wagon driver, who had left the horse and cabbages at the curb and was leaning on the plank counter.

The two men turned toward Louise, both of them smiling. "I'd like a cup—" she said, her voice sounding constricted and weak, but the cabbage man interrupted.

"How much?" he growled, reaching out to grab her elbow. She was paralyzed for a moment, shocked by the gesture and perplexed by the question, and then remembered the shadowy woman. "No!" She yanked her arm away, hearing the seam of her coat rip at the shoulder, and ran down the side street, away from the avenue. Behind her, the tea man and the cabbage man laughed.

After she had run a long block, the grip banging against her knee, Louise slowed to a walk. The street was lined with narrow but prosperous houses, each with a gated garden in front. Although the neighborhood was not well-lit, it looked too respectable to hold the dangers of the avenue.

She walked fast, panting, along the grid of streets that became a maze of curves. Soon she couldn't tell which way was south, and panic grabbed at her throat. She walked faster. Abruptly, the residential street spilled into another district of shops. She paused at a low building with a sign that read "Le Ragtime Parlour." The sidewalk was brightly lit, but she wasn't sure if light made her safer or more vulnerable. A policeman strolled around the corner, a block away, and headed in her direction. She felt an instant of relief and almost walked toward him. Then she realized that if every person on the nighttime streets mistook her for a whore, surely a policeman wouldn't think twice about arresting her.

She stepped into the alley alongside the building and leaned against the wall, hoping he hadn't seen her. Muffled music came from inside. As she listened to the cheery skip and hop of the piano, her pulse gradually slowed, along with her breathing. An alto voice crooned along with the piano, singing words she couldn't make out.

Her mind drifted into worry that she shouldn't have run off in the night. Why hadn't she waited till Charles went to work in the morning? Surely his mother could not have kept her in the house. But what if he stayed home from work? She couldn't bear to spend even one more day with him, subject to his unpredictable temper. A spurt of anger energized her, and she was just bending down to pick up the grip, when a door on the side of the building opened. The music had stopped, and a flood of chatter poured out from the customers inside. Preparing to flee whatever new danger was coming through the door, she straightened, holding the grip, but paused at the sight of a slim young woman in a silvery dress with long sleeves and a yoked collar of white lace. The woman's wavy black hair rested on her shoulders, and her face, shining with sweat, was a tawny brown.

The two of them stood and examined each other. Then the woman in silver stepped forward with a fluid stride, holding up a cigarette. "Got a light?" she asked.

"No."

The hand fell to her side. "Running away from home?" She nodded at the suitcase.

"Yes." Louise's hand went to the bruise turning to yellow on her cheekbone. Was it visible in the dim light from the streetlamp?

"Hmm." The woman leaned against the wall, twirling the cigarette between her fingers. A possum rustled among a pile of trash in the alley and scampered away.

"Was that you singing?" Louise asked.

"Yes. Mabel Mead." The woman stepped forward, thrusting out a hand, and Louise shook it. The fingers were warm and smooth.

"Louise . . . Kelley. Pleased to meet you, Miss Mead."

"Not safe out here for a woman at night."

"I know."

"Where are you headed?"

"The el station at West Farms. But I'm lost. Can you direct me?"

"Better yet, I'll drive you. My manager has a motor. In fact, we'll take you wherever you want the train to take you. Much safer."

"Oh, I couldn't—"

"I'm about to go home, so I can drop you. Going into Manhattan, yes?"

Shouts and babble came from men leaving the club through the front door. Louise said, "East 29th Street."

"It's practically on our way. I'll be back in a minute."

Mabel Mead glided inside, and Louise debated whether to run off or wait. The prospect of getting into a car with two Negroes seemed out of the question. On the other hand, she was lost, exhausted, and in dread of facing more men on the street, not to mention the prowling policeman. Miss Mead was kind and spoke with more cultivation than any of the few colored women she had ever encountered, mostly servants in the college dining hall and washwomen on the street. She had never met a professional singer before, or a woman who moved with such confident grace. Cigarette smoking was an odious habit, possibly pointing to depravity, but she had known a few women at Barnard who smoked. Louise was still wavering when a Ford pulled up at the end of the alley, and Miss Mead leaned out the window. "Let's go!"

White slavery was in the news at least once a week, with warnings to young women to avoid going out alone after dark, especially in neighborhoods where immigrants or colored people abounded. Louise found it hard to believe that scores of white women were being forced into prostitution by a class of people who had little power in society. Moralists were eager to represent her gender as pure and weak, and they liked to stir up fear of non-whites and foreigners.

The white slavery warnings had crossed Louise's mind when she set out on a suburban street in the middle of the night, but she'd been confident she could take care of herself. Now that she had run the gauntlet of White Plains Road in the wee hours and was riding in a vehicle with two black people, she felt she was in a vulnerable position.

Sitting next to the window of the three-seater Model T roadster, she calculated whether she would die if she flung open the door and jumped out, while traveling at such a high speed. That is, if she could figure out how to work the door handle.

"They really have to pave more roads in the Bronx," said the man behind the wheel. "It's a trial to drive up here." The automobile was bouncing over the cobblestones, sending the three of them into the air at every turn of the wheels. Reaching the end of the block, they turned onto asphalt pavement, which diminished the bouncing, but their speed increased dramatically. Louise gasped and clutched at the frame of the open window, a sharp breeze hitting her cheeks.

"I'm sorry," said Miss Mead, who was sitting in the middle of the bench seat, "I haven't introduced you. Miss Kelley, this is Mr. Kendall Stewart."

TO MARCH OR TO MARRY · 57

"Pleased to meet you, Miss Kelley."

Louise leaned forward to catch a glimpse of the man's face in the intermittent light from the street-lamps. He was darker-skinned than Miss Mead and at least ten years older. He wore a black suit, with a high collar and tie, and his speech was just as urbane as hers. Still, confidence men were good at playing a part. Louise lurched against the door as they turned a corner.

"Kendall owns four nightclubs," said Miss Mead. "That one in the Bronx, two in the Tenderloin on 35th Street, and one in Harlem."

"The Loin is dying, though," Mr. Stewart said. "The clubs are moving north. I'm looking to sell those two and buy more in Harlem. It looks like Harlem is going to be big."

"When I sing at the club in Harlem," said Miss Mead, "the crowd is just wild about the music. It's better than anywhere, except the Hotel Marshall. That's my favorite place to sing."

They were back on cobblestones, and Louise's teeth rattled against each other.

"Where exactly are you going?" Mr. Stewart asked.

"45 East 29th Street."

"Do you have friends there?"

"No, it's an office. I'm looking for work."

"Oh, you're a secretary, then?"

"No." Louise wasn't planning to say more, but she became aware that she had brought the conversation to a halt. These people were polite, and they were, she hoped, trying to help her, so she cautiously added information. "It's the Women's Political Union. I'm going to help with the suffrage parade."

"That's marvelous," said Miss Mead. "We need the vote, that's for sure. Men are doing a terrible job running this city. The way they treat black people—"

"You shouldn't complain, Mabel," Mr. Stewart said. "You have a good life."

"Yes, but what they did to my sister—"

"There's nothing you can do for your sister. She's out of reach."

They turned onto a bridge, and Louise could see water below, a few streetlamps reflected in the lapping darkness. For a moment, she was afraid they were taking her across the Hudson, but it didn't take long to reach the other side. She decided it must be the East River, which meant they were now in Manhattan.

"It wasn't her fault," Miss Mead was saying. "Those nosy social workers got everything wrong."

"Is your sister in trouble?" Louise asked.

"She's in a reformatory up at Bedford. Just because they caught her in a man's bedroom. The social workers had come to check on his younger brother. I hired a lawyer, but I couldn't get her out of the reformatory. It's a prison, really."

"Oh, I'm sorry."

"I don't mean to burden you with my problems. Like Kendall says, I am damn lucky to have a job that isn't washing floors or working in a factory."

"How did you get to be a singer?"

"When my mama died, my little sister and I came up from Virginia with our aunt. We got work on a chorus line in one of Kendall's clubs. When he found out I could sing, he got me voice lessons. It's my sister's bad luck that she can't sing and got involved with a fast fellow. I was the lucky one."

"It's not your fault," Mr. Stewart said.

"But she's my sister. I feel bad." Louise didn't know what to say, but she liked Miss Mead's spontaneous, unguarded quality. The women she knew seemed stiff and reserved in comparison.

Manhattan had more paved streets than the Bronx, speeding their progress. With dawn lightening the sky, the automobile turned down a wide avenue, where a few wagons were out. A street cleaner shoveled horse manure into the back of a wagon, even as the horse hitched to the front deposited fresh droppings.

"Here's 32nd Street," said Miss Mead. "Slow down, Kendall."

"I'm so sorry about your sister," Louise said. "Do you know when she's getting out?"

"Supposed to be in July, but only if she's on good behavior, and if you knew my sister . . ."

"When we get the vote, we'll find a way to help young women stay out of trouble." The roadster stopped in front of a building with the words "Women's Political Union" on the window.

"That's a kind sentiment, Miss Kelley."

"It's Louise. I'm so grateful for the ride."

"I couldn't leave you out there with the wolves."

Louise struggled with the door handle, and Miss Mead reached over to unlatch it. On the sidewalk, Louise bent over to the window. "Do you know that was my first ride in an automobile? I thank you, Mr. Stewart." He touched his hat and nodded. "And thank you . . . May I call you Mabel?"

"Absolutely. You take care, Louise."

As they drove away, she stood, suitcase in hand, looking at the window of the WPU office, with its

"Votes for Women" flyers facing out through the glass. She felt like Odysseus finishing a leg of his perilous journey and girding himself to learn the ways of a new land.

Chapter 6

HARRIOT STANTON BLATCH

I found her asleep on the front stoop when I came to open up this morning." Miss Gambrill, broad-shouldered, in a white waist with puffy sleeves and a tweed skirt, nudged Louise to stand up. The woman who had just come through the door had iron-gray curls and wire-rimmed glasses and was wearing a black coat with embroidered lapels. "I wouldn't bother you, Mrs. Blatch," said Miss Gambrill, "but you wanted to know when a woman with college education volunteers."

Louise had read in the news about Harriot Stanton Blatch, the daughter of suffrage crusader Elizabeth Cady Stanton, who had worked alongside the famous Susan B. Anthony. Mrs. Blatch spent much of her time in Albany, the state capital, pressuring lawmakers to pass a bill allowing women to vote in New York State. Each time the measure failed to pass, she returned to New York City to organize a parade in protest. This year's parade was her third.

At the word "education," Mrs. Blatch gestured toward a door at the back of the room. "Come to my office, both of you."

They walked past three rows of desks and chairs, still empty at this early hour, and entered a corner room lined with bookshelves. Mrs. Blatch hung her coat on a carved coat-rack and sat down behind a massive wood desk. "Now then. What sort of volunteer work are you interested in?"

"Actually," said Louise, "I can't volunteer. I'd like a job. I mean, I need a job." The woman's eyebrows went up. "I . . . I want to help women get the vote, and I can work full-time."

"Your name?"

"Louise Kelley."

"Mrs. Kelley—"

"No, it's Miss."

"Why are you wearing a wedding ring?" Louise, though unnerved, explained quickly, avoiding self-pity and tears. She knew strength would be valued in this situation, and the woman did not look like someone who invested in sympathy. "And your education?"

"I went to Barnard College."

"When did you graduate?"

"I didn't. I only went for two years."

"Why?"

"My father . . ." She couldn't bear to lie to Harriot Blatch, and it occurred to her that she didn't have to. "My father left my mother, and I had to work."

"College student, housewife, and working girl, all in one. Superb. What did you study?"

"I especially liked English literature."

"Then you can help with writing."

"And last year I joined a women's club, so I'm accustomed to addressing a group of people."

"Oh yes, the clubs." Mrs. Blatch's eyes clouded over for a moment. "Well . . . in any case, we have an immediate task for you. It won't use your college learning, but it requires the self-confidence you speak of. If you spent much of the night walking through the Bronx, I take it you have nerve."

"Oh, yes."

"And you're good-looking, which serves well for this stunt. Miss Gambrill, send her out with Mrs. Merwin to the storefront for today. If you can handle this little job, Miss Kelley, we'll have work for you at least through the end of the parade next week, and perhaps beyond."

Louise's nerve did not extend to asking this imposing woman what rate of pay or hours she might be offered. She suspected requesting such details would suggest lack of enthusiasm for the cause. Desperation, however, made her inquire, "One more thing. I need a place to stay. I can't go back."

"Miss Gambrill will send you over to the Margaret Louisa. The Protestants run a nice clean boardinghouse. Just don't tell them you're running away from your husband."

"Thank you. I can't tell you how much I appreciate your . . ."

But Mrs. Blatch was already absorbed in the stack of papers on her desk. On the way out of the office, Louise removed her wedding ring and left it at the bottom of a coat pocket.

Two hours later, having watched how the stunt was done, Louise was standing in the window of an empty shop on Fifth Avenue, holding a stack of handwritten signs, one of them facing out so pedestrians could stop and read it. Mrs. Merwin, who had taken the first hour, was standing on the sidewalk, giving Louise a signal when it seemed the audience was ready for the next sign, at which point she swapped the sign to the back of the stack and displayed the next one. She had read them earlier, as Mrs. Merwin went through the sequence.

Half the population of our nation is not permitted to express their views in the way that really counts—that is, at the ballot box.

Women must take up their rights and insist on representation in the government.

Men must honor the rights of women, moral keepers of home and family, if we would form a just society.

Join the members of the Women's Political Union as we parade up Fifth Avenue on May 4 to protest the refusal of the New York State legislature to pass a woman suffrage resolution.

Change our country for the better!

Passersby stopped to read. Some cheered, others jeered, and then there were those who leered. Not quite so many men had bothered to stop when the heavyset, middle-aged Mrs. Merwin was holding the placards. Louise felt uncomfortable at the thought, but she reminded herself she had been hired for her boldness. If she was going to be a suff, she would undoubtedly face plenty of male boorishness. Enduring discomfort was a way to prove how much women wanted the vote. But how much did she want the vote? Or did she just want the companionship of sympathetic women and an escape from her husband?

The crowd on the sidewalk was growing. As people finished reading and walked away, some of them took handbills from Mrs. Merwin, and more spectators took their places. Louise's arms were getting tired, and she was just thinking her hour might be up, when two policemen approached the crowd. They dispersed the watchers, including Mrs. Merwin, who tucked the handbills into her bag before disappearing. One of the policemen tried to open the door of the shop and then banged on the glass.

Louise put down her signs and rubbed her aching neck. "Open up!" shouted the officer. She went to unlock the door. "Come along, missy," he said.

"What? Why?"

"You're under arrest."

"For what? I'm not doing anything wrong."

"For obstructing traffic on the sidewalk. You're coming down to the station with us."

Louise looked around for Mrs. Merwin. How could the woman have deserted her? The officer reached out to take her arm. She sidestepped him. "I'm coming."

The station was only two blocks away, but every step made her feel self-conscious as she walked between the two men. People stared, but she kept her chin up and looked straight ahead. At the station, she sat on a bench while the officer at the desk dealt with two drunks who had been brought in on charges of public disruption. The men, both of them bruised around the face, looked sullen as two policemen joked about them.

Louise's instinct for self-preservation led her, as usual, to cope with fear and shame by working up righteous anger. She directed it primarily at Mrs. Merwin for running off and Mrs. Blatch for sending her on this insane mission, with a dose of resentment reserved for Miss Gambrill, who should've warned her what might happen.

At that moment, Miss Gambrill marched through the front door. She hastened to Louise. "Are you all right, dear?"

"I . . . I don't know. How did you get here?"

"Mrs. Merwin came straight back to report. Don't let these ruffians scare you. They have no right—"

"Madam, can I help you?" asked the officer, who had just sent the two drunks off to a cell.

Miss Gambrill stepped up to the desk. "Yes, you can immediately release this young woman. She's done nothing wrong."

"She's charged with obstructing foot traffic."

"All she did was stand in a shop window and make use of her First Amendment rights. There's nothing illegal in that. If anyone broke the law, it was the people on the sidewalk."

The policeman frowned. "You suffs think you can get away with anything."

"Just because you're not accustomed to women expressing themselves doesn't mean it's illegal. When men play ball in the street and gather a crowd, you don't arrest them. How can you possibly victimize this innocent girl? If you book her, I'll be back with a newspaperman in ten minutes, and the whole city will find out what barbarians you fellows are."

The policeman turned to look at a man in gray flannels who had stepped out of a side office. The man nodded and went back into his room. "All right. You can go," said the officer. "But next time you send someone along to keep the sidewalk clear. You hear me?"

"Mrs. Blatch was all for calling up the *Trib* and sending a reporter to meet me at the station," said Miss

Gambrill on the way back to East 29th Street. "But I reminded her you're just escaping from a marriage, and it wouldn't be fair to have your name in the papers. We might lose you, at a time when we need all the help we can get. There's still so much to be done to get this parade together."

"Oh. Thank you." Louise shuddered to think of Mama and the Blakes reading that she'd been picked up by the police. "You know, I'm awfully tired. I didn't get much sleep last night."

"All right, we'll pick up your grip and find someone to walk you to the Margaret Louisa. The Silent Speech was a big assignment for your first day. I think Mrs. Blatch was testing you."

"Testing me?"

"By the way, I think she's wrong about the clubs."

"What do you mean?"

"She thinks they're naïve and frivolous, but some of our best street-corner speakers are club members. Not everyone is born with the self-confidence that comes from having money."

"Mrs. Blatch is wealthy?"

"Her husband was. She inherited heaps of money when he died. And of course, she came from a highly respected family."

As they approached the office, Louise was reminded of the way ants bustle in and out of an anthill, pausing just outside the entrance to consult each other for a moment, then continuing on their way. She had to wait while a tall young woman stopped Miss Gambrill at the door to tell her the office was out of parade pledge cards. "There's a stack in the corner of Mrs. Blatch's room," came the instant reply. "After that, we'll have to print up some more."

They walked into the main room, where they saw, draped over a desk, a purple banner with white lettering that read, "We Dimand Justice for Women." Mrs. Blatch held it out to Miss Gambrill. "It's spelled wrong. A batch of thirty, and they're all wrong."

"I'll take care of it," Miss Gambrill said.

"Ah, Miss Kelley, I'm glad you're back. We need you to return these to the printer. The address is on the box. Miss Gambrill, come into my office so I can show you the changes to the parade line-up. We have to contact the laundry workers union immediately." Before Louise could remind them how tired she was, the two women were gone. She stood there, worker ants scurrying around her. "Excuse me," she said, as a girl in a yellow dress passed by, but the girl was moving too fast to stop. Everyone was so intent on their typewriting or discussing or telephoning that Louise, in her weary state, couldn't bring herself to interrupt. Finally she folded up the purple banner, put it in the box, read the address, and carried the box out the door.

The brown stain on the ceiling traced the pattern of a river delta across a fan of cracks, and whenever the resident upstairs tromped across the floor, white flakes fell onto Louise's rough gray blanket. The room smelled of mildew, and there was barely a foot of space alongside the bed. Her suitcase stood upright at the end of the narrow aisle, just under a tiny window with cracks that matched the ones in the ceiling. The window framed the view of a brick wall, stained white with bird droppings. But she had a place to lie down, safe from her husband's wrath.

The Margaret Louisa was full up. After tramping around to three other boarding-houses, each more shabby than the last, Louise had landed in this one, just in time for a dinner of undercooked potatoes, over-cooked peas, and gristly beef with watery gravy. She had collapsed into bed expecting to fall straight to sleep, but she was in that ironic condition of being too tired to sleep. Her overstimulated mind ranged over the day, and she wondered if she would ever adapt to the blistering pace of suffrage work. Of course, it was only a week till the parade, and probably activity would slow once the parade was over. But could she stand it till then? Surely a night of rest would change her outlook.

Her thoughts drifted back to her mother, and guilt swept in. Mama must be worrying. Louise sat up, lit the lamp on the little table at the head of the bed, and pulled up her suitcase. She had taken a few sheets of paper and a pencil from the office. Using the suitcase as a desk, she wrote out a note, reassuring her mother that she was fine, had a job and a place to stay, and would be in touch as soon as she had enough money for a little apartment where they could live together. She gave no return address, not wishing Charles to come looking for her. Certainly Mama would show the letter to the Blakes. Louise had nothing to say to Charles.

She laid the letter on the floor so she'd remember to buy an envelope and stamp in the morning. A drunken song drifting down the hall turned her mind to the night before. She had avoided dwelling on the night-mares of her journey, but now she thought of Mabel, the guardian angel of that dream world. Had she really ridden in a motor with two Negroes? There was no concrete evidence of her trek through the Bronx except for the ripped shoulder of her coat. Oh, that rip! She'd have to borrow needle and thread from the landlady in the morning. Her immediate concerns resolved, Louise dropped off to a sleep so deep, no new dreams came to disturb it.

In the morning, Louise's first assignment was to fill out cards telling each person or group who had promised to march where they were to line up for the parade. "You just have to enter the name and the starting location, then address the other side," Miss Gambrill said. "You do know how to typewrite, don't you?"

"Oh, yes." How hard could it be? thought Louise, who had never touched a typewriting machine. She'd just find the right keys and press them down.

"All the cards have to be done today and posted by five o'clock," Miss Gambrill concluded as she whirled off to her next task.

Louise picked up a notification card and placed it behind the rubber roller of the machine, as she had seen other women do. She turned the knob at the end of the carriage and was pleased to see the top of the card appear in front of the roller. Now she had to move the carriage to make the blank for the name appear in the little triangle where the keys would strike the card. She pushed and pulled at the carriage, and it shifted to the right, but she couldn't make it move left. Looking around at the other typewriters, she saw how a girl across the room squeezed a lever at the back of the carriage, and it moved. Louise did the same, and the carriage zoomed to the left with a bright ping that made her jump. She carefully nudged the carriage right and left until the card was lined up.

She started typing the name. But the letters appeared on the same spot as the printing of the second line, instead of just above. Furthermore, all the letters came out lower-case, and the method for obtaining capitals was a mystery. Finally, she went over to one of the girls and asked for help.

An hour later, when Miss Gambrill came back to check on her, five notification cards had been completed, and ten false starts were hidden in the trash can. Miss Gambrill frowned. "I thought you said—"

"It's a new model of machine to me," Louise said, half-truthfully. "I'm afraid I've never been very fast."

"All right, we'll have someone else do the cards. We're going to try you out on street corner speaking. I'll give you a booklet of common objections to suffrage and how we respond to them. Study the booklet, and you can go out with Mrs. Merwin this evening, just before dinnertime."

Louise walked across 29th Street to Madison Avenue and down three blocks to Madison Square Park. She sat on a bench under a crabapple tree, which occasionally released a flock of pale pink petals to decorate her shoulders, and she read the entire booklet. When she had finished, she went back to her boarding-house for a lunch of cold beef on stale bread, then returned to the office, where Miss Gambrill tossed her more pamphlets to read.

Four hours later, she was standing on a wooden crate at the corner of Madison Park and Broadway, looking out at a sprinkling of workingmen and shop girls. Along the curb, cabbies leaned against their hansoms, listening as they waited for fares. Mrs. Merwin had attracted this motley group by ringing a school bell. After delivering a rambling speech that Louise found dull, she introduced "the fiery Miss Kelley," no doubt thanks to some stereotype of Irish women, since Louise hadn't emitted a single spark in her presence. She wondered how to work up a flame. Again she felt cross with Miss Gambrill. Shouldn't she have conducted a rehearsal before sending a raw recruit out in the field?

Just pretend you're speaking to the clubwomen, she told herself. She fixed her eyes on a worn, fiftyish lady wearing a patched brown shawl over a rumpled dress of tan cotton. Not a shop girl, this one, but perhaps a laundress or seamstress. Possibly she had a Charles at home, waiting to beat her for stopping to listen to a crazy suffragette. Louise had better make the beating worth her while.

"Let me ask you a question," she began. "Under a democratic form of government such as ours, who should make the laws?"

"The lawmen!" shouted a man in overalls, provoking laughter.

His neighbor, a thin fellow carrying a tool box, poked him and said, "Nah, the Congress!"

"The legislature," said a young woman.

"And who chooses the legislators?" asked Louise.

"The people," said the man with the tool box.

"And do the people choose the legislators in New York State?"

"The ones who bother to vote do," he said.

"But only half the people are even allowed to vote. Nearly all women in our great nation are denied that fundamental right. What about the laws that are made by the legislators? Must women obey those laws?"

"Of course," said a cabbie.

"Then why may women not vote for the people who make those laws?"

"Same reason children can't. They ain't fit!"

Louise frowned. The booklet hadn't dealt with this objection. But words sprang to her tongue. "You would compare the intelligence of a mature woman with the intelligence of a child?"

"No, women ain't stupid. They're too emotional."

Now the discussion was returning to the script. "And you believe men are not emotional? When the men of our government send aid to people starving in India, do they do so out of hard, cold logic? When laws are passed to protect small children from slaving in factories, do not the men who make the laws have compassion for those children? And is it not the unfeeling factory owner we prosecute for exploiting the children, due to his preference for money over concern for their welfare? If anything, a small increase in emotion will make better laws, not worse."

The woman in the brown shawl clapped, and a few others joined in. "That's right," a thin woman called from the back. "My husband says I cry too much, but he's a cold bastard."

More people were stopping to listen, and Mrs. Merwin made an effort to shepherd them onto a grassy triangle so they wouldn't block the sidewalk. When Louise had stood in the shop window, she had felt ridiculous, but now the use of her own words gave her a thrill of power. Even if she had derived those words from a booklet, she was adapting them to individuals who were paying close attention to her, not reading from a bunch of cards in her hands. And the individuals were responding.

The woman in brown had a fit of coughing, and Louise felt a surge of concern toward her. She was inspired to veer away from the script. "In fact, once we have the vote, our compassion will lead us to make laws about issues that men overlook or do not wish to deal with. How many of you in this crowd know men who beat their wives?" Mrs. Merwin cleared her throat, but Louise ignored her. Hands sprang up, the brown-clad woman's among them. "Suppose there were a law against men beating their wives, as there are laws against men beating strangers? Would that law be a good one? Would it protect us?"

"Yes!" shouted many of the women in the still swelling crowd. The men, however, had gone quiet, some of them shaking their heads.

"Do you think men will pass such a law on their own?"

An undercurrent of masculine grumbling could be heard, and a cabbie yelled, "Those women get what they deserve."

"What an ass!" said the thin woman. "Men are brutes. You're right, young lady. We need a law."

Men began to trickle away. "That's right, men!" called Louise. "Hang your heads in shame and slink off."

"Hey lady, don't you know you need our votes for you to get the vote?" shouted the cabbie. "You're an idiot!"

Louise raised her voice even more. "Go home and think over how much women suffer at your hands or the hands of your brethren. Then show your humanity and join us, instead of oppressing us. Together we can create a just, fair society!"

A number of women cheered. Mrs. Merwin made a rolling gesture with her hand and held up a sheaf of yellow bills.

"If you agree with us," said Louise, "sign up to march in our parade on Saturday. Or at least come out and support us as we pass by. Let's unite and get the vote!" And she punched a fist toward the sky.

Many women, and one nervous-looking man, took bills from Mrs. Merwin. Seven women, two of them pushing baby carriages, signed parade pledge cards. The lady in brown, however, drifted off with a troubled look in her eyes, and Louise feared she'd only reminded the woman of pain. Nevertheless, battling and seducing an audience had left her exhilarated, with a brand-new sense of power.

"You're a natural," exulted Mrs. Merwin on the way back to headquarters. "I feared those men would start a fight, but you shamed 'em. And we got seven pledges, pretty good for a weekday crowd."

At the office, they reported to Miss Gambrill, who was, for once, seated at her desk in the back of the big room. "Excellent," she said. "We'll send the two of you back out tomorrow. I think we've found your niche, Miss Kelley."

As they were making plans for the next day's expedition, a receptionist interrupted. "There's someone up front asking for you, Miss Kelley." Fear skittered up Louise's spine. Had Charles tracked her down already? But when she looked toward the front desk, there stood a brown-skinned woman in a simple but stylish green dress.

"Mabel!" She went up front, smiling. "What a surprise!"

They sat down on a bench at the side of the room. "Quite a busy place," Mabel commented.

"The parade is in a few days. There's a lot to do."

"That's why I came. To talk to you about the parade. You want as many people as you can get to march, don't you?"

"Of course."

"My friends and I would like to join in. We're all singers and dancers, and we agree that women should get the vote."

"Oh, that's wonderful! How many are you?"

"About twenty are interested so far. But we don't know where to meet the parade."

"We have a whole roster of where each group will join. Let me check on the list. I'll be right back."

Louise went to report to Miss Gambrill, wondering aloud where she should tell the singers and dancers to gather before the parade. "They ought to fit in at 11th Street, with the artists, don't you think?"

She went to the chart on the wall, then looked at Miss Gambrill, who had a sour expression on her face. Mrs. Merwin's hands went into a nervous flutter. "Let's put them at 16th Street," said Miss Gambrill.

"But that's almost at the end, with the Men's League. They'll be insulted."

"We already have a group from the National Association for the Advancement of Colored People all set to march there. These women will be in good company with their . . . their peers."

"Do you mean the black women can't march with the white women?"

"Of course, we welcome the support of our colored sisters. But some elements of society are not as progressive as we are. We don't want to scare those people away. We're just placing the Negroes away from the heart of the march in order to . . . to make them a bit less visible."

Louise was stunned. "But that's not fair."

"Fairness has nothing to do with it. We can't afford to alienate supporters over the issue of race."

"This woman is my friend. I can't tell her she has to march with the men."

"Then I'll tell her."

"No! Don't you dare. I'm going to speak to Mrs. Blatch." Louise headed for the closed door of the corner office.

"You can't go in there. She's meeting with someone."

But Louise was already knocking at the door. A voice told her to come in. When she stepped inside, she saw a young, dark-haired woman dressed in lustrous blue bombazine, sitting across from Mrs. Blatch. The woman was neither attractive nor homely but had a memorable face, with small eyes and narrow lips that seemed to pinch together in the direction of her short, pointed nose. She looked up at Louise and exclaimed, "Why, it's her! The one who was speaking."

Confused, Louise was tempted to back out the door, fearing she was being accused of some error. But Mrs. Blatch said, "Come in, Miss Kelley. Meet Miss Damaris Oakley, just back from Europe. She's a graduate of Vassar, my alma mater, and her mother was one of my classmates. She's been telling me about a galvanizing speech she just heard at Madison Square."

"You were most convincing, Miss Kelley," said the young woman, "and you handled the hecklers superbly. If I hadn't been already on my way here, I would have decided to join up immediately."

"Why, thank you," said Louise, feeling her talents were being exaggerated. "That's kind of you to say."

"It's the absolute truth."

"Did you wish to see me?" asked Mrs. Blatch.

"I . . . yes, I did . . . I do." Louise took a breath to recover her composure. "You see, there's a young Negro woman who . . . who helped me out that night I was walking through the Bronx. She and her friends are performers who want to march in the parade and Miss . . . that is, I'm being told they have to march at the end, behind the men, and it seems wrong to me." Miss Oakley was watching Louise's face with interest.

"Ah." Mrs. Blatch placed her elbows on the desk and tented her fingers. "Miss Gambrill only has the interests of our movement at heart. Many suffragists believe there's a danger of defeat from conservatives who fear giving the vote to black women. But I think—"

"That's absurd! It's not worth losing a few supporters if we lose the respect of people like Miss Mead, who is a fine, upstanding—"

"And I completely agree with you, my dear." The tent of Mrs. Blatch's fingers collapsed and thumped on the desk. "My parents were abolitionists. I find these judgments about race unjust. I will speak with Miss Gambrill. Tell your friend her group will line up at 11th Street, with the other occupations. I'm afraid they'll have to be at the end of that section, though, as we've already sent out cards establishing the order. But they'll be smack in the midst of the parade." Miss Oakley smiled.

"Oh, thank you, Mrs.—"

"You will tell her they should dress simply and all in the same color, preferably white, and on no account are they to leave the ranks before the end of the march. Now close the door behind you."

Louise, gratified by her success, conveyed Mrs. Blatch's instructions to Mabel, who thanked her and left. Then she entered the label "Singers and Dancers" on the chart at the 11th Street block, unseen by Miss Gambrill, who was off putting out another fire. As Louise was putting on her coat to head back to the boarding-house, Miss Oakley emerged from the corner office. "Miss Kelley," she said. "May I walk with you?"

They left together in the waning light. Heads turned as they stepped onto the sidewalk. Louise wasn't sure if people were curious about two young suffragists or if Miss Oakley's raccoon coat was the attraction.

"Mrs. Blatch told me a bit about you," Miss Oakley began. "She gave an impression of boldness, which I observed at the park and then again when you came into the office. I have a lot of respect for women with fighting courage."

"But it turned out Mrs. Blatch agreed with me. I didn't have to fight her at all."

"You took a risk, though, walking in on us to speak your mind. Not everyone would've done that."

"I had to defend my friend."

"I admire loyalty too. In any case, I have a proposal for you. I discussed it with Mrs. Blatch, and she gave her approval. I'm here to help out with the parade, and when it's over, she has asked me to canvass my friends and my parents' associates and convince them to donate to the WPU. I'd like to hire you as my assistant."

"Really?"

"I'll have to write letters and practice speaking about suffrage. But I studied mathematics at Vassar. I was never strong in composition or literature. So I desperately need your help."

"And you would pay me?" asked Louise.

"Yes. I hear you don't know typewriting, but I'm hoping you could learn. I'll buy you a machine so you can practice. I'm living in a townhouse a few blocks away. It would make our work easier if you would move in there."

"Oh! How much would the rent cost me?"

"Not a penny. There's plenty of extra room, and you'll get board for free as well, in addition to your salary. Say, fifty dollars a month?"

Having struggled to make thirty a month with piecework, Louise was astonished by this offer. Although she wouldn't start her new job until after the parade, she immediately packed her few possessions and moved precipitously up in the world. She marveled at the quick and efficient way the suffrage movement had conspired to take care of her most pressing needs. It seemed the turn of events was proof she had made the right decision in leaving Charles so promptly.

Miss Oakley's father owned a steamboat line and several choice bits of Manhattan real estate. The newly built townhouse had been furnished by an interior designer, and Louise was given her own bedroom with a four-poster bed, a thick mattress, and a pile of quilts.

Her new employer insisted on being called by her Christian name.

That night they had a late dinner in the spacious dining-room, at an oval table spread with a white linen cloth. Louise felt uncomfortable as a Polish servant set down a meal of thinly sliced London broil, gravy, salad, and whipped potatoes with butter. After the woman left, she asked, "Tell me, what made you decide to work for suffrage?"

Damaris cut a tiny piece of meat and held it on her upright fork until she finished her reply. "I was in the same class as Inez Milholland at Vassar."

"Who's she? I've heard the name."

"She's my idol. She does everything she wants. In college, she played Romeo in *Romeo and Juliet.* She was in the Socialist Club, and she played basketball, tennis, and field hockey. I played tennis too, so I got to know her."

"And she's a suffragette?"

"The Vassar president tried to 'protect' us from suffrage and wouldn't let it be discussed on campus. So Inez brought a whole crowd of us to the cemetery next door for a meeting. She even got Mrs. Blatch to come up from New York and speak to us. Then we kept on meeting off-campus, but the president still wouldn't allow anyone to talk about suffrage on the college grounds. You'll never guess what Inez did then."

"Tell me."

"She set up a series of tableaux about suffrage in the Main Building, all of us in complete silence, no talking, observing the letter of his stupid law. And students walked past to see us. I was the Statue of Liberty."

"What is she doing now?"

"She's been studying law at New York University. Yale, Harvard, and Columbia all turned her away because she's a woman. Can you imagine?"

"And you've been in Europe since college?"

"Yes. It was my parents' idea that I go to Switzerland with my aunt. I studied painting."

"You're an artist?"

"No, I'm not that good. And how am I to use a degree in mathematics? If I wanted to be a professor, I could get a doctorate somewhere. Yale's graduate school lets women do mathematics but not law. How ridiculous! But I don't want to go back to school. I want to live. I want to do something meaningful. More whipped potatoes?"

Damaris was slimmer than Louise, who felt momentarily embarrassed by her appetite, but it was hard to stop eating. "I've never had such delicious food," she said. "My mother's not much of a cook."

"And where is your mother? Mrs. Blatch mentioned you left your husband."

"Mama's still living with his family. I'll be able to send her money now. I'm grateful to you."

"Are you going to divorce your husband?"

"Well . . . yes, I suppose. I haven't had a chance to think about it yet."

"I can talk to my lawyer for you. It takes a while, so you ought to get started, in case you ever want to marry again."

"There's no rush. I'm not interested in men right now." And divorce was a big step, especially for a girl who had grown up Catholic. She would deal with it after the parade.

Chapter 7

TO MARCH

L ouise checked the watch Damaris had loaned her. It read 4:54. Six more minutes. What were the odds the parade would start on time? With the punctual Mrs. Blatch and the rest of the WPU executive committee leading the column, they would probably step through the Washington Square arch and onto Fifth Avenue at precisely 5 o'clock.

Damaris, who had donated a bundle of her father's money to the WPU, was going to march with the Vassar contingent, lined up on Ninth Street, but Louise wasn't allowed to join the Barnard women. She had been appointed a marshal and assigned to a group of nurses. Over a white dress, she wore a purple, green, and white sash, with the word "Marshal" in gold. A brass whistle hung on a chain around her neck, but she wasn't supposed to use it unless spectators grew rowdy.

Louise looked at the four columns of nurses lined up on East 11th Street, their starched white uniforms, complete with bibs, aprons, and perky folded caps, standing out bright against the brownstone buildings. The nurses were chatting and cheerful, a good deal louder than the smaller ranks of women doctors ahead of them.

Farther up the block towards Fifth Avenue were lawyers and businesswomen. She would've preferred to
marshal Mabel's section, at the opposite end, but she
didn't want to cross Miss Gambrill again.

She looked back at the watch. 4:58. Her feet were already aching from standing in her worn boots for
almost an hour. How was she going to survive walking
43 blocks to Carnegie Hall? After the parade, when her
job with Damaris began, she must buy new boots with
her first wages.

A roar went up from the crowds along Fifth Avenue,
and the watch she was holding confirmed that the parade had started on time. A brass band started playing a
march tune. "All right now," Louise shouted to the
nurses, clapping her hands for attention. "We'll be
moving in just a few minutes. Don't forget to pay attention to the women in front and on either side of
you, so can stay lined up in your row and column. We
must present an impression of uniformity and discipline." She could hear a girl up ahead, shouting the
same instructions to the doctors and lawyers. "No
more chatter," Louise went on. "And no waving to
friends in the crowd. We're here on serious business,
affecting every woman in New York State, and maybe
the whole country."

"There they are!" said a nurse. Louise, craning her
neck, saw the top of the purple banner held high over
the first marchers as it bobbed through the intersection. She couldn't see the white letters, but she knew
they said, "Women vote in Wyoming, Idaho, Colorado,
Utah, Washington and California. Why not New York?"
The executive committee, including Mrs. Blatch in her
academic gown, were walking beneath and behind the

banner, but Louise's view of them was entirely blocked by the line-up waiting on 11th Street. Then she saw the ears of the horses and the shoulders, heads, and hats of the mounted phalanx, all WPU members, known to the girls in the office as "the cavalry." Next came the shiny curves of tuba horns and sousaphones, as the strains of the "Marseillaise" wafted across. Soon the tops of signs on wooden sticks appeared, no doubt carried by the unions. "We're next!" Louise called out, and the nurses stopped their residual whispering.

Like an ocean liner easing out from the dock, the lines of marchers shuffled forward. As they negotiated the turn onto Fifth, Louise felt a surge of excitement. With this great mass of women marching, surely people would see their strength, and minds would be changed. The vote was on its way.

As the lines straightened out after the turn, she was amazed to see a huge crowd gathered along the sides of the avenue, cheering and waving. She looked back at the stenographers coming up behind the nurses. The stenos all wore purple and white "Votes for Women" sashes and 39-cent suffrage hats, round white hats with folded brims, which the department stores had sold in recent weeks, at Mrs. Blatch's command.

Louise made sure the nurses were marching in even rows, eyes front. They had gone one block when the parade halted. "Keep your discipline, ladies," Louise called out. "We're still on display."

A young woman came running from 13th Street, stopping to speak briefly to each of the marshals. "Make two lines," she panted to Louise. "They're crowding the street at 14th," and she sped onward.

"All right, nurses," yelled Louise, who had been prepared for this contingency by Miss Gambrill. "Column One, move to your right and join Column Two. Column Four, move left to Column Three." The nurses, accustomed to taking orders, stepped neatly into their new lines, although they had to stand head to nose until the parade moved forward again. Up ahead, the ranks of doctors and lawyers were more ragged and less quiet.

Louise studied the crowd of people who had given up a Saturday afternoon to watch the parade. They were a mix of men and women, mostly middle-class, some with babies in arms or in carriages. The people leaning out the windows along the avenue were undoubtedly more affluent. Many were waving handkerchiefs.

The doctors stepped forward again, and the nurses followed smoothly. They reached 14th Street, which was twice as wide as the other side streets. To the east, the road was packed with people coming from the Broadway intersection at Union Square, where a subway stop was located. Unlike the orderly sidewalks of Fifth Avenue, the entire width of 14th Street was a humming, pulsing mass of people trying to get closer to the parade. Three policemen stood with their arms out between the mass and the marchers, but the officers couldn't cover the width of the street, and they looked fearful as the crowd bore down on them.

A wagon was parked at the corner, a cluster of men standing on it, one of them with his face glued to a camera. A shout made Louise look over her shoulder. A man, pushed from behind, came stumbling straight at her. She held out her hands and thought of the whistle, but it was too late. She and the man tumbled to the ground, and pain stabbed through her leg. People towered over her as she lay with her leg bent at an unnatural angle, while the man squirmed on top of her, trying to get up. An instant of terror gave way to a sense of profound acceptance, since there was nothing on earth she could do. Then a boot, pivoting next to her head, struck her temple, and she passed out.

The photographer had caught Louise in profile, just as she was about to be tackled by the hurtling spectator, but it looked more like he was being thrown into her arms. The photo landed on page two of the *New York Tribune*'s parade edition.

Charles was clutching the newspaper, folded open to the photograph, when he walked into the hospital ward where Louise lay amidst a long row of beds, her leg in a cast. The sight of her bandaged head halted him at the foot of the bed. Seeing her disheveled and agitated husband might have sent Louise into a panic if she hadn't been groggy with morphine. Damaris, who was sitting at the bedside, reading aloud the *New York Times*' sarcastic account of the parade, rose and demanded, "Who are you?"

"I'm this woman's husband," Charles replied in a gravelly voice. "I've come to take her home."

His words penetrated the morphine haze, and Louise grabbed Damaris's hand. "No. Don't let him. Please don't."

"Of course I won't," Damaris assured her. "She's in no condition to go anywhere, Mr. Kelley. And when she is, I'll be the one taking her home."

"Mr. Kelley?" Charles threw the newspaper onto the bed. "How can you . . ."

Louise shrank back against the pillows and raised a protective hand.

"Oh, pardon me," Damaris said. "I wasn't thinking. What's your surname?"

Charles shook his head and pitched himself into the chair at the other side of the bed. "Are you mad, Louise? It's dangerous, this suffrage business."

Up close, he looked pathetic, eyes bleary and hair rumpled. Her mind was sharpening as the reality of the situation became clear. "Do you think I felt safe in our house," she asked, "living with a man who could strike me anytime he got angry?"

A querulous voice came from the woman in the next bed. "He did that? Shame on you, young man!"

Charles ignored the comment. "Where is your sense of Christian forgiveness? I'm your husband!"

"That's not for you to ask."

"I'll say," the woman remarked, then broke into a bout of coughing.

"Come home, Louise. We need you."

"We? You and your mother miss having me as your servant?"

"What about *your* mother? You've abandoned her."

"Oh, that poor woman," said the neighbor. "It's always the aged who suffer."

"Please be quiet, Mrs. Halford," said Damaris. "It's not any of your business."

"Well, I can't help hearing," the woman protested, "if you're going to shout at each other."

"How is Mama doing?" Louise asked, her guilt deftly provoked by his words.

"How do you think? She's hurt and upset."

"I'll take her to live with me when I've saved some money. Or do you plan to kick her out on the street?"

At the rise in her voice, Damaris put a hand on Louise's arm. "I think you need to rest."

"And who are you?" Charles asked.

"Miss Damaris Oakley." She extended a hand across the bed, but he didn't take it. "A suffragette."

"The suffs are a bunch of man-hating crazies," Mrs. Halford muttered.

"How did you find me?" Louise asked.

"I saw the photograph," said Charles, "and I went to the office of your . . . that group that did the parade, and they said you were here."

"What photograph?" He shook the newspaper in front of her eyes. "Oh, my! I'm newsworthy. How exciting!"

"I can't believe you, being glad for this unladylike—"

"Oh, Charles, you need to find another wife. I'm not the right person for you, if you expect me to be lady-like. Don't you see I'm done with all that?"

"And what's this? Entertaining a gentleman in the hospital?" Mrs. Blatch walked up with an armful of flowers. "On behalf of the WPU, for the noble Miss Kelley—"

"Now see here," said Charles, "she's Mrs. Blake."

"Miss Oakley, please go find the ward nurse and see if they have a vase. Don't worry, Miss Kelley, the WPU will pay all medical bills, and we're having a talk with the chief of police tomorrow. The police protection was pathetically inadequate. But some of the papers have estimated we had as many as 15,000 marching, and the spectators were over 100,000."

"Yes," Louise said, "we've been reading the *Times*. Did you see my picture in—"

"It's shameful, that's what it is." Charles shook the *Trib* at Mrs. Blatch. "My wife being—"

"Of course I saw it," Mrs. Blatch said. "We'll be showing it to the police as evidence of their—"

"You're showing my wife to the police? I object—"

"And who are you?" Mrs. Blatch finally turned her head to address Charles.

"I'm Charles Blake, the husband of this poor woman who has been corrupted and then injured by your disgusting organization."

Mrs. Blatch laughed. She handed over the flowers to Damaris, who had returned with a vase. "Mr. Blake, do you know how daring 'this woman' has been? She walked through the Bronx, alone, in the middle of the night, to get away from you."

"You don't know what—"

"She has learned to speak on street corners and convert complete strangers to our cause. And she faced a formidable crowd during the parade and did her best to keep order. If it wasn't for the police being understaffed and disorganized . . . In any case, her talents would be completely wasted as a housewife. Surely you understand, the women of the United States of America need her far more than you do."

"See here, you can't—"

"Mr. Blake, what line of business are you in?"

"I'm . . . in construction. But dammit, that's not—"

"Please, no need for profanity. It happens that our office requires renovation. Why don't you come along and let me show you what we want?"

"What?"

"Are you up to a really large job? We have so much that needs doing."

"Yes, of course. I've done—"

"I'd like to get an estimate from you. Now I must go. I'm leaving for Albany on Friday to do battle for the state amendment. Rest well, Miss Kelley, and I'm sure you'll be recovered in no time."

"Thank you, Mrs. Blatch. The flowers are lovely."

"Let's go, Mr. Blake, I have a lot of work today."

"But I'm here for my wife. She's been—"

"We'll discuss that down at headquarters. Right now your wife needs to rest. What would you say is your specialty in the building field?" She took his arm and steered him down the aisle between the beds.

"I'll be back," he called over his shoulder before the two of them disappeared.

"My, what a fierce woman!" said Mrs. Halford.

"She certainly is," said Damaris. "Those politicians up in Albany had better watch their step."

If anyone could handle Charles, Louise thought, it was Mrs. Blatch. Perhaps she was safe from him at last.

TO MARRY

There was a time when Abbie thought she might never marry. She liked the independence of earning her own money and being answerable to no one but her mother, who kept house for them both and made few demands. Abbie just had to love and respect her and earn enough to supply her with food and clothing. Work at Dodd, Mead was energizing, and the daily trip from the Bronx into Manhattan made her feel part of the great city's ceaseless, colorful movement.

The men who courted Abbie either shared her literary interests but were arrogant, or else they were kind but couldn't comprehend a poem by Keats and fell asleep at the symphony. She had a brief flirtation with the editor of *The Bookman*, Mr. Crowninshield, who was exactly her age but from a loftier social class. For a few weeks, she permitted herself to imagine marrying him, until the day he returned to work from his lunch break with a young lady in mink clinging to his arm.

Abbie's mother fretted that she was going to remain a spinster, provoking indignation in her daughter, who objected to the word. But as she was turning twenty-eight, babies on the street became magnets for her attention. Could she endure growing old without ever having held her own baby in her arms? If she was going to have a child, time was running short.

Then she met Walter, who was both generous and literary. Within a week, he was declaring his love for her. When she told him she couldn't return his feelings, his reply shocked her: "What's that to me? You don't have to love me back. My love is more than enough." His willingness to adore her without recompense was so illogical, so lacking in ego, she grew curious about him.

Each week, when he had finished teaching Sunday School at the Methodist Episcopal church, she would meet him in the classroom, and they would sit together, reading Shelley, Byron, or Browning. Then they walked the streets for hours, discussing the poets' language and their elevated ideas. Walter often became incoherent as he explained his responses to poetry, but by the end of each discussion, it seemed to Abbie that she could feel what he was feeling. Her love of poetry was heightened by the exhilaration she absorbed from him. With each Sunday session, her attraction increased, until one rainy afternoon, on a visit to the Metropolitan Museum of Art, he kissed her in a secluded corner of the Greek sculpture room. His lips, so tender and delicious, conquered her reserve at last.

As their courtship proceeded, she told him about her parents' divorce, and his matter-of-fact acceptance made her feel safe enough to confide her deepest feelings. However, she kept one secret from him. Early on, he had revealed he was twenty-three, and she was afraid to tell him she was five years older. The day he proposed marriage, a year into their relationship, she took a deep breath and revealed her age. He tossed it aside as irrelevant. She, however, recognized the possible problems. She explained her reservations, asking for time to think about his proposal. That night, after his tearful sixty-block walk through Manhattan, he wrote her a seven-page letter, parts of it illegible from emotion, as he argued for their compatibility.

With God's help, I'll race with time and cram ten years in one and find me 33. Ten years I fling away for you, joyfully and with sweet gratitude. But in what must I overtake you? Is not my heart growing softer, tenderer, less callous, and in the very nature of things are we not one? God-given love is sempiternal and that soul is "mature" be it five, fifty, 28 or 23 or 99 years of age, there is no age, no time—only Eternity.

He declared his readiness to have a child with her as soon as she liked. It was true that money might be an issue, given the slightness of his employment, but he was sure their love would overcome any financial lack. Abbie, conscious that her own pragmatism needed a leaven of passion for balance, was so moved by his letter that she wrote him back with a single word: "Yes."

Over the next year, they let their engagement ripen into an easy companionship, until Abbie felt confident about marrying. Walter's wedding present to her, a small diamond-and-pearl sunburst brooch, was accompanied by a card with a line from a Tennyson poem: "Ring out, wild bells, to the wild sky."

Once they were wed, just after Abbie turned thirty, she felt an urgency to have a child as soon as possible. Both she and Walter rejoiced over the pregnancy.

Six weeks before the baby was due, Walter's mother arrived. She had been making the rounds of her five children who still lived in New York, staying with each one for a few months before migrating to the next. She had thought to be on hand for the birth, so she was sleeping in the sewing room at the back of the Bergholtz apartment. Walter heard a rasping sound from the room late one night when he went to the kitchen for a glass of water. He went in and found his mother breathing her last.

After watching her face turn ashen and slack in the lamplight, he went to report the death to Abbie and sobbed in her arms. Then he took his violin to the sewing room and played Mozart to his mother through the rest of the night.

At dawn, Abbie awoke and heard the notes of the violin still drifting down the hall. Heart aching for her husband, she went to the room, stood behind him, and reached over the hard curve of her belly to wrap her arms around his waist. He lowered his bow. "One goes and a new one comes," he said. "That's how it is."

The baby lay between them, sucking on her thumb, the tiny body encased in a long-sleeved barra-coat that kept her feet enclosed and warm, even when she kicked.

"Look at her smoking her pipe," Walter whispered.

"I didn't know it was possible to be so in love," Abbie murmured. Even though she had longed for a baby, the magnitude of motherly passion took her by surprise.

If she had been looking at Walter's face, she would have seen the flicker of an emotion he felt did not belong to him. If he had been honest, he would have named it, but he was too dutiful a husband to lay claim to anything but adoration of mother and child.

The baby hiccupped in her sleep.

"Our sweet Dolly," Walter said.

"Darling, I'm so tired and hungry."

"I'll make you an omelet and toast."

"That would be lovely." As he got up with his usual abruptness, the bed creaked and bounced, jarring Ivy awake. She mewled and rolled her head. "It's all right," Abbie told him. "Go get me a piece of ice."

He left. Abbie gathered up the baby, bared her breast, and prodded the tiny mouth. The gums parted. Abbie squeezed her breast, trying to push out the inverted nipple and put it deep into the baby's mouth. Pain slashed through the nipple as Ivy sucked for a few moments, then stopped and whimpered again. Walter arrived with the ice. Abbie rolled the nipple between her fingers, trying to get it to stand out. She applied the ice for a few seconds, but it didn't have the drawing-out effect it was meant to have.

"Not too long," Walter said.

"I know, dear." She handed back the ice and drew the baby close. "Darling, go make me those eggs."

He left again. The baby groped with her mouth, then tossed her head side to side. Abbie put a pinky finger in Ivy's mouth, and the baby worked it with her gums until she fell back asleep. Abbie eased out of bed, piled a barrier of pillows along the edge, and padded to the kitchen. She stroked each of her swollen breasts over a bowl, filling it halfway with her milk. "I'm making less and less," she told Walter.

"It's been ten days."

"That seems too long."

"Do you think we should give up?"

"I feel like a failure. Nurse says if the baby keeps trying to suck, it will help."

"Dr. Shirmer's coming tomorrow. We'll do whatever he says."

Walter put the eggs on the table, and Abbie ate while he boiled water to sterilize the bottle. At least Ivy would get the little bit of breast milk she'd expressed. "Would you like me to feed her when she wakes?" Walter asked.

"Yes."

He waited for her to thank him. Maybe she was just too tired.

Walter adored Abbie beyond life, beyond music, beyond, he sometimes thought but did not say aloud, even God the Father. She was his rescuer and his queen, the only woman he'd ever had all to himself. He'd had to share his loving mother with thirteen older and two younger siblings, a warm but chaotic family.

Walter had been a hyperactive child, a strange adolescent, and a young adult obsessed with music, his primary source of joy. Awkward with women, he'd feared he might forever remain a bachelor. Then along came Abbie, who saw through the streams of verbiage and the paroxysms of self-doubt that he could not hide, who skirted the treacherous crevasses of his being and nourished the blossoming of an expansive self whose existence he'd only suspected. Abbie had brought him into a world of love, comfort, conjugal joy, and profound sympathy, though he had never been able to be truly intimate with anyone but God. Abbie was his savior, his queen, his Virgil. Motherhood had made her even more lovable, more elevated in his perception. When he watched her hold little Ivy, his heart became twice its size, and he thought he might explode into a thousand pieces, but he knew if he did, she would gather them all up and put him back together.

And so he was startled by the glimmer of fear that she loved Ivy more than she loved him. Of course, mothers had to love their babies that much, or they would never have the endurance to take care of all the endless needs of a helpless creature. Or so he told himself. And surely grief over his mother made him more needy of Abbie's love. The word "jealousy" never crossed the threshold of his consciousness.

When Dr. Shirmer came the next day, he declared the baby underweight and advised switching to a mixture of cow's milk and barley water. He recommended sage tea to dry up Abbie's milk and an ointment to soothe her cracked nipples. "You should have sent for me sooner," he told them. "Discharge that nurse immediately." Abbie felt ashamed of her error but more relieved than regretful about giving up the painful duty of breastfeeding.

Each morning she boiled barley in water, mashed the cooked grain, then strained out the liquid to combine with milk. Ivy sucked avidly at the bottle, which made Abbie fear she must be starved. But more often than not, the baby threw up afterwards.

"All babies burp up milk," Walter pointed out.

"But she's spitting up so much. I can't tell if she's keeping any of it down."

"But she's bright and happy. Aren't you, little Dolly?" He stroked a finger down the side of her face as she lay in Abbie's arms. Ivy turned her head toward the finger.

"She's too quiet. She hardly ever cries."

"She's well-behaved. What's wrong with that? You worry too much, my darling."

Abbie, sitting on the parlor sofa, propped her feet up on the hassock. Walter sat on the hassock and began to massage her feet. "I got another letter from Uncle Al," Abbie said. "He wants me to bring the baby out to visit. And of course Mama wants to see her."

"I'd love a trip to Chicago, but the baby's much too young for that."

"I don't think you should go, deary, we simply couldn't afford to lose your income."

"But how would I stand being apart from you?" He slipped to his knees on the floor and laid his head on her lap.

She stroked his thin, dark hair. "It wouldn't be for long. Poor Uncle Al, losing his child and then his wife. It would be such a comfort for him to spend time with us."

"But your mother's looking after him. Why does he need you too?"

"It's not about me, it's the baby." Walter was right, it was too soon to take a newborn on the train, but Abbie had a yearning to see her mother, who would give her that luxurious sense of being cared for. Maybe in a few months she could go.

He looked at his watch. "Oh goodness, I'm late for a lesson! I must get up to Stephen Reif."

"You'll come straight back, won't you?"

"Of course." He kissed her and left at a run.

But on the way back, he bumped into Jeremy Morgan and had to hear about Jeremy's wife's operation and tell Jeremy about his own darling baby. Then he decided to stop in a flower shop and buy a rose for Abbie. There happened to be a second-hand book seller on the street outside, and he never could resist a book seller. Francis Bacon's *Novum Organum* was only twenty-five cents. He read the first two pages while walking down the street, causing him to collide with a woman and making her spill her shopping, so he helped her pick up her onions and potatoes and acorn squash, while she ranted at him for his carelessness. He arrived home flustered and had to tell Abbie the whole story, while not even apologizing for being an hour late. She was lying in bed while the baby napped beside her.

"Did Stephen pay you?" Abbie asked.

"No, he's short this month, but he promised to pay next week."

"He owes for a whole month of lessons."

"I know, but his . . . he's had a lot of expenses with his father being ill."

"Walter, we have to pay the rent. We're already a week late."

"Oh, I almost forgot to give you the rose! I had to fold it up in my pocket to help that woman with her groceries." He took out the rose and broke off the bent stem, then offered the rumpled crimson ball on his palm.

Abbie took it and inhaled its sweet musk. "You are a dear one, but you really should not have spent the money when we're so short."

"It's only one, and I so wanted you to have it. I'll get a paper tomorrow and look in the help wanteds." But she could see from his lowered eyes that her reproach, though mild, had wounded him.

"The rose is lovely. I'm so lucky to have you, darling." She leaned forward to give him a kiss.

"Shall I make us some lunch?"

"I already had some."

"Oh, I'm terribly late then. I didn't think . . . I'm so sorry. What a poor excuse for a husband I am. It's a wonder you don't give up on me. Please, please forgive me, darling."

"You know I love you to the ends of the earth," she said. "It's just that I'm a practical person, and I dwell on our needs more than I ought. You are . . ." It was tiring, all the reassuring she had to do. Whatever had happened to the self-sufficiency he had expressed when they were first together, when she did not yet love him? Ivy whimpered, and Abbie stroked the baby's forehead. "I think she's a bit warm. I hope she doesn't have a fever."

Walter put his hand next to Abbie's. "She feels fine to me." He cupped his wife's hand in his and smiled at her imploringly.

She disengaged and picked up Ivy, who was still fussing. "I think she needs a fresh diaper. Would you mind?"

"Not a bit!" He took over, and she sat back with her eyes closed, thinking how lucky she was to have a husband who worshipped her and was willing to deal with diapers. Sometimes his need for her was touching and made her feel special. Other times . . . It wasn't in her nature to complain, but she wished she had Louise to tell her worries to.

Chapter 9

TO DIVORCE

M rs. Lappe has laryngitis and can't read her paper," Mrs. Fulton announced. "Who would like to read it for her?"

No one wanted to read a paper they'd never seen before and hadn't practiced. Abbie, who liked reading, wasn't fearful, but she had delivered her own paper at the previous meeting, and she didn't want to hog the spotlight. Mrs. Fulton tapped her foot. "How about you, Mrs. Bergholtz?" So Abbie read Mrs. Lappe's paper on Thomas Edison, happy in the confidence that she was considered a good reader, perhaps the club's best.

As chair of the Program Committee, she had convinced the club to forgo the custom of picking the culture of a country as the theme this year. Instead, she proposed they study inventions and innovations. The subjects had included photography, electricity, gunpowder, steam engines, the Brooklyn Bridge, and people involved in the creation of such wonders. Everyone agreed it had been a stimulating season of reading. Abbie had missed only six meetings after Ivy's birth, having returned last week to read her paper about the city's subway line.

The doorbell rang twice in the midst of the reading, but she didn't let the interruptions throw her off. The first arrival was Mrs. Everett, who breathlessly apologized that her sister had come late to look after the children. She slipped in and sat down to listen. The second person to arrive told the hostess, Mrs. Varian, in a whisper, that she would stand in the foyer until the reading was over.

As Abbie finished the last paragraph and raised her head to acknowledge the applause, Louise swung into the room on crutches, a white cast peeking out from under the hem of her tailored beige skirt. She looked more vibrant than ever, if a bit thinner than Abbie remembered, a new aura of maturity and self-possession making the crutches seem less a support than an accessory. The ladies flocked around her, asking questions, while Abbie stayed seated, carefully aligning the pages of Mrs. Lappe's report.

"There was an accident at the parade. I don't believe it was deliberate," Louise told them, nodding her thanks to Mrs. Varian, who had brought in an extra chair. "The crowd was out of control."

"Are you still with the suffs?"

"Yes, I'm fundraising for the Woman's Political Union."

"Are you interested in rejoining the club?" Mrs. Fulton inquired. Abbie detected an apprehensive tone.

"I . . . well, no . . . I'm living way downtown. Actually, I came to ask you all a favor. It's a big favor."

"We are not joining the next suffrage parade," said Mrs. Lowitz. "No, absolutely not."

"It's nothing to do with suffrage. I'm divorcing Mr. Blake. He's claiming I'm at fault for abandoning him, so I have to show cause."

"You did abandon him," Mrs. Fulton observed.

"Yes, but for good reason. I have to prove he assaulted me. I need you ladies to go to the central courthouse and give a deposition that you saw me . . ." She drew a paper from her purse. ". . . on April 23, 1912. I had a black eye and a cut on my cheekbone. I told you he had hit me simply because I wanted to go to a woman's club meeting. You just have to swear to those two statements."

"All of it's true," Abbie said, rising from her seat. "Of course, I'll go and swear, if it will help you."

"Thank you," said Louise, sounding surprised and relieved. "Thank you so much."

"I'm happy to do it. Who will go with me?" In fact, Abbie was daunted by the prospect of her first visit to a courthouse. However, she had been horrified by Mr. Blake's violence and appalled by the club members' response on the day in question. They had to make it up to Louise. All the other ladies looked uneasy. No one raised a hand. "It's the least we can do for Mrs. Blake," said Abbie. "We'll go all together, and we'll have an exciting adventure."

There were coughs and rustlings but no volunteers.

"Surely we're all interested in justice, are we not?" Abbie demanded. "As women, we have to help other women if the men will not. That's why we have a woman's club."

"I'll go," said Miss Fulton. It was as if an armchair had spoken. Although the club's youngest member read a short paper from time to time, she did so in the softest and most halting of voices, and she rarely contributed to discussions.

"Jessie!" Mrs. Fulton exclaimed.

"I think it was beastly of Mrs. Blake's husband to hit her. I want to help."

"You are an angel," Abbie said. "Don't worry, Mrs. Fulton, I'll take good care of her. All right, who else will come? I hope you ladies aren't going to allow two of your youngest members to go to the courthouse without mature chaperones."

Mrs. Flint raised her hand. "I've always been against divorce because it undermines the social fabric. But since Mr. Flint died, I often regret the years I wasted living in fear of that so-and-so. I will go to the courthouse."

"I'll go," said Mrs. Everett. "My daughters need to see women band together and help each other."

"It's out of the question for me," said Mrs. Caterson. Her baby had been stillborn the year before, and she was now three months pregnant.

"My husband's on the city council," Mrs. Hoag said. "I'm sure if I go, it will lend weight to the testimony."

"Won't he object?" asked Mrs. Varian. "How will it reflect on him?"

"It's my decision. It's not up to him." Mr. Hoag may have been running the city, but Abbie knew Mrs. Hoag was the one running the family.

Mrs. Lappe was prevented by her laryngitis, and Mrs. Fulton stood her ground, but Mrs. Crump, Lowitz, and Varian all agreed to go. Louise thanked them and wrote down the date and the address for giving the depositions.

"Mrs. Everett," said Mrs. Fulton, "as you arrived late, we skipped the Reception Committee report. Would you like to give it now?"

"Do you mind if I stay?" asked Louise, and she settled back in her chair.

"The Reception Committee," said Mrs. Everett, "has made great strides with the planning. As previously announced, we will meet in the basement of the Presbyterian. Each person will receive a pink carnation upon entering. The table decorations will be clusters of fern with pink bows. We'll serve ice-cream in forms shaped like roses. There will be fancy cakes, candy, nuts, and coffee. Mr. Bergholtz has agreed to bring his quartette and play for us. Mrs. Caterson and I will act out a short farce we wrote, but we're not telling the theme, as it's to be a surprise. Did I leave anything out?"

"Finger bowls," said Mrs. Caterson.

"Oh yes, we'll have finger bowls after the food. Please try to arrive promptly at eight o'clock."

"Ferns as table decorations?" said Mrs. Lowitz. "Don't you think that's going to look silly?"

"We got an excellent price on ferns from the florist on White Plains Road. Flowers are much more costly, and we want everyone to wear a carnation, for the visual effect."

A lengthy discussion ensued, and Abbie saw Louise looking out the window. With the fern issue resolved at last in favor of Mrs. Everett, the meeting broke up. Louise offered to walk Abbie home.

"On crutches?" Abbie asked.

"Oh, it's nothing. I've gotten so strong in the arms, I can walk miles on these things."

Abbie was ready to forgive and forget. So much time had passed since their disagreement. She hoped Louise felt the same way, especially given Abbie's response to her appeal for the deposition. But they walked in awkward silence for three blocks, the crutches tapping rhythmically on the sidewalk.

"You haven't seen my baby," Abbie said finally.

"Is she wonderful?"

"Oh, yes. I adore her. Motherhood makes me happy. And Walter is so gentle with her and so attentive. He even changes her diaper in the middle of the night." She stopped speaking, worried it wasn't polite to brag about her husband when Louise had had such bad luck with hers.

"I'm glad for you. And you're still enjoying the club?"

"Yes, it's so nice to be back the past couple of weeks. It was my idea to have papers on inventions. I'm chairman of the Program Committee."

"That's nice."

They stepped around a group of boys playing marbles on a ring chalked onto the sidewalk.

"I suppose you thought it was silly," said Abbie, "the arguing about ferns."

"We argue too," said Louise, "but about . . . other things . . . how to respond to men shouting that we're ugly spinsters or . . . threatening to knock sense into our heads."

"We are rather frivolous at times."

"Well . . . you're training yourselves."

"Training ourselves? What do you mean?"

"I mean, it's good practice—discussing topics, reading out papers, arguing about anything at all, really."

"Practice for what?" Abbie couldn't keep the sharp edge out of her voice.

"I just think . . . see here, Abbie, it's all well and good to study history and the arts. It's important, in fact, and everyone learns how to speak up in a group. But don't you think clubs should eventually get around to social issues? A lot of them do, you know."

"We've joined the New York Federation of Women's Clubs this year. At the convention in the fall, we're going to collect money to send a fourteen-year-old girl to school and pay her parents the money she would have earned in a sweat shop."

Louise halted and stared at her. "One girl gets to go to high school. You think that's social justice?"

"Of course it is! It'll change her life."

"Yes, it will. It'll alienate her from her illiterate family and leave her friendless, since the high school girls will have nothing to do socially with a girl from the tenements. Meanwhile, every other fourteen-year-old girl on her street will be slaving away in a hot, airless room for twelve hours a day, with no alternative but marriage to some dolt even worse than my husband. And you ladies get to feel good about your heartfelt generosity because each of you invested a dollar in social welfare."

"Mrs. Blake, I can't believe how hard and mean you've become. If that's what being a suffragist has done, I pity you."

"Please don't call me by that name. I'm sorry, Abbie. I really appreciate what you did just now at the club. I don't mean to insult you. It's just that I've had to talk to so many people who understand so little about women and our place in the world. I've learned not to pretend everything is all right when it's so frightfully wrong and unfair. When I speak on street corners and at factories, I meet young women who are scared, poor, exhausted, lots of them pregnant at fifteen. We need laws to help them, to make sure they can *all* go to school. The legislators men elect are not going to make those laws."

"But the families need the money the girls earn. That's why the Federation is raising a scholarship."

Louise sighed. "You're a good woman, and you're doing your best, but you need to research topics besides literature and inventions."

Abbie felt both mollified and condescended to. She had been thinking she might confide in Louise about her problems with Ivy, but now she didn't feel safe. What if Louise was horrified that she had let the baby go ten days with just dribbles of breast milk? They walked on without speaking. At Abbie's front door, she asked Louise, "Will we see you at the courthouse?"

"No, I'm not allowed. But my attorney will be there. He'll explain what to do."

"I hope the depositions will help you."

Abbie was debating whether it would be rude not to invite her in, but Louise said, "I have to go. I'm scheduled to address a group of women at a boot factory on the Lower East Side."

"All right then. Good luck with the divorce." She thrust out her hand, and Louise shook it.

"Thank you. I hope you're very happy with your baby."

Abbie went in, her heart wringing inside out. Why did Louise have to be so critical? Why were husbands so difficult? And how on earth was she supposed to protect fourteen-year-old girls?

Chapter 10

IVY

Ivy went from barely ever crying to wailing for hours each day. She spit up after every bottle and woke hungry two or three times a night. Because she was so small, Abbie didn't dare refuse her a nighttime bottle, but the baby wasn't putting on much weight. At five months, she was only nine pounds.

Abbie stopped going to the Athenaeum Club. She was just too tired, and she didn't feel right about leaving the squalling baby alone with anyone, not even Walter. He had been helpful with Ivy at first, but when he wasn't able to stop her crying, he quickly grew agitated and found excuses to hand her over to Abbie. He made it up to her by doing most of the housework.

With her tenderest parts recovered from the trauma of childbirth, they had resumed sexual relations. Although her desire was much diminished, she felt sorry for Walter, who was tormented by his frustrated passion. She held him off during her fertile time of the month and let him explore her weary body as he wished on other nights, comforted by his affection. Although she was unable to match his ardor, the gentleness of his touch sometimes roused her to unexpected pleasure.

When Ivy learned to sit up by herself, the crying abruptly lessened, and Abbie's life began to right itself again, just as June came, and with it the end of the club season. Instead of having meetings to look forward to, Abbie was still alone in the house with the baby, except when Walter took over to let her go out for a stroll or to do the marketing. One day she dropped by to see Gwendolyn Hoag, and a neighbor informed her the Hoags had gone on vacation. Abbie felt acutely her loneliness without the structure and camaraderie of the club. And still Ivy was not gaining.

At last Abbie talked Walter into letting her go to Chicago, where the fresh air that babies need would be abundant in her uncle's suburban back yard, and she herself could focus all her attention on Ivy's health.

"You must put your foot down," Uncle Al said. "He's got a child now. He has to give up this foolish music career and find a real job. That's all there is to it."

Abbie looked out at the manicured yard, with its yew hedges, three spreading basswoods, beds of coneflowers and black-eyed Susans. The afternoon heat that embraced the porch was made just bearable by ice-cold lemonade and a sultry, intermittent breeze. Ivy was asleep in the go-cart Uncle Al had bought her at the Marshall Field department store on their trip downtown the day before. The cart was a great convenience for walking the city streets and even folded up for train and tram rides. Abbie was grateful but felt each gift from Uncle Al as a reproach aimed at Walter for his failure to provide.

She looked at her mother, hoping for support, but Margaret Robbins stared into her lemonade. Obviously, she and Al had discussed this issue before. "He worked with his brother-in-law for a few months, and they were doing quite well," Abbie said. "Four days a week, he went into the office for at least part of the day. But there was some problem with a demolition Johnny did, and we realized he wasn't entirely on the up-and-up. Walter was really quite good at finding them jobs, though. A letter he wrote was highly praised by a customer."

"And since then?" Uncle Al's eyes were warm with affection as he leaned toward his niece, touching her arm. She was so fond of him, with memories of childhood visits where he had called her his little "What say" and they had joked about keeping their ears clean. She hadn't seen him for twenty years, except when he came East for her wedding, bringing a silver platter as a gift. He had telegraphed his delight on the arrival of Ivy and then sent a long, loving letter. But she had hoped this visit would be relaxing, and she was annoyed at both Al and Walter that she now had to defend her husband.

"Since then, he's been helping with the baby. Really, I don't know what I would do without him. Ivy is so devoted to her papa. And he's gotten three new pupils since May. But it's summer, and all at once, half of his regulars went up to the Catskills on vacation. He's been trying to get work. Really he has."

"I know these musician types. They *live* for their music, supposedly." The word "live" made his hands rise along with his voice. "But they're really just lazy. If they weren't, they'd have real jobs. And you are the one who must make him."

"I do encourage him to look out for work." She chose not to describe how crestfallen he was whenever she brought up work, how his self-loathing set in, and then she had his depression to handle. His reaction didn't stop her from giving him a nudge now and again, but she had to be tactful.

"I can find him a position, you know," said Uncle Al. "It would be in Chicago, or somewhere else in the Midwest. My clients are always looking for bright young men." Al sold office furniture, and his business trips took him to all the states that bordered Illinois.

"I did tell him I was going to consider what it would be like to move West. It's part of why I wanted to come, and I told him that."

"Good girl. All right, then. We'll work on it. And meanwhile, we'll fatten up this darling child of yours."

Relieved by the change of subject, Abbie said, "Do you know I scorched the barley this morning and couldn't use it in her bottle? I had to feed her plain water and milk, and she didn't throw up one bit. I'm wondering if the barley is too heavy for her."

"I think she's looking a bit more plump today," Margaret said.

"Yes, but I don't trust looks. I must weigh her soon."

"Didn't you say you knew a neighbor with scales, Al? We must get hold of them."

"Yes, the Schryvers have got scales," Al replied. "I'll go ask them tonight."

"I think all this fresh air is making her cheeks more pink," said Abbie. "I am so thankful to be here, truly, Uncle Al."

The baby stirred. When Al bent over the go-cart and held out his hand to her, she grabbed his finger, gurgling. "Oh you little packet of sweetness," he said. "As pretty as your mama, and that's saying something." He lifted her up with the ease of a man who has been an attentive father. When he carried her over to Abbie, Ivy clung to his neck instead of reaching for her mother.

"Look how she adores you," said Abbie, thinking of the daughter Al had lost, glad there was something she could give to him.

Walter wrote to her at least once a day. She knew if she did not write back just as often, he would be crushed, and she did want to write. They had never been separated for more than a night since their marriage, two years before. She missed their evenings cuddling together with the baby, the way Ivy fell asleep so trustingly on his chest, the notes of endearment he left under the salt-shaker. So her writing was essentially sincere, but sometimes it was an effort to make her declarations of love approach the intensity of his.

The first few letters to arrive were long, breezy accounts of his hikes around the city ("Walked my self tired"), the meals he cooked for himself ("Potatoes sweet, Potatoes common, Beans—I've strung them!!!!—and Milk omlet"), and a train ride to Bridgeport with Johnny, an unsuccessful attempt to collect money for a job they'd done. Then Walter sent a rambling, incomprehensible essay he'd written on Bacon's *Novum Organum*, asking her opinion, and Abbie wrote that she'd rather respond in person. He clearly had too much time on his hands.

Once he received her first letter, his own became ardent and plaintive.

O my sweetheart your dear letter is only as a sprinkling on a parched longing heart.

The letters became increasingly dramatic.

Cycling home from Mount Vernon, I saw that beautiful Moon—Crooked Faced old Fellow as yellow as Butter as he lazily squinted over eastern hill tops. But now how changed, a bewitching Diana—O yes I think of you my love if I can't see you, I can think you as I please, I can cause my sweet to lay aside her conventional garments and gracefully mount those silvery clouds, tripping nimbly beneath the dark blew star-studded canopy, Her flowing drapery half revealing lips, body, neck . . . well, you see me smile as I whisper to you that your bad, bad boy may have a little Fancy in his soul—O Abbie, what an expression you used! how big with meaning: "My love is all around you."

She read his baroque prose with pleasure, flattered by the yearning declarations of love. And yet, she felt alienated from him. She couldn't tell him about the gentle sparring with Uncle Al over their money problems, nor the anxious shame she felt whenever Al bought her presents—shirtwaists and a summer jacket, things she needed and could not afford. She did write out her relief when the Schryvers loaned her scales that showed Ivy had gained just over a pound in two weeks. She also suggested Walter learn typewriting and shorthand to increase his chances of employment. He picked up a stenography manual at a second-hand bookstore and wrote her postal cards in Pitman shorthand. He sent a letter that included the pleasing line:

I want our Ivy to love a father such as her mother (not like a simple doting mother and wife but as a strong progressive mother, she is).

She left her conflicted emotions unresolved by escaping into the lulling life of the suburbs. Uncle Al continued to dote on Ivy, and her mother's easy-going company was a comfort. Most evenings, they played Flinch, a card game that was sweeping the country. Al, gratified by the baby's progress, urged Abbie to stay through the end of August, and she agreed. Then, when he was off in Michigan, selling desks and filing cabinets, a cry of distress arrived from Walter.

Your uncle Al wrote a letter to me setting a date for your arrival here. Sweet one I do not believe it is selfishness that prompts me. But do not forget that my absolute lonelyness may not be best for you and for Ivy. It may affect my health, and to no purpose. Your dear good uncle, I love for what he is to you, but his simple, inconsiderate arbitrary riding through a bed of roses (that need you, that will not grow when plucked from your bosom) I don't think it would ever be forgiven for you to remain till Nov. 23 Thanksgiving. The thought—four more months—has stunned me, it almost stops my heart.

Abbie showed the letter to her mother. "What is Uncle Al thinking? He never asked me to stay that long. Is he trying to upset Walter?"

Margaret inspected the hem she was stitching. "I suppose he sees how well Ivy is getting along here. And he does love having both of you around."

"Well, I appreciate his hospitality, but he's going to wreck my marriage. What am I going to do about this letter from Walter?"

"Tell him Al was joking and reassure him you won't stay that long."

Abbie took her advice, writing back immediately. She spent the evening helping her mother in the kitchen and playing Flinch after dinner, trying not to think about Walter.

Three days later, she answered the doorbell in the morning, expecting the postman, and there stood her husband, grinning. She lost control. It was their first out-and-out fight, and she was glad Uncle Al wasn't there to witness it.

"How could you spend all that money on the train when we have so little, and now you're losing the income from your pupils besides! Don't you care about our family?"

The grin collapsed. He looked like he was going to cry, and she immediately felt regretful, but it was too late. Her true feelings had come out, and they would not go back inside. "Aren't you glad to see me?" he asked.

She pulled him inside and shut the door. Standing in the foyer, she hissed, "Walter, I love you, but you're not behaving like an adult. You're a father now. Where is the maturity you promised when you asked me to marry you?"

"But . . . but I'm worried I'll lose you. If I am to do battle with your uncle, I'm at a distinct disadvantage being at a far distance. He's trying to take you away from me."

"No, he's not." But she realized, in that moment, that maybe he was. Her confidence flagged.

"It would be unmanly of me not to come and claim you. And I miss you terribly. And Ivy."

"I wrote to you the moment I received your letter about Uncle Al. How many times do I have to tell you I love you before you believe me?" The long-hidden resentment flared in her voice.

"You don't sound like you love me!" His voice was rising, and Abbie worried fleetingly about her mother overhearing, but she decided she didn't care. It was too much effort to hide her feelings.

"I do love you. But I need you to pay attention when I say you're not taking our finances seriously."

"I came all this way out of love for you, and all you can think about is money."

"No, all I can think about is our daughter, who is the reason we need money, so we can take care of her. But you don't worry about her, so I must."

He looked down at the floor, dark hair falling over his eyes. Abbie felt as though she were crushing a tiny, unprotected creature, and she felt terrible. "I'm sorry, my love," he mumbled. "I'll go back." He turned toward the door.

"No. It's silly to go back now."

A voice called from deeper in the house. "What's wrong, Abbie?"

"Nothing, Mother Robbins," Walter called back. "It's Ivy's papa, come to see her."

Margaret came into the foyer with the baby in her arms. "Why, what a surprise!"

"My sweet Dolly!" Walter said.

"Da!" Ivy responded, reaching out her arms.

"You remember me!" Walter gathered her close and crooned, "I was so afraid you would forget your Da-da."

Abbie watched them nuzzle their hellos, like a lion and his cub. Then she said, "Mama, take her out on the

porch, please, and we'll be there in a few minutes."
When Margaret and the baby were gone, she faced
Walter. "Now that you're here, we'll make the best of it.
I'm sorry for what I said." She lifted her hands to his
face. "Let's begin again. Give me a kiss."

He stooped to reach her mouth, and her body
pressed into his, savoring the touch she had been missing. "I'm sorry for wasting our money," he said. "What
can I do to make it up to you, sweetheart?"

She studied the brown eyes, so liquid and beseech-
ing, and knew exactly what to ask for. "While you're
here, you can look for work. If getting a decent job
means moving to Chicago, and being near Mama and
Uncle Al, we just have to consider it. That's all there is
to it."

"Whatever you say, my love. You're in charge of me
now." The sense of power his words gave her was unexpectedly gratifying.

Uncle Al was happy to help set up a series of job in-
terviews for Walter at the offices and emporia of
downtown Chicago, but none of them panned out. After three weeks, Walter went back to the Bronx and
threw himself into cleaning the house in preparation
for Abbie's return. His letters this time were short, protesting his inability to write because of the depression
that had come over him just before leaving. She stayed
another two weeks in Chicago and then took the train
home, bringing a pudgy, lively child and high hopes
that she would be able to shape her husband into a
good provider at last.

Chapter 11

DAMARIS

The ladies of the progressive branch of the New York City social set were no match for the team of Oakley and Kelley. Before calling on a target, Damaris researched the woman's background. Through inquiries, often using her mother as a resource, she inevitably found a personal connection, whether it came through Vassar, marriage to a distant cousin, her father's work contacts, or vacations in Newport. She made a list of people she and the target might know in common, found out the situation of the woman's offspring, and discovered the status of her husband's business. By the time she arrived in the parlor, she was ready to bond over innumerable confidence-provoking topics, and she knew just how much money to ask for.

Louise, meanwhile, prepared a speech on suffrage tailored to the target's interest. To the mother of school-aged children, she pointed out how the Colorado legislature had refused for years to introduce kindergartens into the public school system. When Colorado granted equal suffrage, the kindergarten measure was passed the following year. A target who was in business would hear complaints about the obligation of women to pay taxes despite not having the right to elect the men who imposed those taxes.

For the first month, Louise's arrival on crutches made their dedication to the cause all the more convincing. Nine times out of ten, they left with a check or at least a pledge to consider a donation. Some of the women were so enthused, they promised to speak in favor of woman suffrage at charity events and other occasions. Nearly all of them wanted to be in on the next parade, whenever that might be. Louise kept careful notes of the names, addresses, and research on each woman, as well as the outcome of every visit. However, on the occasions when a woman turned them away without a donation, Damaris went into a funk, and Louise's job included cajoling her into a better mood by listening to a rant about the faults of the woman in question or suggesting a visit to the sweet shop.

Each failure inspired Damaris to take a day off from fundraising, and Louise took advantage of those breaks by going to speak at garment factories, so she could keep up her practice with working-class people. Irish women responded especially well to her speeches, sometimes coming up to her in tears afterward to thank her for trying to get them the vote.

Fundraising was less arduous than organizing a parade, and without a deadline, the two women felt entitled to spend evenings out on the town. Although Damaris had lived in Manhattan as a child, she had boarded elsewhere for most of her schooling, so she had few friends in New York City. Louise became as much a companion as an employee, and without Manhattan friends of her own, she was glad of the company. Nevertheless, she remained aware of the hierarchy of their relationship.

They went to motion pictures and vaudeville shows, which had been an occasional pleasure for Louise in the past, but Damaris introduced her to many other delights of the city. At the Hippodrome, the vast theater on Sixth Avenue, they paid seventy-five cents a seat to see a spectacle entitled *Around the World.* Though billed as a travelogue, the show managed to work in gaudy costumes, a chorus of five hundred, a troupe of acrobats, three live elephants, and a horse that dived into a tank of water.

Another treat was the occasional meal at Horn and Hardart, the automat that had recently opened at Times Square. Each customer gave the cashier a dollar and received a roll of nickels in return. Then she perused the walls of little glass boxes to pick out a sandwich or a hot dish. After inserting the proper number of nickels into a slot next to the box, the customer would hear a click and could then open the glass door of the box to remove the plate of food. The cooking was surprisingly good, and the novelty was amusing.

Two blocks from the automat was Rector's, one of several local "lobster palaces" where they dined one September evening. Louise felt out of place among the pillars, chandeliers, potted palms, and statuary. As they were eating, to the sound of cracking lobster shells, a band came onstage and struck up a ragtime number. All the musicians were black, as were the waiters, although all the customers were white.

"Isn't this fun?" said Damaris, her chin dripping with drawn butter. She picked up the cracking tool and attacked a claw. Louise had to admit she was enjoying the childlike pleasure of destruction, as well as the creamy texture and distinctive, mild flavor of the lobster meat.

"The food is expensive, but these people are not rich," she observed, looking around at the middle-class dress of the customers.

"I think a lot of them are tourists. Or people from New Jersey."

"But on the streets around here, I saw lots of nicely dressed black people. Why don't they eat here?"

Damaris laughed. "You are so naïve. Most white people don't want to eat with Negroes. They aren't allowed in."

"I know that. But if they want to listen to Negro music, why are they afraid to eat with Negroes?"

A baritone voice from the next table replied, "You should go to the Hotel Marshall. White and black people eat together there." The man turning toward them had unruly dark hair, deep-set brown eyes, and heavy eyebrows over a squarish chin and jaw.

"I've heard of the Hotel Marshall," Louise said. "Mabel Mead sings there."

"That's right. What a splendid voice she has! I'm sorry to intrude, but I'm alone tonight. Would you mind if I joined you?"

Louise's impulse was to refuse, but Damaris was smiling. "Please do," she said, "Mr. . .?"

"Jonathan Harris." He shifted his nearly empty plate to their table. "May I buy you ladies some champagne?"

"Oh, no," Louise said. "I don't drink."

"I do," Damaris said. "I'd love a glass."

Mr. Harris ordered a bottle from a passing waiter, then told his new table-mates, "The Marshall has better music than this place, and the crowd over there is first-class. All sorts of famous people are regulars."

Damaris put her chin on a hand and leaned toward him. "For instance?"

"Well, the best Negroes in the city go there. W.E.B. Du Bois, Williams and Walker, Eubie Blake, Paul Laurence Dunbar." He was looking at Louise, checking to see how impressed she was, and it must have showed that she had no idea who these celebrities were. "They're mostly musicians and poets," Mr. Harris said. "Du Bois is a writer. Very intelligent. I've spoken to him a few times."

"Are there famous white people too ?"

"Quite a few actors and singers. Do you know Lillian Russell?"

"Of course. I've seen her in vaudeville shows, and she's always in the papers. She got married for the fourth time just a few months ago."

"She comes in with her good friend Diamond Jim Brady, one of the richest men in America. Oh, do those two love to eat! They shovel it in, the both of them."

"It sounds like you spend a lot of time at the Marshall," Louise said.

"I'm a real estate agent, representing properties in Harlem. Quite a few Negroes have bought apartment buildings up there, and they're renting to other Negroes, a lot of them from this neighborhood. My clientele and my competitors go to the Marshall, and I have to keep up with 'em, don't I?"

Mr. Harris kept addressing his remarks largely to Louise. She found him attractive, but she didn't want to compete with Damaris, who was now sipping champagne and bidding for his attention by saying, "Yes, I heard there was a real estate boom in Harlem."

He turned toward Damaris. "It's becoming a popular neighborhood for Negroes of a decent class. Rich people used to live there, so there are big buildings, beautiful parks, and wide streets. Now that the poor Italians and Jews are moving away, new stores and nightclubs are opening. There's a lot of opportunity for a smart businessman." He looked back at Louise. "I can take you up there someday if you'd like to see my buildings. They're pretty sharp-looking."

"I'm finished eating," said Louise. She hoped to reconfigure the situation and prevent Damaris from downing too much champagne, which she was not in the habit of drinking. "I'd like to go over to the Hotel Marshall and see if Miss Mead is singing."

"I was just about to go there myself. I can drive you over." While Mr. Harris waved for the check, Louise exchanged a look with Damaris, who was glowering. Louise tried unsuccessfully to signal that she had no designs on the fellow. Mr. Harris insisted on paying their tab, and the women went out front, waiting for him to bring his automobile around.

"You're flirting with him," Damaris accused.

"Not a bit. I'm not interested in him at all."

"Don't lie to me."

"I'll admit he's good-looking, but men right now hold no—"

"I just don't want to see you get hurt."

"Hurt? What do you mean?"

"I mean he's probably interested in a certain social class, and when he realizes where you come from . . ." Louise, although offended, said nothing. Damaris paid her salary, and Louise wasn't going to point out that she herself was obviously more attractive to Mr. Harris. "Just find some way to bow out, all right?" Damaris said, as the motor pulled up. "Oh my, how fancy!"

Mr. Harris leapt from the shiny maroon Pierce-Arrow and ran around to pull open the door to the back seat. "Why don't you sit in front, Damaris?" Louise suggested, sliding onto the seat. She was gratified by his look of disappointment. It served Damaris right, although at that moment, she wasn't looking, engrossed as she was in admiring the automobile.

The sleek Pierce-Arrow was luxurious compared to the Model T that had conveyed Louise to Manhattan a few months earlier. Unless Mr. Harris had rich parents, he must be making a bundle up in Harlem. Louise settled into the spacious back seat, determined to remain silent through the nine-block ride up Broadway and then across 53rd Street. Their progress was slow, as they veered around wagons and braked for heedless pedestrians. Mr. Harris drove with casual skill and confidence, one elbow out the side window. "So what brings you ladies to Times Square?" he asked.

"We're in need of entertainment," said Damaris. "We've been working for suffrage."

"'Votes for Women!' Yes, you ladies certainly deserve to have a say in the government. I'm all for woman suffrage."

"I'm so glad to hear that, Mr. Harris. So many men have a pig-headed attitude about giving us the vote."

"Are you out speaking on street corners, trying to convert the pig-headed?"

It was hard for Louise not to mention that she had, in fact, spoken on street corners, and quite successfully.

Of course, Damaris would not report that fact. "No, we're raising money for the organization. In fact, maybe we could induce you to give a donation. Surely you have a bit of cash to spare."

Mr. Harris laughed, a bit nervously, Louise thought. "We'll see about that later."

"Mostly we call on society women my family are acquainted with, and tell them about the importance of getting the vote. We've done quite well so far."

"Tell me, Miss . . . oh, but I haven't found out your names yet."

"I'm Miss Oakley, and Miss Kelley is my secretary."

"Pleased to meet you both. Miss Kelley, how did you hear of Mabel Mead?"

"Oh . . . she marched in our parade," Louise replied.

"I see." A tense silence stretched for the last block, and then they pulled up in front of a five-story building. It had stepped cornices under the lip of the roof, arched windows, and a line of automobiles out front. "I'll have to park down the street. I'll meet you inside."

As Damaris got out, she slammed the door, then stalked on ahead. Louise, taking pity on her companion, decided to make peace. She caught up and murmured, "I think he likes you, but he's shy about it. And he doesn't want me to feel left out."

Damaris halted. "Do you really think so?"

"Oh, yes. I see it in his eyes."

Damaris gave her hand a squeeze. "I doubt it, but you're sweet to say so. Let's go in." Relieved, at least for the moment, Louise followed her through the double wooden doors.

The Marshall was elegant in an understated way, less pretentious than the lobster palace. Crimson velvet draperies muted the chatter of a roomful of people sitting at round tables with white cloths. The air was thick with laughter and cigarette smoke. Glasses clinked at the long, curved bar as four bartenders served a steady stream of customers. The small stage was empty except for an upright piano. A maître d' escorted Louise and Damaris to a table off to the side of the room. At the next table, a dark-skinned man with rimless eyeglasses was telling two white men, "I'm sorry, my orchestra only plays music written by black composers."

"But Mr. Europe, Antonin Dvořák based parts of his Symphony Number Nine on Negro spirituals," said one of the white men. "If a Negro orchestra were to play it . . . why, we could get you into Carnegie Hall."

"Where do you yokels come from? We've already played Carnegie Hall."

A black waiter appeared. Damaris asked for red wine, and Louise ordered lemonade.

They spotted a man worming his way through the crowd in their direction, having a difficult time of it because of the paunch that poured over his belt and kept catching on chairs. He never bothered to excuse himself but plunged onward until he was standing over the two women. He took off his rolled-brim hat and said in a scratchy voice, "Allow me to order you lovely ladies a drink." He was dressed smartly enough, but the paunch and the strings of hair combed over his bald head interfered with his dignity.

"No, thank you," Damaris said. "We're just fine. We've already ordered."

"Well then, let me pay for your drinks." He plunked down into a chair and took his wallet from a jacket pocket. He laid the wallet on the table, open so they could see the tens and twenties on the corners of the slightly fanned-out bills.

"Her gentleman friend will be back from parking his automobile any moment now," said Louise. "I don't think he would be happy to see you sitting with us, and he has a terrible temper."

The man glanced around, then put the wallet back in his pocket and placed both hands on the table to support himself in the effort to stand up. As he walked away, Louise heard him mutter, "Snooty dames."

They waited till he was well across the room before they started to giggle. "So clever of you," Damaris said.

"What an unsavory character!"

Damaris pointed. "Oh, there's Mr. Harris."

Louise turned to see their escort, who was walking past the bar. He was intercepted by a willowy black woman in a flowing, pale blue gown. She was about to embrace him when a middle-aged, impeccably suited black man touched her shoulder. She stepped back. The three of them had a whispered conversation, and then she drifted off to the other end of the bar. Mr. Harris threaded his way to the table.

"Is that woman your girlfriend?" Damaris asked.

"She's a singer with the band. And that was Jimmie Marshall, who owns the place. He was warning us about a spy."

"A spy?"

"Have you heard of the Committee of Fourteen?"

"I have," said Damaris. "It's group of rich people, a self-appointed vice squad. My father knows two of their members."

"They try to shut down hotels that rent rooms to prostitutes."

"Isn't that the job of the police?" Louise asked. "Prostitution isn't legal."

"The police have no problem taking bribes in this part of town."

"Well then, it's a good thing, isn't it, if this committee could stop prostitution at the hotels?"

"I suppose. The problem is, now they've decided to shut down places where whites and blacks socialize."

"But that's not a vice."

"Not to you. But suppose a white man and a black woman decided to have . . . well . . . relations. And suppose they had a child. Wouldn't that be terrible?"

"I don't think so."

"Well, the Committee of Fourteen thinks so. After all, when those tan kids grow up, people might get confused about whether they're white or not, and then how do you know who's on top? They've sent inspectors, that is, spies, trying to find a reason to shut down the Hotel Marshall. This is a respectable place, and Jimmie is a law-abiding fellow, so they've always failed. But now he says they're trying again."

"How does he know?" asked Damaris.

"The man just has a look about him, you know? Fat man with an automobile and a fat wallet." Louise and Damaris started to giggle again. "Excuse me, there's someone I have to talk to." Mr. Harris headed back through the sea of tables and sat down with a young black couple.

Damaris shifted into a chair next to Louise so she could whisper. "Do we look like whores?"

"No, of course not. Why?"

"Because if that man was from the Committee, and he was showing us his money, it's because he hoped one of us would make him a proposition, and then he could shut down the place."

"Oh. Well no, we don't look like whores. It's just that we were sitting here without a man."

"Dammit. When we get the vote, we've got to—"

The waiter arrived with their drinks. A pianist and a guitarist appeared onstage and launched into a rag, prompting several people to head for the dance floor. The second number started out easy and languid, like slowed-down ragtime. Louise had never heard music with just that slide and skip, with a light coolness. Half the dancers sat down. Among those that remained, the women draped themselves over the men and swayed to the beat. Then Mabel stepped onto the stage, and her silky alto flowed out over the tables.

The chatter in the room had not lessened for the other musicians, but Mabel's voice quieted the crowd with mesmerizing, gliding tones. She sang about love and yearning, or she just sang sounds, "aaaah" or "ooooh." Heads nodded along. As Louise listened, she had the sensation of walking underwater, swayed by rippling currents. After four songs, Mabel left the stage to enthusiastic applause.

"Wasn't that strange music?" Louise asked.

"Quite unusual," Damaris agreed.

Mabel slipped into a chair next to Louise. "What are you doing here? I'm so happy to see you."

"You were wonderful!" They embraced briefly. "But what was that music you were singing?"

"Did you like it? This place is great for trying new things. A fellow from Memphis came through last month, and we've been bringing in some of his ideas too."

Mr. Harris returned to greet Mabel and report, "Patrick told Jimmie he knows that big fellow, and he says he's all right. So I'm allowed to give you a hug, Mabel."

"Isn't he sweet?" Mabel said to Louise. "I'm glad you met Jonathan. Anyway, I'd love to chat, but I have to go sing at another club. Come see me again some time."

The band went back to ragtime and were joined by another singer, the woman in the blue gown. On the dance floor, Louise noticed a white woman clinging to the shoulder of a black man. She looked around for Jimmie Marshall and saw him relaxing at a table, smoking with a group of men. The volume of conversation rose as the liquor continued to flow.

"So what do you think of the Hotel Marshall?" Mr. Harris asked her.

"I like it here. It's so . . . alive. Although many of these people seem drunk. That's just not to my taste."

"I see, you're an innocent."

She wondered if he could be reformed in terms of alcohol, then remembered she wasn't supposed to be interested in him.

When Damaris said she wanted to go, Mr. Harris drove them home. As he opened the back door of the automobile for Louise, he slipped her a business card. She didn't mention the card to Damaris, who said, as the motor disappeared down the block, "Oh, darn, we forgot to get his donation."

Then she hiccupped and wove her way from the sidewalk into the townhouse.

Each month, Louise sent her mother money, giving the WPU office as a return address. The letters she received in reply were plaintive but full of the

neighborhood gossip Mama relished. She never mentioned Charles or his father, although she did refer
often to Mrs. Blake, sometimes as a conspirator in the
realm of gossip, other times with a critical tinge, due to
the woman's bad temper or harsh remarks about the
Irish. But overall, Louise felt her mother was in better
hands with the Blakes than she would have been living
with a daughter whose lifestyle was straying leagues
away from her Catholic upbringing. She put aside the
plan to live with her mother.

Once a week, she went with Damaris to the WPU office to deliver their latest haul of checks. No
renovations had occurred, and Louise wondered how
Mrs. Blatch had managed to get rid of Charles. Women
at the office conveyed encouraging news from Albany.
By the end of the summer, the WPU had secured
promises from the Republicans, the Democrats, and
the Progressives that all three parties would include
suffrage planks in their campaign platforms. Surely the
legislature elected in November would pass a measure
calling for a popular referendum on suffrage for New
York State. Furthermore, there were six other states
about to vote on suffrage, and they all looked promising.

Mrs. Blatch was so optimistic, she decided it was
time for another parade, one of celebration rather than
protest. She and her lieutenants were worn out from
the summer of lobbying, so she let the Woman Suffrage Party take the lead. The WSP were, in Mrs.
Blatch's opinion, too mild-mannered to be effective as
suffragists, but they could handle a celebration. Harriet
Burton Laidlaw, who had just been made WSP's Manhattan borough president, took charge of the planning.
Damaris's father was second cousin to Mrs. Laidlaw's

husband, a financier and president of the Men's League for Women's Suffrage. Damaris brought Mrs. Laidlaw the names of the society ladies who had expressed interest in a parade. In return, she was welcomed to help out as organizer.

Thus Louise found herself seated at a strategy meeting in the Fifth Avenue office of the National American Woman Suffrage Association, known as "the National," which offered its space to affiliated groups such as Mrs. Laidlaw's WSP. In the light admitted by windows overlooking the bustle of 42nd Street, Louise placed her notepad on the vast table of carved black walnut in the National's reception room and waited to hear Mrs. Laidlaw's directives. Their glamorous leader, an energetic, curly-haired woman in her late thirties, stood at the head of the table, dressed in white silk, and waited for the dozen women seated in the walnut chairs to stop their chatter. Without preamble, she launched into her shocking pronouncement.

"We're going to have a torchlight parade. We'll start just after sundown and march with lanterns, candles, miner's lamps, automobiles, searchlights. It'll be vast and brilliant, one long blaze of glory. The world will have to take notice."

The women sitting around the table looked at each other. "But women don't go out on the street at night," said Miss Winston. "It's not respectable."

"Who knows what kind of ruffians will be out and about?" Mrs. Tillinghast said. "It could be dangerous. And afterwards, women will have to travel home in the dark, possibly alone."

"I walked through the Bronx alone at three in the morning once," Louise declared. She was only there as a secretary, so she wasn't really supposed to speak, but after all, she was a suffragette, meant to be forthright with her opinions. "I was frightened, but I survived. Anyway, we should have the right to be out at night if we want. We're not prostitutes." The two middle-aged ladies who had just spoken stared at her.

Mrs. Laidlaw gave Louise an appreciative smile. "The point is, if we hold it at night, the industrial workers will be able to come. We'll get an extra five thousand marching, and who knows how many spectators. And just think how spectacular it will be."

"It will prove to people how serious we are," Damaris pointed out. "Just that we're willing to put up with the risk shows how much we want the vote."

"Exactly," said Mrs. Laidlaw. "And the newspapers will give us lots of coverage. We can't have a parade just like the one six months ago. We need something fresh."

The discussion went on for three days, and Mrs. Laidlaw got her way. Once the police chief was talked into granting a permit, he vowed to station twenty officers per block along the parade route, plus a cadre of mounted police, to prevent the May parade's disaster.

Five thousand paper lanterns were ordered from Paris. Damaris went back to her donors and signed most of them up either to march or to bring their automobiles. Louise went back to street corner speaking, accompanied by Miss Winston to hand out bills and pledge cards.

She was at the office one evening, looking through the thirty-three pledges collected that day, when Damaris burst through the door and hurried to her side. "You can't possibly guess what I just heard!"

"What's happened?"

"Inez Milholland is coming on the parade. She's going to be Wyoming." Mrs. Laidlaw planned to have six golden chariots, one for each of the states that already had suffrage. Wyoming had been the first to give women the vote, so it was an honor to drive the Wyoming chariot. "I haven't seen Inez since graduation day," said Damaris. "And there's more—she's also going to the National convention."

When women in the office were not talking about the parade, they were discussing the annual convention of the National American Woman Suffrage Association, to be held in Philadelphia in late November. Damaris had considered attending but told Louise it would probably be terribly dull. Now she exclaimed, "Everyone is going to be there. Jane Addams, Anna Howard Shaw, Alva Belmont. And Mrs. Blatch is going."

"I thought Mrs. Blatch despised the National. She thinks the members are timid and lack imagination."

"True, but it's the biggest suffrage organization in the country, and of course she's a member."

"I didn't realize that."

"She has to keep an eye on them. Some people think Anna Shaw is going to lose the presidency. Mrs. Blatch wants to have her say."

"So you wish to go?"

"Yes, I'd like you to arrange train reservations, a hotel room, and tickets to the convention, as soon as possible."

"I'm coming along?"

"Yes, of course! I couldn't manage without you."

In late October, Damaris took a day off to visit her parents on Washington Square. Louise was not invited, so she found the business card for Harlem Homes and called Jonathan Harris, using the telephone Damaris had just had installed at the townhouse.

They met at a nearby Italian restaurant. Over *zuppe di pesce,* he told her what had happened to the Hotel Marshall. "The fellow with the big wallet did turn out to be a spy for the Committee of Fourteen. A few days later, their chairman called Jimmie Marshall into his office and threatened him. I didn't find out exactly what was said, but he was forced to sign a paper promising he'd make separate facilities for blacks and whites."

"But New York State has laws against segregation," said Louise.

"They don't care. They're going to find some way to shut him down, I just know it."

"That's so sad."

She told him about her suffrage work, and he talked about real estate. Louise relaxed in the restaurant's homely atmosphere. With the weight of steady parade work momentarily lifted, she was enjoying his company.

"I asked Mabel about you," he said. "She thinks you're a courageous woman."

"Hm. That's nice."

"But she wouldn't tell me why. I got the feeling she had met you somewhere besides that parade."

Louise ate the last of her soup and laid down the spoon. "So?"

"I'd like to hear how you met."

"I think it's impertinent of you to ask."

"No doubt it is."

Louise stared down at the soup bowl, as her relaxation turned to annoyance. "Why do you insist on asking then?"

"Because you interest me, and I want to know more about you. I'm sorry. I've ruined your mood. Why don't you ask me some questions?"

"All right." She paused as the waiter removed their bowls from the table. "Tell me where you grew up."

"In the Tenderloin, on 30th Street. It was a rough neighborhood, and it still is."

"Where are your parents from?"

"Raleigh, North Carolina."

"Why did they come to New York?"

"Ah, now I could make up a story. I could say they came for wider opportunities. The real reason is something I don't usually tell."

"And why is that?"

"Not everyone is sympathetic. I'm willing to tell you because . . . I think you're different. But if I tell you, then you must tell me how you met Mabel."

"You are a most unusual man, Mr. Harris."

"I suspect you are an unusual woman. Shall we share our secrets? Or should we go home not really knowing each other?"

She felt breathless, seduced by his directness. She remembered Mabel had called her courageous. "All right, if you tell me, then I will tell you."

"Do you promise?"

"As long as your secret is worthy of mine."

He laughed. "I'll bet it is."

"You tell first."

He looked straight in her eyes as he told his story. "My father's family came over from Scotland generations ago and set up a whisky distillery. My father worked as an accountant in the family business. My mother was the daughter of a plantation overseer and a

slave, his wife's maid. After the war, when my grandmother was freed, she took my mother to Raleigh, and
they got work in the kitchen at my father's family's
house. When my parents fell in love and announced
they were going to marry, his family disowned him.
That's why they came to New York. The question is,
what about me? I have one Negro grandparent and
three white grandparents. Am I a Negro?"

She considered his deep brown eyes, his curly but
not kinked hair, his skin just a shade darker than her
own. "I never suspected. I thought you might have Italian blood, or Greek."

"The U.S. of A.'s one-drop rule says I'm black, without a doubt."

"One-drop rule?"

"One drop of African blood does it. But to look at,
I'm white. Are we who we think we are or who other
people think we are? I ponder that question a lot."

"I think I know what you mean. Women often find
themselves in a similar dilemma. But I suppose it's
even harder for Negroes."

"Have I shocked you?"

"You've surprised me, but . . . well, I liked the Hotel
Marshall. Now I understand why you seemed so comfortable there."

"I'm not that comfortable anywhere, but at least
there I have some sense of belonging."

"Do they know? At the Marshall?"

"If I want them to know, I let them know. But otherwise, most white people don't."

"But I don't understand why you've told me such . . .
such a deep secret. Aren't you afraid I'll reveal it to
people who might . . . mistreat you?"

He shook his head. "A year ago, I was courting a white woman almost as beautiful as you. We had been together for six months, and I felt it was time to tell her the truth because I wanted to marry her. When I told her, she was angry, not about my Negro blood but because I hadn't told her about it. She broke it off with me and married another man. If I'm going to keep company with you, as I wish to do, it will be on the basis of clear honesty. And I saw how much you liked Mabel and the scene at the Marshall."

"I see." Louise was flattered and moved.

"All right, now it's your turn."

"I'm afraid my secret isn't nearly as dramatic as yours. My husband hit me, and I ran away in the middle of the night. I got lost and met Mabel. She and her manager drove me to where I was going, the suffrage office. Now I'm trying to get a divorce. That's all."

"In the middle of the night. I'd say you certainly *were* courageous."

"I was more desperate than brave. But very few people know about my marriage. Please don't tell anyone."

"Of course not. We'll both be pledged to silence." His somber look gave her a thrill of pleasure, suggesting they were already bonded in secrecy.

The waiter served their *manicotti*, and they turned to more mundane topics. By the time the *cannoli* arrived for dessert, they were laughing together. As he walked her home, she realized she had never felt so close to a man, her husband included. In the shadows at the front door, he put his arms around her, and before she could think twice, they were kissing. Even though it was only their second meeting, she ached for a deeper physical union, but such behavior, without marriage, was outside the realm of possibility. She didn't mind that Mr. Harris was one-quarter black, but the risk of pregnancy loomed large, and besides, Louise was not a loose woman.

The November 5 election results brought euphoria. Voters in Arizona, Kansas, Oregon, and Michigan passed suffrage referendums, making a total of ten states where women could vote. The New York legislature tilted toward the Democrats, the party most staunch in their support of suffrage, virtually guaranteeing that a law would be passed calling for a New York referendum on the woman vote. On the other hand, Woodrow Wilson had been elected president, and although he was a Democrat, he had so far failed to endorse suffrage. Nevertheless, the parade would truly be a celebration.

On November 9, at 8:15 in the evening, Louise, in a white dress with a yellow muslin shawl across her shoulders and a purple sash around her waist, was stationed at 41st Street and Fifth Avenue, holding a bucket of candle stubs. Her job had been assigned by Mrs. Tillinghast, who was in charge of the spherical orange paper lanterns, which resembled pumpkins by day and were meant to become harvest moons when lit by candles at night. Louise had at least been allowed to select her post, in front of the main public library, guarded by its alert pair of marble lions. Although she was apprehensive about the crowds after her previous parade debacle, there were eight policemen within her line of sight, and she felt, against pure logic, that the library lions would protect her. Besides, she had made it a policy, after surviving her nighttime trek through the Bronx, that fear would not rule her.

So far, the crowds appeared orderly, at least on this corner. They stood five deep under the electric arc lights of the streetlamps, many people with umbrellas raised against the drizzle. Others held small purple and yellow "Votes for Women" pennants, sold for ten cents apiece by street urchins who normally hawked wilted violets or penny candies. Seventeen blocks to the north, the parade had already begun, and strains of the march from *Aida* drifted down the avenue. All eyes were turned uptown as the horse brigade took shape in the distance. Every horse in the parade was white or the palest of gray. The cheering of the crowd rippled south as the horsewomen progressed.

Soon Louise could see the lights of lanterns on sticks, held by over a hundred National members, who marched just behind the horses. It was, as Mrs. Laidlaw had predicted, a breathtaking sight, the darkness broken by bright bobbing globes that cast an orange glow over the women in white. As the marchers passed the library, her focus shifted to the scattering of globes that were dark. Instead of paying for five thousand brand-new candles, Mrs. Laidlaw had sent out a call for households to contribute the stubs of used candles, although they were bound to expire right in the midst of the march.

Louise darted through the ranks and fell into step alongside a woman with an unlit lantern. The woman lowered her globe. Into the puddle of wax in the tin socket suspended within, Louise pressed a stub from her bucket and reached in to light the wick. Without waiting for thanks, she sidled over to the next dark lantern. For the next two hours, she marched with the National women, all the way to Union Square, spotting lanterns as they went out and restoring light from her bucket.

Occasionally she looked back at the gold chariots, which were next in line. Miss Milholland, wearing Grecian robes and handling the reins of a white mare, was a marvelous specimen of feminine strength and beauty. She ignored the crowd, gazing straight ahead as if looking into a transcendent future. Behind the chariots came floats for each of the new suffrage states.

The band took a break, and Louise could hear the hundred fifty members of the chorus singing "The Woman's Battle Song." Their united voices soared overhead, as she continued to march in the midst of a sea of women in white. She gloried in the sense of being part of a movement, as if she were both a speck being swept along by an irrepressible tide and an element of that tide, contributing in small ways that were nevertheless essential to the success that would undoubtedly come.

As the National group poured into Union Square, the horses, chariots, and floats went onward, and the ranks of marchers gathered in a steadily growing crowd around the speaker's platform. Louise dropped off her bucket behind the platform, then watched the other suffrage organizations flood in, followed by the Men's League, the Prohibitionists, the Socialists, and the Progressives. Wandering through the crowd, she marveled at the number of women and men who had come together to support the right for half the country's population to vote.

She listened to the speeches for an hour, thinking how circumstances—college, her father's departure, the Athenaeum Club, marriage and violence, a chance encounter with suffs—had all conspired to bring her to this place and time. A conviction was growing that she had not fallen into this path by chance but had been led to a true purpose for her life. Someday, she would study literature again. But it would have to wait until this great goal had been accomplished.

Chapter 12

PHILADELPHIA

"M"ichigan" was the word on everyone's lips the day Louise and Damaris arrived at the Hotel Walton in Philadelphia for the National convention. "Did you hear? After we won in Michigan, liquor interest shenanigans stole the vote."

"The scoundrels in Michigan are terrified voting women will bring about Prohibition."

"They contested counties in Michigan and reversed the decision by 762 votes."

"Irregularities in Michigan" . . . "stuffed ballot boxes" . . . "ballots marked both yes and no" . . . "anti literature right in the booths."

"Michigan proves it—men are incorrigible."

Louise was barely listening, so awed was she by the brick-red turrets of the Hotel Walton, the massive double arches of the entrance, the marble and onyx walls of the lobby. The curved vault of the lobby ceiling was pierced with a long skylight, and every inch of the room that was not windowed was carved with curlicues and floral motifs. Her feet sank into a deep burgundy carpet, passing plush-seated benches and leather armchairs arranged around enormous mahogany tables.

Damaris, accustomed to such luxury, was focused on the women. "Look, there's Alva Belmont." She pointed out a broad-shouldered woman in a purple satin fur-trimmed suit, surrounded by fawning women.

"Who is she?"

"The richest, most scandalous of all the suffs. She divorced her husband, a Vanderbilt who had been unfaithful. Then she married a Belmont, and now she's widowed and has made suffrage her new project. She financed the National headquarters in New York."

"Who's that, talking to Mrs. Blatch?"

"Dr. Anna Shaw. She always wears black. Oh my, there's Inez!" Damaris grabbed Louise's hand and dragged her over to Miss Milholland, who had just descended the marble stairs from the balcony. Her alabaster skin contrasted with her navy blue cloak and a round blue hat with a few pink feathers. She had large blue eyes, one slightly higher than the other, a straight, patrician nose, and full, rose-colored lips. "Hello Inez, you're looking fabulous!" Damaris gushed.

"Why, thank you," replied Miss Milholland with a puzzled look. "And you are . . . ?"

"Damaris Oakley, from Vassar. I was the Statue of Liberty in your tableau."

"Yes, of course, so good to see you. Are you a member of the National?"

"I've been working with Mrs. Blatch and the WPU. I helped organize—"

"Thank you so much for your service to the cause," said Miss Milholland, turning to a woman who was clutching her sleeve with an urgent request.

Damaris slunk away, muttering, "Of course, Inez always was a bit of a snob." She went into a sulk. Louise took over the decision-making. She towed Damaris to the front desk, inquired for their room number, and indicated their luggage to the bellhop. They crowded into the elevator with women discussing Michigan, and Damaris found an outlet for her frustration by adding more outrage to the general conversation.

At their room, Louise tipped the bellboy. When he left, she was about to flop onto one of the beds when she heard Damaris, still in the hallway, say, "Oh my, Edward, I haven't seen you since Cousin Lawrence's wedding! What on earth are you doing here?"

Louise went to the door and saw a young man in a brown suit with a starched collar. He had blond hair parted in the center, a short, sandy mustache, and an underbite. "I'm in town on business. My father has me selling office equipment—typewriting machines, adding machines, telephones. I'm sure I know why you're here—the suffs."

Damaris laughed in agreement, her mood thoroughly altered. "We had such good fun at that wedding. Although my gown was quite ruined when I fell into the pond."

"It was lucky my sister was your size."

"And had packed an extra dress. That was so long ago. Look at us now, being so serious and boring—you a salesman, me a suffragette."

"Oh, I heard the suffs can be pretty wild. And who is this lady?"

Edward nodded to Louise, and Damaris glanced back. "My assistant, Miss Kelley. Louise, meet Mr. Edward Jones, the nephew of my cousin's wife. We're here for a week, Edward. I hope to see you again."

"Inquire for me at room 311." He gave Damaris a coy look. "From the hotel desk, I mean."

"I certainly shall."

The next day, during the opening ceremonies at Independence Square, Damaris lasted only half an hour before she complained of a headache and said she was going back to the hotel. All week long, she met Louise for breakfast in the hotel dining-room, then jaunted off to visit college friends who lived in the Philadelphia suburbs. Louise went to the Witherspoon, an eleven-story office building, where she sat in the great hall and listened to a bewildering succession of reports, speeches, and debates.

The women wrangled over how to make use of donations, whether to keep the headquarters in New York, and whether to censure Jane Addams. The renowned founder of Hull House in Chicago, the first of the settlement houses established to help poor people, Miss Addams had dared to venture into party politics, against the policy of the National. Apparently she had endorsed and even campaigned for Theodore Roosevelt in his effort to take back the U.S. presidency as a candidate for the new Progressive Party. She was too famous and respected to earn a formal reprimand, but the debate over her action took up an entire afternoon. Louise wondered why the members spent so much time arguing about how to run the organization, rather than discussing strategies for winning the vote.

Each night, Damaris returned to the hotel for dinner, then went out dancing with Edward Jones. He

offered to find a date for Louise, but she was determined to obtain an education from the convention and
did not want to be bothered with men.

Two days before the convention ended, she woke up
at dawn and found her roommate had not slept in the
other bed. Alarmed, she was on the verge of calling the
hotel's security force when the door opened. Damaris
slipped into the room, dreamy-eyed, dress wrinkled,
hair in tangles, hat missing, coat draped over one arm.
She tossed the coat onto a chair and sprawled on the
undisturbed bed.

"Are you all right?" Louise asked.

"Oh, yes, I certainly am."

"Are you drunk?"

"Drunk with . . . joy."

"Where have you been?"

"In room 311. A wonderful room." She flung one
arm up in the air and let it drop to the bedspread.

"You spent the night with Mr. Jones?"

"Ah, yes. Mr. Jones."

"But did you . . . I mean—"

"That's right. I'm no longer a virgin. At last."

"But . . . but . . . is he going to marry you?"

"Of course not. It's nothing like that. Anyway, I don't
want to get married." She went to the dresser and started brushing her hair, wincing as she hit the knots.

"But what if you get pregnant?"

"I won't. He used a condom."

"Oh. Are you sure they really work?"

"As long as it's made right, and it doesn't break. This
one seemed fine."

"But where did he get it?"

"He was in England a few months ago." Damaris caught her eye in the mirror. "I've scandalized you, haven't I?"

"Well . . . I'm not accustomed to the idea of . . . of relations without marriage."

"If Inez can do it, I can too. I just had to find the right man. Do you think I should get my hair bobbed?" Damaris threw down the brush and tied a ribbon at the base of her neck instead of braiding the still knotted hair. "I am in desperate need of a nap. I'll see you tonight at dinner."

Louise wanted to ask more, but she had been dismissed. She dressed and went down to breakfast, trying to decide whether Damaris was immoral or simply modern.

That midnight, Louise was awakened by her roommate tiptoeing into the room.

"You're not staying with Mr. Jones tonight?"

"No!" Damaris lit the bedside lamp and began to undress, flinging clothes onto the floor.

"What happened?"

"He was awful. He brought a flask of whisky to the dance hall and got himself drunk. Then he made fun of me for not drinking as much as he did, even though I told him about the terrible hangover I had last time. When we went back to his room, I was so annoyed with him, I almost didn't go inside, but he pulled me in and started to paw at me."

"How unpleasant!"

"Even so, I wanted to lie with him, just from the memory of last night. But when we got our clothes off, it turned out he had no more condoms. Can you believe it?" Damaris wriggled into her nightgown.

"I'm so glad you left."

"And he didn't want me to go. He got a long scratch on his cheek for trying to hold me there. Men! They are disgusting."

"I'm so sorry for you!"

Damaris turned out the light and slid under the covers. The sound of soft weeping prompted Louise to reach a hand across the gap between the beds. Damaris gripped her fingers for a few minutes, sniffling in the dark. Then she whispered, "Thank you," and they both went to sleep.

The next morning, the final day of the convention, Damaris came along to hear the closing remarks by Dr. Shaw, who had been reelected president, although by a narrower margin than in the past. While crossing the Witherspoon's expansive foyer, as the three hundred delegates trickled into the main hall, Damaris spotted an elderly woman surrounded by a cluster of attentive ladies. "Isn't that Jane Addams?" Damaris asked.

"Yes, I believe it is."

"And who is that young creature standing next to her?"

"That's Alice Paul, the Quaker who was in England with the Pankhurst women. She spoke about Susan B. Anthony on the first day of the convention."

"I wonder what's going on. Let's go listen."

They burrowed through the crowd until they were close enough to hear Miss Addams declaring her intention to support Miss Paul in her plans to create a mammoth parade in Washington, DC, on the day before the inauguration of Woodrow Wilson as president.

"I agree with Alice Paul," said Miss Addams. "We have to go back to demanding a national suffrage amendment, as Susan B. Anthony proposed. Our state-by-state efforts will never give all women the vote. Ohio and Wisconsin just defeated suffrage legislation, and their liquor interests will continue to obstruct us. And we ended up losing Michigan, showing how erratic the state process can be. I believe we should give Miss Paul all the resources she needs to mount a momentous parade in Washington on March the fourth."

Louise could not picture the short, slender Miss Paul, with her ethereal grace and huge doe eyes, leading the organization of thousands into a parade or pressuring legislators to give women the vote. Compared to the overbearing Mrs. Blatch, she was a delicate spring blossom. Yet she stood with absolute assurance, nodding appreciatively to Jane Addams and linking arms with her.

"She's only twenty-seven," Louise murmured to Damaris. "They say she spent several years with the Pankhursts picketing for the vote in England."

"Mrs. Blatch used to live there. She was good friends with Emmeline Pankhurst."

"But she didn't get arrested with them and go on hunger strike like Miss Paul did."

"She did? With the government forcibly feeding them and all?"

"Yes. Can you imagine? That little woman being held down and a tube put down her nose? They say it's terribly painful, and she kicked and screamed each time."

"And the English claim to be civilized," said Damaris. "They would never do that in America."

"And then when the women were released, they went right back out and got arrested again."

Damaris shuddered. "What do you think, though? Is she right? To work for a national amendment?"

Louise studied Miss Paul and her faint, relaxed smile. The woman made her think of Abbie, who was only a few years older. What would it be like to work under this enigmatic woman instead of under the thumb of the imperious Mrs. Blatch? Louise had never been to Washington and was eager to see more of the world. She leaned over and murmured to Damaris, "I think she's absolutely right."

ALICE PAUL

It may have looked like she was organizing a parade, but Alice Paul was digging trenches for battle. She was delighted to welcome two energetic, experienced young women who were willing to work full-time for the Congressional Committee, the long-neglected branch of the National that was focused on passing a federal amendment. Damaris had heard Miss Paul was bent on having lots of floats and a classical tableau, so she offered her services as a designer.

"Mrs. Blatch tells me you've raised over a hundred thousand dollars for the WPU," Miss Paul said. In the office on Washington's F Street, in an unheated room, she wore a floppy purple hat pulled down over her ears. Her chin nestled in the high fur collar of an otherwise plain wool coat. Both hands were encased by a black fur muff resting on a huge desk that had once belonged to Susan B. Anthony, author of the amendment the Committee was trying to push through Congress. Miss Anthony's former secretary had donated the desk when she heard of Miss Paul's mission. The piles of papers on its surface were stacked so high, they almost hid her from view. The tiny office held no other furni-

154

ture except the rickety slat-back wooden chair on which she sat. Damaris and Louise were forced to stand.

"Yes, we were quite successful," Damaris said. "But we grew weary of raising funds. I'd like to take charge of the tableau. I've studied art, and I was in Inez—"

"But you see, right now, we will have no tableau unless we can acquire funds," said Miss Paul. Her low voice had a curious ring to it, a brassy undertone that Louise found alluring. "Dr. Shaw gave me charge of the Congressional Committee on the condition I do my own fundraising. The National's budget for the Committee has previously been ten dollars a year."

"But I don't know the society women in Washington. My family is based in New York."

Miss Paul sat quite still, fixing her dark eyes on Damaris, who remained uncharacteristically silent as the stillness went on for almost a full minute. Finally Miss Paul spoke. "Mrs. Horace Kittel is the daughter of a senator and knows everyone in Washington society. She will help you. Raising money is terribly important, and so few people know how to do it." She extended a delicate hand for Damaris to shake, then Louise. Miss Paul bent over her papers again.

The pair returned to the clatter of typewriting and hum of voices in the main room. "I suppose it will be different here," Damaris said. "We'll be dealing with politicians' wives. A new challenge! And we already have a system set up." Louise marveled at the persuasiveness of Miss Paul. She herself was willing to do almost any kind of work, but she could hardly believe the fussy Damaris had simply caved in.

The Washington women proved to be hard nuts to crack. With the authoritative help of Mrs. Kittel, Damaris applied herself diligently but was frustrated at the slow pace of the inflowing funds. Louise, feeling superfluous, was glad when she received another summons to Miss Paul's office.

"I hear the fundraising team might be able to spare you for another project," Miss Paul began. The weather had turned sharply cold the night before, and the women's breath formed mist in the air.

"Certainly," Louise said. "Although you know I am paid by Miss Oakley. I'm not sure she will continue my salary if I'm working separately, and I can't afford to eat without receiving wages."

"I'll speak to her." Miss Paul removed a hand from the black muff to wave aside the concern. "You are needed to help with the capes. We've ordered three thousand, in several colors: white, red, rose pink, and three shades of blue. Mrs. Street is in charge of the color scheme. She will help you assign capes to specific groups to create blocks of color in a pleasing sequence. You will see to it that they are kept and distributed in an orderly fashion." She went back to scribbling notes.

After a few minutes of silence, Louise realized their meeting was at an end.

If organizing the New York parades had been a whirlwind, then the work in Washington was a tornado, for time was short, and such an ambitious event had never been mounted before in the nation's capital. Miss Paul had spent all of December negotiating for a parade permit from the police superintendent, who was concerned about the nearness of the saloon district. Men in town for Woodrow Wilson's inauguration, to take place the following day, would be at loose ends and bound to be going in and out of those saloons. Miss Paul wore down the head policeman with her repeated visits to his office, in the company of legislators' suffragist wives. In early January, he finally gave in, leaving her only two months before the March 4 inauguration in which to conjure up a spectacle that would imprint upon the national mind an image of beauty, order, and feminine power.

It took Louise only a day to complete the organizing of the capes, bringing her to the notice of the float designer's assistant. With her writing talent and hard-earned skill as a typewriter, Louise was put in charge of correspondence regarding floats, of which there would be many more than in New York. Then a rumor circulated that college boys were planning to release a thousand mice along the parade route. Miss Paul composed a statement insisting suffragists would not be diverted from their course by anxiety about rodents. Then someone came up with the idea of inviting the Boy Scouts to the procession, to keep an eye out for men with boxes of mice. Louise took on the task of typewriting a letter to the police superintendent with this suggestion.

A week before the parade, she had yet to be assigned a job at the actual event, until one of the participants fell ill. The float representing the Bible lands, where women were currently working for suffrage, featured three Old Testament prophetesses, Deborah, Miriam, and Huldah. A rebellious Nashville debutante, who was scheduled to portray one of the four daughters of the evangelist Philip, had come down with the mumps. Louise was sent to the costumer to be fitted for a Biblical daughter outfit.

Thus it was that she watched the unfoldment of the day's calamity from the relative safety of a wagon bed, which also afforded a view of more than just the heads of the horses and riders leading the procession. Inez Milholland, the most glamorous of the parade's many glamor girls, sat regally upon Grey Dawn, a luminous white charger. Louise could see Miss Milholland's dark curls cascading from a tiara, down over the long cape, sky blue to represent freedom, despite Miss Paul's request for yellow. But Gray Dawn, his rump and flanks overspread by blue, was not charging forward to freedom, as he was hemmed in by a horde of men pouring onto Pennsylvania Avenue.

Many of them were drunk, shouting obscenities. As they surged alongside the Bible lands float, one of the Philippian daughters, who was seated on the edge of the wagon, leaped to her feet when a man tugged at and spit on her robes. He tore a swag of bunting from the side of the float and lifted it overhead. A policeman, wading among the swirl of spectators, saw him carry it away and not only didn't interfere but laughed. A perspiring Boy Scout in military khaki grabbed the bunting and squeezed his way back to the float to return the cloth. Huldah accepted it with thanks.

Louise felt an impact and a brief burning sensation on her cheek. She looked down to see a lit cigar butt fall at her feet. She crushed it with her cork sandal so it wouldn't ignite the bunting or the makeshift desert tent. Furious, she was tempted to throw the stub back, but it might hit an innocent person, if there were any in that crowd. She calmed herself, remembering Miss Paul had impressed upon the marchers the importance of maintaining their professional poise, even if men chose to misbehave. The possibility had been foreseen, but no one expected this level of crassness.

Up ahead at the Treasury Plaza, she knew an assembly of women were waiting in their filmy Grecian costumes. Damaris was among them, having wormed her way into the tableau as Charity. "I certainly deserve to represent Charity," she had pointed out. "It's what I've been asking for from the women of Washington these past two months." As soon as Miss Milholland and Grey Dawn were able to pass the plaza, the figures of the tableau would begin their dance, warming up Columbia, Liberty, Justice, and several cohorts, but with the parade stalled, they were no doubt shivering in the March breeze. Except for her sandaled feet, Louise was comfortably warm, robed in draperies and shawls.

At last, a group of cavalrymen appeared. The horses shouldered the crowd away from the marchers, and the parade moved forward again.

Huldah, standing next to a palm tree made of lacquered paper, said to Louise, as they jolted along, "These rowdy men are the best thing that could have happened to the movement."

"What do you mean? They've behaved horribly. They've ruined the parade."

The prophetess gestured with her menorah, the branched candelabrum of the Hebrews. "The newspapers will go on and on about the rudeness of the men. Then we'll demand an investigation into how and why the security failed so miserably, and we'll be in the news for weeks."

"Really? Is that how it works?"

"Publicity is everything. The suffragettes will look saintly and innocent next to those boorish men. We'll take a big step closer to the vote."

And every word of Huldah's prophecy came true.

"My mother must be going crazy with worry. She's been writing every day, and I haven't had a single moment to write back," Damaris said. She was sorting through the mail accumulated over the past week, when they had been too busy even to look at the letters, much less open them. Now that the parade was two days in the past, and the celebrating had wound down, they were slowly putting their unkempt apartment back in order. "Here's one for you." Damaris tossed an envelope across the table. Louise nodded and went on sweeping out the corners of the parlor, knowing it was probably another gloomy note from her mother, who had grown increasingly reproachful in the last few months.

"I need a vacation," Damaris declared. "And I never want to be cold again after standing around in that tableau. I've been thinking. I have an aunt who lives in Miami, right on the beach. Let's go south and get warm."

"Miss Paul asked if I would stay on and help gather information on congressmen. She has a strategy for getting them to vote for suffrage."

"Oh, she asked me too, but it sounds tedious."

"It seems much like what we did in New York, to set up for fundraising. There's a file system of cards on the congressmen's backgrounds."

"But I know hundreds of people in New York. Why do you think the fundraising here went so miserably? I told Miss Paul I wasn't the right person."

"I'm curious to know how she'll proceed." Louise bent down with the dustpan.

"Oh, maybe in a month or so we'll try it, when Miami gets too hot. What do you say?"

"Well, if you're sure your aunt won't mind having a complete stranger in her house. It would be lovely to get some sun. I've never seen the ocean."

"What fun, to show you the beach! You'll love it. I'm going to write my aunt this minute and ask." Damaris took out a pen and paper.

Louise dumped the contents of the dustpan and sat down across the table. She looked at the return address on the envelope awaiting her. "It's from my husband's mother. How odd. She's never written me before." With foreboding, she opened the letter and read it through. Then she tossed it across the table. "I have to go back to New York." Damaris picked up the single sheet and read:

Louise,

Your mother is not well. Her forgetfulness and melancholy have increased to the point where we can no longer be responsible for her. It's time for you to cease your self-indulgent behavior and either return to your husband or take your mother away to live with you. Otherwise, we will contact the poorhouse next month.

Yours truly,
Lavinia Blake

Chapter 14

FAMILY LIMITATION

The chicken was stubborn even though dead. Later, when Abbie served the cooked meat, it was tasty and tender, but when raw, it clung to the bone, and the joints simply refused to separate. Meanwhile, Ivy, who had learned to pull herself up to standing, cruised and crawled underfoot in the kitchen.

A wing finally broke loose. As Abbie was working at a thigh, she looked down and saw Ivy kneeling by the garbage pail, bringing a bouquet of turnip peels to her mouth. "Oh sweetheart, give those here!" Abbie bent down to take the peels and set the pail in the one empty corner of the counter.

Abbie and the chicken resumed their battle as Ivy pulled open the refrigerator door. Her hands went deep in the butter. She pulled them out and licked her fingers, one by one.

"Ivy, darling, let's clean you up, or the whole kitchen will be covered in butter." The stubby fingers were wiped, and Abbie's hair was sticking to her cheeks, when she finally gave up on the chicken and dumped the entire bird into the pot. She set to making a cornstarch pudding for dessert. As she was giving it a final stirring, Ivy, who was making a circuit of the kitchen by pressing her palms against the wall, let go and took a wobbly step toward the cast-iron stove. She pitched forward, threatening to bash her head against it. As her mother lunged to grab her, the sleeve of Abbie's dress caught the handle of the saucepan. The pudding landed on the rug beside the stove.

Abbie's urge to cry was halted by the sight of Ivy crawling over to dabble her hands in the pudding. Soon the child's face and dress were smeared with pudding, and Abbie couldn't help laughing. She plunked Ivy in the high-chair, just outside the kitchen door, and lowered the little tray-table that held her in the chair. The baby grabbed the table and rocked back and forth, so Abbie feared the whole chair would fall over, but she knew confinement in the dining room would cause Ivy to scream. Working fast, Abbie managed to get the pudding mopped up.

Finally, the kitchen was clean, the baby was clean, and the mother sank, exhausted, into an armchair in the parlor. Ivy snuggled up on her lap. "You are a dear, and you make a huge amount of work for Mama," Abbie said, stroking the fine, reddish hair. "But that's what babies are meant to do, isn't it?"

The front door opened with a bang. "I met with Dr. Judson," Walter shouted from the hallway. "He's hired me to play at four services a week for the next two months." He hung up his coat and hat and came into the parlor.

"That's wonderful, deary! Oh, I am so proud of you." Abbie had been urging him for a month to contact Dr. Judson. Well, she wasn't going to complain now. It was a long tram and subway ride to Judson's Baptist church downtown on Washington Square, but the pay was good, and the minister was a progressive, good-hearted man, always organizing programs for the poor.

"I'll get two dollars on Wednesday and Friday, but five for the two Sunday services, which makes nine. And I've got lessons with Miss Ice, Stephen Reif, and Dr. Shirmer, plus his daughter and the two new boys, which makes fifteen dollars a week altogether. We'll have enough to hire a washwoman to come in twice a month. Won't that make you happy?"

He was like a puppy, so eager to please her. Their rent was twenty-six dollars a month. If the price of food didn't go up, yes, they could just afford a wash-woman, which would certainly bring relief. Abbie rose, with the baby in her arms, and gave her husband a kiss. "Thank you, my darling. Thank you so very much."

The washwoman was a gift from God. Abbie still did the clothing, but Kate, a hardy woman from County Clare, took care of the towels and linens. Each time she came, she also washed a couple of blankets or curtains. Kate, although pregnant, was diligent and strong. She lifted wet quilts effortlessly from the vat and sent them speeding through the mangle. Abbie had to insist she take a break at noon for a sandwich. The first day she came, they sat together over tea.

"When is your baby due?" Abbie asked.

"In three months, ma'am. I'm sorry I'll have to quit then, for I hate to lose the money. But I should be back on my feet in a few weeks."

"Is this your first baby?"

"Oh no, it'll be number nine. My oldest is fifteen, and she's a good worker, she is."

"Nine children! How on earth do you take care of so many?"

"The older ones look after the little ones. We get along all right. But clothing costs so much these days. It's hard to find the money to keep us all dressed. The hand-me-downs wear out till they can't be mended."

"What does your husband do?"

"He works in a cigar factory. It's nasty work, with tobacco dust all up his nose, so he's got a cough most of the time. But he rolls fast, and he's paid by the piece, which means we do all right. He can make a hundred fifty cigars in a day."

Abbie felt helpless, thinking of those many children and a mother who had to work outside the house full-time. She looked at Kate's dress, which was worn so thin, it looked like her shoulders might break through at any moment.

"I have an idea," Abbie said. "My mother lived with me before I was married, and I still have some of her old waists. She gained weight, so she didn't take them when she moved to Chicago. They're taking up room in my closet, and I'm sure they'll never fit me. May I give them to you?"

"Why sure, Mrs. Bergholtz. That's very kind of you."

At the end of the day, relieved that Kate had not been too proud to refuse, Abbie paid the woman's daily wage of $1.25 and added four lightly worn shirtwaists, plus an old skirt of her own and two yellow ribbons for the baby. She only wished she could do more.

That night at dinner, she told Walter about her gift to Kate. "You are so thoughtful," he said. "My generous girl. This stew is delicious."

Ivy banged a spoon on the table of her highchair. Abbie reached over to wipe mashed potatoes off the elfin face. "It makes me sad to think of those poor children who don't get their mother's attention all day. And look at our dear one, who never has to hear a hard word, with one of us always here to help her and keep her safe."

"Your heart is so tender," Walter said. "I grew up in a big family. I got my sisters' attention quite a lot. They kept me safe enough."

"But you had to share your mother with all those brothers and sisters. I feel for Kate's children. Just think, nine of them, and the oldest only fifteen!"

It was a few weeks later that Abbie's morning sickness revealed how soon Ivy would be sharing her own mother. But two children were a far cry from nine.

"Gave in to him at the wrong time of the month, did you?"

The words murmured in Abbie's ear gave her a shock, not just because of their crudeness but because, over the rumbling of the streetcar wheels and the clop of the horses' hooves and the chatter of people swaying around her, she recognized the voice. "How dare you!" she whispered through gritted teeth, turning to glare at Louise. "Don't be vulgar."

"You shouldn't have to worry about such things," Louise replied. "That's all I mean to say."

"I have no idea what you mean." Ivy tried to crawl onto Abbie's lap, but there wasn't room alongside her bloomed-out belly. "Ivy, sweetie, sit still in your seat. There's a good girl."

"I mean you must have heard of Margaret Sanger."

"Wasn't her writing banned for indecency?"

"She's only trying to give women control over their own bodies. There's nothing indecent about using a method that stops one from getting pregnant. You might want her help after this one's born. Or was that your plan, to have two children under the age of two?"

Ivy stood up in her seat and put her plump arms around Abbie's neck and her candy-sticky fingers in Abbie's hair. The child's breath smelled of milk and peppermint. "Here's a kiss, sweet one, but then you must sit," said Abbie, her eyes stinging for a moment. Louise's words had struck a nerve. "What are you doing in town? I thought you were in Washington."

"I've moved back. My mother and I are living in a boarding-house on the Lower East Side, and I'm working as a secretary at the Henry Street Settlement."

"You've learned typewriting?"

"Yes. Alice Paul wrote me a recommendation to Lillian Wald, who runs the settlement house."

"So you're quitting suffrage?"

"For now. I have to look after my mother. She's gone rather dotty these days. I take her to work with me, and she's all right playing with the children in the nursery."

"I'm sorry to hear that. It must be difficult." The streetcar made a turn that flung Louise against Abbie's shoulder, just as Ivy gave her hair a painful yank. "Sit down, Ivy, and I'll give you a cracker."

"Yes, well, I left Mama with the Blakes for almost a year, so I have to make up for it. I don't mind, really. I like working at the settlement house. I'm learning a lot about the problems of immigrant women. When my mother came over from Ireland forty years ago, there weren't nearly so many factories and slums, and conditions were quite different."

Abbie dug in her handbag for a cracker. "But what brings you uptown? Still working on the divorce?"

"Yes, the court won't grant it without grounds of adultery. My lawyer thought the violence might be taken as grounds, but it didn't work. Charles is being perfectly horrible, trying to put all the blame on me. Maybe I'll give up and live in sin with some other fellow. What about you? Are you still an anti?"

"I've never been an anti. I just don't care to sacrifice my dignity by marching in the street when I don't believe women having the vote will make so much difference in the world."

"You're just lucky you married a man who respects your right to make your own decisions. I envy you. Still, once you have a pile of children, you don't know how Walter will handle it."

"I don't intend—ow, Ivy! Now you really must sit, my sweet."

"You should get hold of Mrs. Sanger's newspaper, *The Woman Rebel.* She came by the settlement house a few weeks ago. What a lovely, gentle person, a little slip of a thing, not at all the demon the newspapers make her out to be. But here's my stop. If you want a copy of *The Woman Rebel,* write me care of the Henry Street Settlement. Good luck with the new babe."

And Louise slipped away, leaving Abbie to think over what she had said. Mrs. Sanger was a controversial figure, but if there was a way to stop a third baby from coming on the heels of the second, it might be well worth finding out.

Abbie knew women who hated being pregnant, but she was not among them. The morning sickness was difficult, but after the third month, it was over, and then she reveled in the sense of carrying a little sea of life within her everywhere she went. Shopping, visiting friends, meeting with the club, caring for Ivy, even cleaning the house—all activities were underlaid by the secret sense of a wordless, invisible bond with an unborn being. Like a sacred rite conducted day and night, the growth occurring inside her body lifted her spirits whenever her awareness glanced upon the new child.

But in the eighth month, as her belly grew even bigger than it had been just before Ivy's birth, anxiety plagued Abbie. Was she overeating? Was this baby a giant? Was she carrying twins? The muscles and tendons of her small frame ached with the weight, and she imagined a huge baby ripping her apart on its way from the inner to the outer world. This pregnancy exhausted her more than the first one. She wondered where she would get the energy to care for Ivy and an infant at the same time. Other mothers did it, so she would too, but now that Walter was playing with the Philharmonic, in addition to one service a week at Judson's church, he'd be less available to help out. Of course, Abbie was relieved to have the income of a steady job, although the flow of money was irregular, since the Philharmonic musicians were paid per performance, not according to rehearsal time. At least she didn't have to scrimp at the end of each month to pay the rent, Ivy had enough clothes, and Abbie could buy a new waist before an old one was quite frayed to bits.

She considered having her mother come out to help after the birth. The two of them were close, but nowadays Margaret's letters were filled with details of her rheumatism, and the stairs to the third-floor apartment would be a trial to her. Dr. Shirmer had recommended a new nurse, and they had enough money to keep her on for at least a few weeks after the baby was born. She had already started Abbie on a course of massaging and pinching her breasts to get the nipples to stand out well in advance of the birth. Hopefully a long period of breastfeeding would reduce the chance of a new pregnancy occurring soon after the baby's arrival.

Abbie didn't really want more than two children. In her own family, she had been the third of four, and she could remember how harried her mother had been after the birth of the youngest. She had a vivid memory of climbing into bed with Mama and the baby boy, who began to wail, causing Mama to push Abbie away. A keen sense of betrayal had lingered from her fall and the knock of her head on the floor. She hoped she would never have to cause pain to Ivy, especially not due to an excess of children. Louise's comments kept coming back to her.

Abbie knew fertility was said to be limited to the midpoint of the female cycle, about ten days after the menses began and for a few days thereafter, assuming a regular cycle. But her own cycle was variable, and it was difficult to time the demands of desire with the hopefully infertile nights of the month. She had to find a more reliable means of preventing, or at least holding off, a third child.

She laid her worries out to Walter as they sat in the parlor late on a Sunday, after Ivy had gone to sleep. Abbie rested her forearms on her belly as she sewed a little white muslin nightdress. Ivy had been born in winter, and this summer baby would need lighter clothing for its first months. The day had been unseasonably warm. Although Walter sat comfortably in his shirtsleeves, Abbie's condition left her damp with sweat, even in the lightest of cotton shifts. She stitched at the nightdress and considered how to broach the topic on her mind.

"So many people came up to congratulate me on my playing tonight," Walter said, unlatching his violin case, "that I didn't have time to wipe down my instrument. I shall never forget this evening. Dr. Judson was so inspired, we were all transported."

"What did he preach on?"

"He gave a bird's-eye view of the Book of Job. He applied higher criticism without pedantry, without being dry or stern or . . . or preachy." He laughed as he took out his violin and the soft cloth stored with it. "He brought the poem alive! On wings of revelation, I got up and played Tartini's sonata with a passion that carried everything with it and yet left my own self behind. I have never played better or with more power. Mr. Norcross felt it too, and he followed me right along, without allowing the piano to dominate. I believe we communicated a taste of divine ecstasy."

"That's marvelous, Walter! I wish I had been there."

"I do too. But at least you are here to share it with me now and let me relive . . . oh, such a joyous moment." He began to rub flecks of rosin off the body of the violin.

Abbie basked in the aura of his joy, happy for him and glad he could communicate those moments of bliss that came more readily to him than to her. She wished she didn't have to interrupt his pleasure by bringing up her problem. He hummed a melody from the sonata. She let a thoughtful minute go by before saying, "I had a quiet time reading to Ivy. She was such a dear. But my legs are quite swollen tonight. It helps if I put my feet up."

"My poor sweetheart. Well, the baby will be out in another month or so. I hope it's quite on time, for your sake."

She took her cue. "How would you feel, darling, if this baby were to be our last?"

He looked up from the violin. "Why? Did Dr. Shirmer say there was a problem?"

"No, no. It's simply that I feel . . . well . . . two children seems an ideal size for a modern family. More would put a strain on our resources."

"Not if I become a famous violinist. If I stick with the Philharmonic, I could rise to first violin. Of course, it would take some years."

"But I don't want to have to divide my attention among a whole pack of little ones. I like being able to give Ivy everything she needs. More than two seems rather . . . a strain. And then I might have to give up the club, which is so important to me."

He nodded, his long fingers turning the violin over. "But I don't see how . . ." The cloth started up again, then paused. "You can't mean . . . my darling, of course I love your pure, sweet soul immensely more than your beautiful body, but I can't fathom the idea of . . . of abstinence . . . that is—"

"No, that's not what I mean at all!" Abbie put down her sewing and laid a hand on his arm. "Of course not!

Our pleasure is important to me too. But there are ways to prevent a woman from getting with child."

"Oh!" The cloth resumed its careful slide along the polished wood. "You mean condoms. But it's illegal to buy or sell them."

"But I know they exist. They're made in Europe, and people smuggle them over. I thought perhaps you could inquire among your colleagues. Surely musicians travel abroad."

He shook his head. "Abbie, you ask too much. I do not want to be known as the violinist who asks smutty questions. It's hard enough being the youngest player in the whole section."

"All right, I'm sorry. I just thought . . . what about your brother-in-law, Johnny? He seems to know some rather shady people."

"Heavens, no! He'd find some way to blackmail me as soon as I asked."

Abbie tied off the stitching, threaded her needle again, and turned over the hem of the little nightdress. "I ran into my friend Louise on the streetcar. She told me about Margaret Sanger, a woman who's trying to help people have smaller families. Louise sent me this newspaper Mrs. Sanger is publishing." Abbie unfolded a copy of *The Woman Rebel* from her sewing basket.

"Such a dramatic title! What does it say?"

"She believes the sex drive is normal, in both men and women, and should be a source of satisfaction, not a cause for worry."

"I agree with her there." Walter replaced his violin in its case and folded the cloth. "It seems we've always been either trying to make a baby or trying not to. It does have an inhibiting effect on . . . on our pleasure."

"She says all upper-class women know how to prevent pregnancy. Middle-class women, like me, have
the means to find out, but lower-class women, who
need it the most, are fated by lack of money and poor
sanitary conditions to have endless babies. Like our
washwoman, Kate, who just goes on and on having babies and has never thought it was even possible to stop."

"And does Mrs. Sanger suggest any methods besides
condoms to prevent pregnancy?" He shut the latches of
the case with two loud clicks.

"No, she doesn't discuss any methods at all, because
of the Comstock law. It makes publishing or teaching
methods of contraception illegal because it says they're
indecent. She just writes about the injustice of the law.
It does strike me as quite unfair."

"If the information would help women, then certainly they should have it."

"She's been to Europe, and she says all the women in
France and Holland know what to do because people
there aren't afraid to talk about their anatomy. I'm going to write to Mrs. Sanger and tell her I must have the
information on . . . she calls it 'birth control.'"

"I don't want you in correspondence with her. What
if she sends you obscene information?"

"Oh no, Walter, it's just medical advice. And I'm a
married woman. It can't possibly corrupt me."

Abbie wrote to Mrs. Sanger but did not receive a reply. Louise sent another issue of *The Woman Rebel,*
which reported that some of the newspapers had been
confiscated by the Post Office, and Mrs. Sanger had re-
lied on friends to sneak copies into the mail at various
points around the city. Her goal was ultimately to chal-

lenge the Comstock law and get it changed. Abbie, although she thought of herself as a law-abiding person, began to hope this woman would succeed in her daring plan, if it meant birth control advice would become available, both to her and to all women who needed it.

Each time Walter brought home his daily copy of the *New York Tribune,* she paged through it, hoping to see news of Mrs. Sanger, but none appeared that spring.

Chapter 15

THE PROGRAM COMMITTEE

My idea for next season's theme is: everything to do with children," Abbie announced. The four members of the Program Committee were gathered in her parlor, sipping coffee. Being chair of the committee for the second year in a row gave her a degree of power, but she knew its limitations. She had to be canny to get her way. Children would make an appealing topic with a wide range of options.

"That's a wonderful idea," Mrs. Caterson said. "We could do children's authors. Kate Douglas Wiggin and Hans Christian Anderson." Her baby was flourishing, a relief to them all after the loss of her first. Of course she loved the topic.

"Oh, yes," Abbie said. "I had also in mind the welfare of children. Education, for instance. The advantages of kindergarten. The training of teachers."

"I'm interested in Maria Montessori's methods," Mrs. Hoag said. "My sister's children go to a Montessori school in Tarrytown, and they are so smart and happy."

"Excellent. Put Montessori on the list with your name." Abbie was glad the committee included Mrs. Hoag, the clubwoman whose friendship she valued the most. They had never grown as close as Abbie and Louise had been, but they called on each other during the summer break and occasionally dined together with their husbands.

"This will be so stimulating," Mrs. Hoag said. "You did well to get us onto inventions last year, Mrs. Bergholtz. The topic of children will be even more relevant."

"But it might become controversial," Mrs. Caterson said. "Do you think it's wise to discuss public policy? We don't want to destroy the harmony of the group."

"I think it's a good idea." Miss Fulton spoke up for the first time. "Children are so important."

"Exactly," Abbie said. "Important and powerless. They need so much protection, and we owe it to them to study what's best for them instead of just treating them any old way. Don't you agree, Mrs. Caterson?"

"Yes, I suppose so."

"And who better than mothers to address these issues?" Abbie looked at Miss Fulton and added, "That is, mothers and daughters," provoking a smile. She was growing fond of Miss Fulton.

"All right then," said Mrs. Hoag. "We have four topics under education. I do think we could have one on children's literature if Mrs. Caterson wants to take it on."

"Oh, yes," said Mrs. Caterson. "And one on fairy tales. They're very psychological, you know."

"I'd like to do a paper on voluntary motherhood," Abbie said, trying to keep her voice casual. "After all, the size of a family has a huge effect on the children."

Mrs. Caterson, in the midst of passing the scones around the table, dropped one on the floor.

"Voluntary motherhood?" Miss Fulton said, her soft voice sounding puzzled. "What's that?"

"It's . . . well, it's not having all your children right in a row, but rather, spacing them out and . . . and not having too many."

"Are you talking about . . . that Sanger woman?" Mrs. Caterson asked.

"Well, yes. I mean, I wouldn't write anything indecent, of course, it would just be about . . . about the idea of it and whether we ought to have such information and why."

"Have what information?" asked Miss Fulton.

"Information on how not to have one baby right after another."

Without thinking, Abbie stroked the curve of her belly. Miss Fulton noticed, and a glint of understanding came to her eyes as she said, "I see. That seems like an important topic."

"Well, to me it sounds extremely controversial," Mrs. Caterson said.

"I like to write about subjects I'm trying to learn about," Abbie insisted. "I would only report what seems positive and helpful."

"I'll put it down with a question mark," Mrs. Hoag said. "What other topics?"

"Childhood illnesses," said Miss Fulton.

"Teaching use of the toilet," suggested Mrs. Hoag.

"I'd like to write on child labor," Abbie said. "That is, unless you think it's too controversial, Mrs. Caterson."

"Oh no, we can all agree that's a social evil. Those poor little dears having to work all day in stuffy tenement houses."

By the end of the hour, they had come up with twenty-two subjects and needed only ten more to fill the thirty-two weeks of the club season. They agreed to meet the next day at Mrs. Hoag's house. As the ladies were preparing to leave, Abbie went to fetch Ivy from the bedroom, where Walter had been entertaining her with books and her favorite dolly. When Ivy caught sight of Miss Fulton, she wriggled down from her mother's arms and ran to the young woman.

"She remembers me from the last meeting," Miss Fulton exclaimed. Walter had been busy preparing for a concert and had not been able to watch Ivy, so Abbie had brought her along to the club meeting. Ivy's good behavior had made her mother proud, until it came time for Abbie to read her paper about the inventing of the telephone. Ivy kept trying to climb onto her already crowded lap, so Mrs. Crump gave the baby a biscuit, not realizing she had a little sing-song that always accompanied her eating. Abbie had to raise her voice over her daughter's and felt the distraction was not ideal for the women's absorption of facts about modern communications. However, they all seemed more amused than annoyed. After the reading, Miss Fulton engaged Ivy in a lengthy game of pat-a-cake, then rode her around on her back, so the exuberance of their reunion was no surprise.

Miss Fulton took Ivy into the parlor and knelt on the floor with her. Ivy extended her doll for a hug and a kiss, then twirled around twice and threw herself, laughing, into Miss Fulton's lap. Abbie sat watching the two of them. "Would you like to come over and look after her sometimes?" she asked.

"Oh yes," said Miss Fulton. "I love children."

"You are naturally good with Ivy. I expect you'll have your own one day."

"I don't know. I have no wish to marry."

"Why not?"

"Men are so rough and uncouth. Except Mr. Berg-holz, of course."

"I don't suppose you get many chances to meet young men."

"That's true, but I don't really care to." Abbie was aware that Miss Fulton, with her receding chin, a bumpy nose, and a large red birthmark on her cheek, was not likely to attract a good-looking fellow, but there ought to be some man who would appreciate her gentle intelligence.

"Well, there's nothing like having a baby of one's own."

"I can look after other women's children."

"You could work as a teacher," suggested Abbie.

Miss Fulton turned her attention back to Ivy, who was swinging the doll around by the foot. Abbie sympathized with the younger woman because they had both grown up without a father, but Abbie's life had been so different because she'd gone to work. Miss Fulton had been only five when her father died, so her mother had started the baking business, leaving the girl to take on housework as she grew up. Abbie had an urge to give her a gentle shove out of her sheltered life into activities more satisfying. But such an effort would have to proceed gradually.

"Let's call each other Jessie and Abbie, shall we?" Abbie said.

"Yes, I'd like that," Jessie said with a shy smile.

Abbie felt they had made a small but significant step.

When, as head of the Program Committee, Abbie presented the topics for the following season, she read quickly through the words "voluntary motherhood," adding, "I'll be doing that one," and spent more time on the other items. She avoided the eyes of Mrs. Fulton, who approached her during the coffee and cakes.

"A word, Mrs. Bergholtz." They were off to the side of the room, where no one was likely to overhear. "Did I understand correctly, that you plan to write a paper on methods of preventing the conception of babies?"

"Not exactly." Abbie had prepared for this moment by rehearsing what she might say to Mrs. Fulton or anyone else who had misgivings. "Not on actual methods of prevention but on the need for such information, which is hardly available at all."

"Mrs. Bergholtz, there is an innocent girl in this club, and she happens to be my daughter. I don't think a discussion of . . . such practices would be fit for her ears."

A year ago, Abbie would have been cowed by Mrs. Fulton's complaint, but her rising status at the club gave her the courage to stand up for both herself and Jessie. "Forgive me for saying it, Mrs. Fulton, but your daughter is not a girl, she's a woman. And she's likely to marry some day and need this information as much as any other woman. Don't you think she ought to be prepared with at least a hint that such knowledge might be available?" Mrs. Fulton opened her mouth and then closed it again. "Don't worry, there will be nothing obscene in my paper. My research will be on the need for information and obstacles to obtaining it."

Mrs. Fulton pressed her thin lips together and shook her head. "I would ask to bring it to a vote, but I don't want to discuss the subject in front of my daughter. I hereby register my objection and hope that your sense of propriety will prevail." And she walked away.

Chapter 16

HETERODOXY

H eterodoxy." Damaris savored the word. "That's a brilliant name for a women's club. It implies so much."

"It's very different from the club I used to belong to," Louise said. "At Heterodoxy, we don't write papers, and there's no rule against controversy. In fact, controversy reigns."

"If they meet in Greenwich Village . . . well, I can only imagine!"

The shouts of children, as they pushed their sailboats out onto the Central Park pond, resounded across the water. One little girl was weeping because she had dropped the string that served as the leash for her boat. A breeze propelled the craft out under the sky, its white sail bellying.

"Some of the members are women I've heard of," Louise said, "although the times I've been to the meetings, they haven't been there. Charlotte Perkins Gilman belongs, and so does Mrs. Boissevain."

"Really? I couldn't believe Inez got married. He's a wealthy Dutchman, I hear."

"Yes, an importer of coffee. She met him on a ship to Europe."

"I met a man on my ship too, a German, but he disappeared as soon as we docked at Liverpool. I had better luck with the French, especially since I didn't have a chaperone this time." Damaris's pinched features wore a misty expression.

They paused in their stroll around the pond to watch the errant sailboat, which had almost reached the opposite shore. The child's mother was running to fetch it, pulling the little one along by the hand. Their progress was slow.

"Did you enjoy Paris?"

"Oh, yes! You should see what's happening in art. Extraordinary work. Picasso, Derain, Matisse. America is so far behind. Of course, there were European paintings at the Armory Show last year, but you and I were in Washington. I so regret missing it. But in Paris, I studied the new masters closely. I may look for a job at a gallery."

"You don't want to go back to suffrage work?"

"I'm still deciding. But tell me more about Heterodoxy. How did you meet them?"

"They held a public meeting at Cooper Union in February, all about the rights of women. Someone spoke on the right to ignore fashion. Mrs. Gilman talked about the right to work, and so forth. They were all so brilliant. Mary Ware Dennett was in the audience. I found the nerve to go over and talk to her, and it turns out she's also a member of Heterodoxy."

"Mary Dennett. Wasn't she the one who spoke up against Miss Paul placing the black women at the end of the parade?"

"Yes, I admired her for that. Of course, Miss Paul still got her way."

"Except for Ida Wells jumping into the Chicago group, right in the middle of the parade."

"I was glad Mabel wasn't in Washington. Ida Wells was humiliated to be treated so poorly. In that respect, Mrs. Blatch is more progressive."

"Did Mrs. Dennett remember you?"

"Oh, no. But we talked about the parade. Then I told her I was working at the settlement house, and she invited me to a Heterodoxy meeting. I suppose I made a good impression, because they asked me to join the club." Louise glanced at Damaris, fearing her envy, and was not surprised to see a crinkling around the eyes. She envied Damaris for getting to visit Europe, so maybe she didn't mind so much being envied. But she hastened to add, "I'm allowed to bring a friend. Would you like to come to the next meeting?"

"I might."

The mother and daughter had almost reached the sailboat, which was rocking on wavelets against the bank of the pond, when a boy, perhaps twelve years of age, lifted the boat out of the water. The little girl extended her arms, but the boy tucked the boat under his elbow and began to walk away. The mother stamped on the trailing string and shouted at him. They stood and argued.

"Oh, dear," said Louise. "We should help them."

"Why? It's none of our business."

"But we saw the boat go astray. We know it belongs to the little girl." She set off around the pond.

Damaris trotted a few steps to catch up. "And what's happening in your life besides the settlement house?"

"Actually," said Louise, "I may quit soon. My mother died last month."

"Oh, I'm sorry! What happened?"

"She had a stroke. The brutal truth is, it's a relief to me. She was extremely unhappy. She couldn't accept that my marriage had ended, and she took every opportunity to make me feel guilty. As if I didn't feel bad enough about leaving her for a year."

"At least you spent her last few months together."

"And I'm seeing Mr. Harris."

"Who?" Surely Damaris was pretending indifference.

"The man who took us to the Hotel Marshall. Which, unfortunately, was shut down last fall."

"That's sad."

They were halfway around the pond when they saw the mother appealing to other women, who gathered around with their children. The boy holding the boat had a sullen look. Finally, he handed it over, but as he did so, he snapped the mast in half, then laughed and ran off before anyone could respond.

Louise gasped. Damaris shook her head. "Males!"

Heterodoxy met upstairs from Polly's, a restaurant on MacDougal Street, in rooms rented by the Liberal Club and furnished with plain tables on bare wood floors. The chairs were painted brilliant yellow or orange. When they walked in, Damaris went straight to the paintings on the walls. "Not as good as Matisse," she declared, looking at a Fauvist portrait of a somber man with a face the color of cantaloupe flesh and emerald green hair, "but not bad at all."

"My sister painted that," said a woman in a jacket and trousers. "She's going to be famous."

"Oh, really?"

Louise led Damaris to a couple of seats near one end of the long table and presented her to Mary Dennett. "Ah, another sister in the fight," said Mrs. Dennett. "Glad to meet you."

"Do you expect to go back to Washington?" Damaris asked her.

"Actually, I'm thinking of retiring from suffrage work. Ever since Margaret Sanger came and spoke to the club, I'm inclined to shift my energy over to birth control. We Heterodites, who need it more than just about anyone, already know what to do, but other women don't. The poorer ones just keep churning out children, and then how will they ever get out poverty?"

"Oh, I agree," said Damaris. "Birth control is critical. But why do Heterodites need it?"

"Free love, my dear. Many of us practice it avidly, so we've learned what to do. But I seem to be the only one with an interest in teaching other women how to prevent pregnancy. Mrs. Sanger complained we're too busy with getting jobs and keeping our maiden names. As if those weren't important too!"

"Did you hear?" said a woman across the table. She had bobbed hair and wore a high, stiff collar and a tie. "The Hendersons are filing for divorce."

"Well, they shouldn't have any problem getting it," came a reply. "They've both had enough lovers to fill a courtroom."

"What about you, Louise?" asked Mary Dennett. "How's your divorce going?"

"Well, I finally committed adultery last week, so that ought to move it along." She didn't feel quite as flippant as she sounded.

"With your uptown fella? Good for you, honey." Louise smiled, hiding her embarrassment.

Damaris whispered, "Ah, Miss Louise is growing up."

"Who's your friend, Louise?" asked the woman with the tie.

She introduced Damaris to the women sitting around them. A waiter distributed menus. Just after all twenty orders had been put in, a tall woman in gray serge swept into the room, saying, "Sorry I'm late."

"Too bad, Charlotte. We just voted to redecorate the room . . . with yellow wallpaper."

Perplexed by the ensuing laughter, Damaris glanced at Louise, who told her, "Charlotte Perkins Gilman. One of her books is a novella, *The Yellow Wallpaper.* Everyone here has read it."

"Vera and Sonia aren't coming," said a redhead who was touching shoulders with a thin blonde. "They're battling over a pretty grad student who came down from Boston to help Vera with her research."

"Is it serious?"

"Vera says nothing's happening between her and the grad student. At least not yet."

The arrival and consumption of the meal did not slow the conversation.

"I'm organizing another demonstration at the Board of Ed," said a woman with close-cropped hair and a purple dress shaped like a flour sack. "Who'll come and carry signs?"

"Another one? I went last time. Can't someone else take a turn?"

"That's Henrietta Rodman," Louise explained to Damaris. "She's a teacher, and she got fired for insisting women who marry should be able to keep teaching."

"The picketing keeps us in the news," said Henrietta. "It's vitally important."

"Well, I think the picketing's getting old," objected a woman with large eyes, her face framed by short wisps of hair. "You need a gimmick, like the Women's Political Union is always thinking up."

"Doris Stevens," Louise murmured to Damaris. "She's become one of Miss Paul's best organizers."

"Oh yes, Mrs. Blatch has wonderful ideas," said Damaris. "I used to work with the WPU."

"Harriot's got lots of tricks. Did you see her motion picture? It's called *What 8,000,000 Women Want*. She plays herself, and she got Emmeline Pankhurst to play in it too."

"Oh Doris, it's a silly picture," Henrietta scoffed. "Harriot Blatch ought to stick to browbeating politicians. That's what she's good at."

"Does anyone know how the New York campaign is going?" asked Damaris. "I've been abroad, and I haven't heard a thing."

"Harriot's fighting with Carrie Catt over who should be in charge of it," Henrietta replied. "They're like two billy goats butting at each other."

"Carrie's a bore," said Doris, "and so is her whole Empire State Committee. They could never come up with ideas like Harriot's."

"What do you think, Crystal? You went to teach in Carrie's suffrage school. That was rather a gimmick."

Crystal, a striking brunette with dark shadows around her eyes, was lighting a cigarette. "Yes, she held one in Poughkeepsie in January. Inez was supposed to give a lecture, but she was ill, so I took her place. It was well-attended, I suppose, but so provincial."

"I remember you," Damaris said. "You're Crystal Eastman, the socialist. I was at Vassar when Inez brought you to speak to the suffrage club." Louise wished she had Damaris's instant confidence around these educated women. Although they had accepted Louise without reservation, she was still shy with them.

"You're a Vassar girl too? I was in the class of '03," Crystal said. "Years ahead of you and Inez. But she's one of my dearest friends."

"Does the WPU have an office in Poughkeepsie?" Damaris asked.

"No. The city has a suffrage group of its own. I think Harriot is concentrating farther upstate."

Damaris turned to Louise. "Let's go to Poughkeepsie. We can visit Vassar, recruit some students, and set up our own office downtown."

"I thought you agreed with Miss Paul that we should focus on a national amendment."

"Yes, but if New York passes the referendum, there'll be so many more women voters. That'll be just the leverage we need in Washington. And I would love to be in charge of my own office."

"If you do go to Poughkeepsie," said Crystal, "you must go to the harvester factory. It has over a thousand workers. It's down by the river."

"Too often the workers get neglected." Henrietta Rodman was nodding in agreement. "That's Harriot's blind spot. She knows she needs them, but she's afraid of them."

"With good reason," said Charlotte Gilman. "Poor people have poor judgment. If you could see the women who have—"

"It's not poor women she's afraid of," the redhead cut in, not intimidated by the author's fame. "It's the immigrant men. The Germans and Hebrews come from cultures where women have few rights, and they're opposed to us getting the vote."

"Then we must educate them, not push them away," Louise said, elated to finally speak up.

"Some things cannot be changed," Charlotte insisted. "Or they take far too long."

"And that Sanger woman is no better." Henrietta was almost yelling as heated side conversations added to the mounting din of argument. "She says she wants to help poor immigrants, but she really wants to reduce their numbers by teaching them to stop having children. It's an insidious—"

"Maybe so," Mary Dennett jumped in, "but it happens to help them at the same time, and it helps the rest of us, so I don't really care."

Louise felt exhilarated. She loved to hear women expressing themselves so freely, even if she was not yet in the thick of the conversation. It still amazed her that she'd had the good fortune to meet these illustrious, capable women, just by pursuing her interest in suffrage and the rights of her gender.

The pounding of a gavel from the other end of the table interrupted the shouting. In the near-quiet that followed, Crystal observed, "We've been here an hour and a half, and that's the first time Marie has used the gavel. I think it's a record."

Chapter 17

MOTHERHOOD

I t was pretty smart of me to give birth in June, just at the start of the summer break," Abbie told the clubwomen. It was October, and they were gathering for the first meeting of the season. "Then I had three months to recover and didn't have to miss a single meeting."

"I don't know who was smarter," said Mrs. Hoag, "you or those babies."

She had been the first club member to learn that Abbie had given birth to twins. Stopping by to enquire after her friend, she was delighted to hold little Samuel and Benjamin just a few days after the birth. Then she went around and collected a dollar from each of the clubwomen, reappearing at Abbie's house two days later with diapers and baby clothes to augment the one-baby supply already on hand.

"I don't know how we would have made it through the first weeks without your generous gifts," Abbie told the women.

"I could hardly believe it," Mrs. Fulton said. "A little thing like you, giving birth to twins."

"I can't imagine taking care of twins," said Mrs. Caterson. "You must be exhausted."

"It certainly is tiring," Abbie admitted. "But they are darling boys. Ivy adores them."

"Is your mother in town?"

"No, she came for a few weeks, but she's gone back to Chicago."

"Well then, who's staying with the babies while you're here?"

"Oh, Walter has them. He's so good with the children. It's my great luck the Philharmonic doesn't rehearse on Tuesday afternoons."

"How I envy you!" sighed Mrs. Caterson. "My husband can barely be bothered with my little one. But then he is quite busy with teaching at the college. He has to read the students' homework in the evenings."

Mrs. Fulton called the meeting to order. During committee reports, Mrs. Crump announced the library collection had reached over five hundred volumes and was outgrowing the room in the church basement. Mrs. Hoag said she had seen a newspaper article about a library fund established by Andrew Carnegie. "Why don't we see if we can get some of the money and set up a public library? He's providing the funds, but it's up to people in the neighborhoods to do the work. Other clubs have done it, and we'd have a head start with our five hundred books."

"But I'm leaving soon to have my baby," Mrs. Crump replied. "Someone else would have to take it on."

"It's a wonderful idea," said Abbie, "but I don't have time just now because of the twins. What about you, Miss Fulton? You love books and research."

"Me?" Jessie looked surprised and flattered.

"Oh yes," said Mrs. Crump. "A young, energetic person like you would be perfect."

"I know an excellent location," Mrs. Hoag said. "Mr. Newsome's dry goods store on 231st Street has closed, and the building is for let. All the walls have shelves, and the lighting is excellent. I know the owner, and I would be glad to introduce him to you, Miss Fulton."

"Why . . ." Jessie looked at her mother. Mrs. Fulton bit her lip and then nodded. "All right. I suppose I could do it." Abbie felt pleased her Jessie project was on the move.

After the committee reports, Mrs. Everett read her paper entitled "Why School Nurses are Valuable and Why We Need More of Them." The discussion following was brief and upbeat.

Over coffee and cakes, the conversation turned to the war in Europe. "I read in the news it's expected to last at least two years," Mrs. Varian said. "There's no chance Germany will negotiate a peace."

"Poor Belgium, occupied by German soldiers," Mrs. Lappe said. "My husband has cousins in Brussels. The Germans thought some civilians had helped out the French, and they massacred a whole group of Belgians."

"A barbaric people," said Mrs. Varian. "Oh, I'm sorry, Mrs. Bergholtz, I didn't mean . . ."

"In fact, the Germans are a highly cultured people," Abbie retorted. "It's just that a militaristic group has taken control of the country. We are so distressed about the situation."

"Does your husband have relatives in Germany?" Mrs. Lappe asked.

"Oh, no . . . that is . . . not anyone he's in touch with. The family came over long ago."

"Are you a pacifist?"

"What? No, although I'm glad President Wilson has declared neutrality. I don't want us sending our boys over there." Abbie saw a nod from Mrs. Lowitz, who had a nineteen-year-old son.

"Of course," said Mrs. Lappe, "you don't want to attack your husband's people."

"Excuse me? I just said he doesn't—"

"Well, I think we ought to help out the Belgians. They declared neutrality too, and they are being torn to pieces." Mrs. Lappe's voice was growing strident.

"Britain is helping out," Mrs. Hoag said. "It's in their backyard, so it's natural for them to respond. They'll stand up for the Belgians. As for us, I don't think—"

"And France is in trouble. Paris nearly fell to the Germans last month. I'm telling you, they need America's help. With all our resources—"

"All right, ladies, we'd better drop this topic," Mrs. Fulton interrupted. "It's not worth our time to fight over politics."

"Well, one good thing has come of the war," Mrs. Lowitz said. "It's stopped those British suffragettes in their tracks. Mrs. Pankhurst and her daughters are no longer demonstrating, and they're telling their women to work in the factories to support the war effort."

"Thank God," Mrs. Varian said. "They were going quite too far with smashing windows and lighting mailboxes on fire. I hope that doesn't happen here."

"Oh, it won't," Jessie said. "Alice Paul is a Quaker. She would never allow violence."

The anxious silence that ensued was broken by Mrs. Everett. "Has anyone been to the new automat on Lexington Avenue? I'm longing to take my children. They'll have such fun putting nickels in the slots."

Abbie had learned her lesson with Ivy. Her nipples, despite methods instigated by the new nurse, again stayed puckered and did not cooperate with breast-feeding. As soon as it became clear the twins weren't latching on properly, the bottles and sterilizer were brought into use.

Before the club's summer break, Mrs. Everett had loaned Abbie a set of scales. She weighed the twins daily, recording their measurements in a pocket calendar. At six months, both boys weighed over 13 pounds, which Dr. Shirmer said was on the small side but three pounds more than Ivy's weight at that age and no cause for alarm, as Abbie was small-boned herself.

Remembering how jealous she had been of her own little brother, Abbie made an effort to include Ivy in activities of caring for Sam and Ben. At bath-time, Ivy rubbed their little arms with a wash-cloth, at first with an excited vigor, but then following Abbie's command to be gentle, with slow strokes and a little crooning song. Ivy was riveted by diaper-changing, as long as it wasn't too smelly, taking a particular interest in the male anatomy. Abbie decided her curiosity was healthy and talked with her about the difference between boys and girls. Ivy leaned her elbows on her knees, chin on palms, as she gravely took in the information.

She was possessive of her sacred Dolly, but when Abbie laid the boys down to nap, Ivy snuggled her second-favorite doll up to Ben's face, as he always took longer to fall asleep than Sam.

"She's such a loving child," Abbie told Walter. He was so busy with the Philharmonic, he didn't have time to be jealous of her attention. During rehearsal breaks, he wrote love poems that she found beside her breakfast plate on Saturday mornings, tied with a ribbon to a long-stemmed rose. She read the verses aloud to the children, cherishing every word.

"My paper is entitled 'The Horror and Shame of Child Labor.'" Abbie glanced at the faces of the women before her in Mrs. Lowitz's parlor, noting both interest and apprehension. Resolutely, she began to read.

"Although slavery has been outlawed in this country, thousands upon thousands of children, many of their families having left desperate conditions in other lands to seek streets paved with gold, are now toiling their youthful lives away with no say in the matter, sacrificing their childhoods for the corrupt gods of mammon." Abbie paused to peek at her audience again. A few of them looked puzzled. Perhaps the sentence was too long to follow. No matter, the rest of the paper would explain.

"Picture a tenement in Manhattan, perhaps on Sullivan, Thompson, MacDougal, or Houston Street. The landlord has bowed to the New York State Tenement House Act of 1901 and has built in a certain quantity of windows for ventilation and light, so his building may be licensed for home work. Never mind that one of the windows is between the kitchen and the parlor—it still conforms to the law. In a two-room apartment, an Italian family of six is engaged in assembling artificial flowers. The youngest child, at the age of three, has the task of pulling apart the petals, which arrive from the factory stuck together. She and the five-year-old boy, who lays the parts out for sewing, are not yet at the age of compulsory education, so they toil from morning to night. The nine-year-old girl, who helps the mother with sewing the petals to the stems, has pale and pasty skin because she spends her mornings and early afternoons at school, and then works from three o'clock to ten o'clock at the creation of the flowers. The fifteen-year-old, being past the age of compulsory education, works alongside the mother and the little ones, also from morning to night.

"In a grotesque fate, symbols of divine beauty are being used to enslave innocents who should be outside playing in the fresh air. The father, who is able only irregularly to obtain work on a street-paving crew, is sometimes present, his large fingers unsuitable for the fine handwork, so he is most likely asleep or drowning his despair in a bottle of the cheapest wine. And what does this family earn for their labors? Sixty cents a day."

Abbie felt again the heart-wringing despair she had suffered while researching her paper. Most of the ladies were now leaning forward, brows creased in shock and concern. Good.

"Furthermore, this family, their landlord, and their employer are perfectly within the law. We know there are many illegal tenements, where children work in rooms without ventilation, or where a family member has tuberculosis but continues to labor nonetheless, despite the risk of contagion, because the family is desperate for money. These tenements are nearly impossible to regulate because there are over 18,000 legal, registered tenements in New York City, each one requiring inspection, so the illegal ones are simply beyond our resources to detect. But the tableau I have described above is entirely legal and a source of shame for all Americans."

Another overly long sentence in that paragraph. She should have spent more time editing, but the twins kept her so busy.

"The law applies to a list of products commonly processed at home, including nuts, the finishing of clothing, brushes, doll clothing, crocheting, embroideries, beading bags and moccasins, and others. Any product not on the list is exempt from the law. One entire industry that is exempt is the cannery industry, since it operates in the countryside, where the fresh air is considered healthful for children. Conditions there are even worse. Families are lured out of the city by a promise of free housing, which turns out to be a filthy shack with no running water. Women and children work from five in the morning to midnight, processing crops from the field, with speed being of great urgency so the food will not spoil. Last year, the U.S. Census of Manufactures recorded over eight thousand children working in the canning industry, again perfectly legally."

She went on to detail the monumental efforts expended by reform organizations to force the passage of laws, against resistance from wealthy manufacturing concerns. Since the reforms of 1910, only minor changes had been implemented, such as the raising of the minimum age of newsboys from ten to twelve. As she listed other recent developments, she saw her audience growing restless. She skipped a few paragraphs, ending with, "The question now lies before us: what is an enlightened society to do in the face of these horrors? How do we restore a childhood of health and play and well-deserved freedom from care to the most innocent of our neighbors? How else can we expect them to grow into responsible citizens? This problem is a hard one but deserves our attention as mothers, daughters, and sisters, steeped in compassion and devoted to care of the family. What shall we do?"

Abbie set down her pages and surveyed the room. Several women expelled loud sighs, as if they had been holding their breath. Others stretched their arms overhead. "What indeed shall we do?" Mrs. Fulton said. "Does anyone have a thought? Or is this social evil simply beyond our control?"

"It's terrible," Mrs. Everett said. "I knew about these tenements, but I had never heard just how awful they were. You've done an excellent job of research, Mrs. Bergholtz." Others echoed her praise.

"It's a systemic problem," Mrs. Flint declared. "Rich manufacturers are greedy for a cheap supply of labor, and scores of desperate poor are willing to work their children for almost nothing. I know my nephew the socialist sees it that way, although I am doubtful about his solution, which is letting the workers own the . . . What do they call it? . . . the means of production."

"It seems to me," said Miss Fulton, "that if women had the vote, we might be able to elect a better sort of man who would make laws to protect children." Emboldened by her success in establishing a popular neighborhood library, she was speaking up more at meetings. And Abbie was aware her protegée needed a new project.

"Jessie," Mrs. Fulton said, "you know we don't discuss suffrage at club meetings."

"But how else are we to help the children? There must be laws made."

"Women have other powers besides voting. Education, for instance."

Miss Fulton's face was red with the exertion of contradicting her mother. "But how are we supposed to educate people?"

"Mrs. Bergholtz has just educated us right here."

"Yes, but who's going to educate the men who make the laws?"

"You heard what she said. The reforms of 1910 came from organizations." She turned to Abbie. "Which ones were they again?"

"The labor unions, the New York Child Labor Committee, and the settlement houses."

"What exactly do they do at settlement houses?" Miss Fulton asked. "I know they take care of poor people, but how?"

"I can answer that," Mrs. Everett said. "My sister is a nurse, and she works at the Henry Street Settlement, where Miss Kelley was working. Their visiting nurses go to people's homes, and they have cooking and sewing classes, English classes for immigrants, nurseries for when mothers are at work—all sorts of services."

"When the nurses go into the tenements, they see how bad the conditions are," Abbie said. "That's what made Lillian Wald start the Henry Street Settlement and then work at changing the laws."

"See? She did it without the vote," Mrs. Fulton observed triumphantly.

"She must be awfully brave. But what can *we* do?" her daughter asked.

"The married women can talk to their husbands about it," Mrs. Lappe ventured. "We can tell our husbands to vote for a candidate who promises to take action on child labor."

"If there *is* such a candidate," Mrs. Hoag said. "I suppose the Progressive Party may take it up."

"We could write letters to newspapers," Mrs. Caterson suggested, "now that we've all practiced writing."

"An excellent idea!" Mrs. Fulton crowed. "Jessie, there's a task for you."

Miss Fulton sat with her shoulders hunched, looking thoughtful.

"I think," said Abbie, "that we should make a list of laws that would protect children. A law that would forbid children under a certain age to work at all, for instance. And laws that would include the canneries. And we should submit the list to the city council and the state legislature and tell them what we want."

"But why would the city councilmen pay any attention to us?" asked Mrs. Lowitz. "Except for Mr. Hoag, of course." There was giggling.

"Well," said Miss Fulton, "if we could vote, the councilmen would have to pay attention to us." Her mother gave her an exasperated look.

"We could make up a committee for proposing laws on child labor," Abbie said.

Miss Fulton said, "I would join that committee." But no one else volunteered.

"All right, Miss Fulton and I will schedule a meeting later in the month."

They broke for coffee. Abbie described how Walter's job with the Philharmonic had made a great improvement in their finances. "Ah," said Mrs. Hoag, "that's such a blessing. I don't know what I'd do if my husband didn't get a regular paycheck."

"And how is little Ivy?" Mrs. Flint asked.

"She's so bright!" Abbie said. "She is a dear. Although she often suffers from digestive upset. She vomits so often, we have to keep a bucket in a corner of each room."

"Have you tried Pape's Diapepsin?" Mrs. Lappe offered. "It works wonders with my ten-year-old."

"What is it?"

"It's a compound of digestive enzymes and herbals, with a bit of sugar to make it palatable. Henry takes it quite willingly."

"Thank you. Perhaps I'll try it."

Abbie went home pleased by the success of her paper and grateful to the club members for listening to her personal concerns and giving advice. Her life would be so difficult and lonely without these stalwart, like-minded women. Three days later, her contentment went head over tail when Walter returned from a rehearsal with an announcement.

"The Philharmonic has decided to join the city musician's union. The players want to negotiate wages for rehearsals and performances, by the hour, instead of receiving a lump sum for each performance."

"Oh, Walter, that's wonderful! Our finances will—"

"Therefore," he said, "I am quitting."

He might as well have punched her in the stomach. Of course, she knew he had always been opposed to unions, but surely in this case, he could see the benefits for his own family. "Are you sure? Don't you think the union would be good for the players?"

"They're giving me no choice. The members voted, and the majority is in favor of the union. Everyone has to join, and I will not be forced against my will."

"But it would be useless for the union to strike if some of the musicians did not belong."

"I know that. Mob rule. It turns my stomach. Europe is at war, yet the musicians are fussing over their wages. If wages go up, so will ticket prices, which will add to the general inflation of prices, and then they'll want another wage increase, and it will just keep going round and round. I will not be party to this dictatorship by the masses. Unions are bullies!"

And he sat down to prepare his letter of resignation. Abbie knew it would be useless to argue further. All she said was, "I hope you will go tomorrow to an employment service and submit an application. The boys will need new coats by March."

Chapter 18

TO PREVENT

I'm volunteering at the Henry Street Settlement,"
Jessie said. She was sitting at Abbie's dining-room
table, and they were both peeling pears, destined
for a tart to serve at that afternoon's club meeting.

Abbie's knife paused. "You're volunteering?"

"I'm helping with a cooking class once a week, and
then I feed the children in the nursery. That is, I did
them both yesterday. It was my first day." Her eyes
grew bright when she mentioned the children.

Abbie's knife resumed its peeling. "And what does
your mother think?"

"She's beside herself. I didn't ask her first because I
knew she would tell me not to. I went for an interview
when she was out delivering cakes."

"And what did she say when you returned?"

Jessie's face went pink. "She called me rebellious and
inconsiderate and selfish."

"Selfish, to go and help the poor?"

"That's what I told her. And I wasn't inconsiderate. I
left a note."

"Rebelliousness is not always a bad quality. Of course, I would not say such a thing to your mother."

Jessie finished the pear and picked up another. "I'm twenty-two. It's hardly rebellion to want to do something outside my own house."

"Well, I think it's a fine thing for you to do."

"Thank you for saying so."

"I would think about volunteering myself if I didn't have these babies. It's a miracle I managed to get both of them, and Ivy, down for a nap at the same time. This is the quietest my house ever gets in the daytime."

"Has Mr. Bergholtz found a new job?"

Abbie went to the sideboard and picked up a business card, which she plunked onto the table. Jessie read:

Reliance Auto Parts Mfg. Co.
Manufacturing and repairing
of all automobile and aeroplane parts in copper, brass
steel and aluminum
<u>*Radiators a specialty*</u>
Office and factory
224-250 W. 49th Street, New York
Near Broadway

Represented by
Mr. Walter Bergholtz

"So he's a salesman?"

"Yes. He works on commission. No salary."

"And does he know very much about automobiles and aeroplanes?"

"Not a thing."

"So . . . this isn't all that good, then."

"It's better than no job at all, he tells me. I think he'd be better off practicing his shorthand or looking for another position. I've borrowed money from my mother for next month's rent."

"I'm sorry to hear it. But do you think . . . maybe you should talk to Mrs. Hoag. Her husband knows the whole city government. He found a job for Mrs. Caterson's brother, cutting grass and pruning trees in the parks."

"The parks?"

"Not that Mr. Bergholtz would do parks, but maybe something else."

"Thank you, Jessie. That's an excellent idea. I'll speak to Mrs. Hoag."

"I have to get back and finish the sweeping before Mother gets home from her deliveries. I just had to tell you about the settlement. I didn't want to bring it up in the club yet, in front of Mother, until she gets used to it."

"I understand." A yowl from the bedroom brought Abbie to her feet.

"Oh, let me have a look at the babies before I go."

The boys were standing in their crib, gripping the rails. Sam, the more verbal of the two, was yammering away, while Ben bobbed up and down, bending and straightening his knees. Ivy rolled out of her low bed and ran to Jessie, who picked her up and started their traditional game of touching noses. Ivy laughed a belly laugh. "I'm sorry I won't have as much time to look after them now," Jessie said to Abbie.

"It's all right, dear. I'm proud of you."

Due to Jessie's volunteer work, Abbie's money worries, and the demands of three energetic children, meetings of the Child Labor Committee fell by the wayside. Besides, Abbie was working on her paper about birth control, of more immediate personal interest than child labor. However, she was perplexed over how to present the topic to the club.

The previous August, the newspapers had reported Margaret Sanger's arrest for sending "obscene" literature through the mail, although Abbie did not see anything obscene about a discussion of whether women ought to have the means to prevent pregnancy. Mrs. Sanger had made the same point at her arraignment, asserting that the Comstock law, which she was accused of violating, was unjust, and she did not consider herself guilty. When the judge refused to allow her several months to prepare a thorough defense but insisted on an immediate trial, she had sat down and written an explicit guide to all the birth control methods she had learned of on her recent trip to Europe.

This booklet, entitled *Family Limitation*, arrived in Abbie's mailbox a few weeks later, when Mrs. Sanger was on her way back to England, avoiding a probable prison sentence. Abbie opened the brown envelope and removed the sixteen-page booklet with eagerness.

There was something breathtaking about the direct, clinical way Mrs. Sanger wrote about the male and female organs, naming them and explaining how to administer techniques to prevent conception. While the words were jarring at first, the information was presented in a way not in the least titillating. Soon Abbie was engrossed in deciding which methods to try.

Mrs. Sanger said it was useless to rely on timing the sex act with the phases of the menstrual cycle. Abbie had to agree, based on her own experience. Should she drink quinine to prevent implantation of the ovum? Insert a sponge soaked in carbolic acid, or a vaginal suppository of citric and boric acids, to kill sperm? Douche with a solution of vinegar or potassium permanganate? In Mrs. Sanger's opinion, insertion of a domed rubber barrier called a pessary was the most effective means of preventing pregnancy. Unfortunately, pessaries, manufactured in Europe, had been outlawed in the U.S., just like condoms, which received her second highest recommendation.

Abbie decided to try a sponge, as well as douching. Maybe once she had experience of these methods, she could decide how to report to the clubwomen, who surely could benefit from such information. But as she wrote down the terms presented so matter-of-factly in the booklet, she couldn't imagine reading them out loud at the club. She decided the topic of her paper should be the Comstock law that prevented women from obtaining the information they needed, and how Mrs. Sanger was trying to challenge the law. Then any club member who wanted to learn about specific methods would be welcome to borrow the booklet.

Still, a prudishness, combined with fear of how her paper would be received, kept her from writing fluently on the topic. She struggled over it late into the night, several nights in a row. Meanwhile, use of the sponge and douche provided a partial sense of security, but as she was overwhelmed by the stress of taking care of three small children, she wished for a more reliable method. Damn that pious Anthony Comstock, who had talked Congress into outlawing birth control! She found curse words entering her thought far more often than she wished.

Then one day, Walter came home from his new job as a motor parts salesman and withdrew a palm-sized tin case from his pocket. On the cover were stamped the words "Rubber Goods—Protection for Gents."

"What is it?" Abbie asked. She took the tin and opened it. Inside were several stretchy little sock-like objects made of thin rubber. She picked one up and stared at it, then hastily put it back and shut the case. "Where on earth did you get those?" she asked, aware that she was blushing.

"The men at the shop are much less cultivated than the musicians at the Philharmonic." Walter put the tin back in his pocket. "I heard them talking about a prostitute, and I ventured to ask if they used condoms with the ladies. They said every pharmacy has a section of rubber goods, only the labels don't tell what they're really for. I had no idea."

There was a long silence, punctuated by a coughing fit from Mrs. Flint, when Abbie finished reading her paper. She was yearning to ask the women if and how they practiced birth control themselves, but she knew such a question would not be welcome, at least not if she asked directly.

Finally Jessie spoke up. "I think Mrs. Bergholtz's paper is very good, and I think the law should be changed. At the settlement house, I see lots of women with far too many children. Their lives would be much better if they had only one or two."

The breeze stirred the curtains at the half-opened window of Mrs. Everett's parlor. The voice of a knife sharpener, calling out his service, echoed up from the street. "Did you ladies know?" said Mrs. Fulton. "My daughter has been hired by the settlement house to work two days a week in the nursery. For money. I'm so proud."

Abbie knew Mrs. Fulton was actually upset by Jessie's growing independence and was forcing her to use the money to hire a cleaning woman. And it was irritating that she had used the opportunity to change the subject. The ladies all congratulated Jessie. Abbie said, "Yes, she's doing good work with the immigrant families, and they need birth control desperately. But so do we. I certainly don't want more than three children."

"I have five," said Mrs. Varian. "I adore them all, and I'm glad to have them."

"But your husband manages a factory," Abbie said. "Imagine if he didn't make a steady wage."

"But my dear, I thought Mr. Bergholtz had a new job. Didn't Mr. Hoag find him work with the subway?"

"Yes, he's been working for over a month now, and we're doing well financially, but—"

"Oh, how wonderful!" Mrs. Caterson exclaimed. "What kind of a job is it?"

"He's an inspector," said Mrs. Hoag. "Not heavy labor, but it's also not a desk job."

"That sounds perfect for him," Mrs. Lowitz said. "I know he's a restless type, can't sit still, isn't that right, Mrs. Bergholtz?"

"Yes, it's good for him," Abbie replied. "I didn't want to tell everyone until I was sure it was going well."

"And what exactly is his function?"

"He examines the work done on building the new subway line and makes sure everything is completed to specifications. He meets lots of people, which suits him well. And we've already paid next month's rent, so I am relieved. But even though our finances are better, I still would prefer not to have more children. Don't you think birth control—"

"Oh, I'm so pleased to hear it," said Mrs. Flint. "You've been waiting a long time for this kind of opportunity. And I'm sure he can still play his violin at home. It's less pressure on him that he doesn't have to do it for money, isn't it? Now music can be pure pleasure for him."

Abbie gave up. The club just wasn't ready for frank conversation on the one issue that seemed most critical to her own well-being. She liked and respected these women, but at that moment, she felt unutterably lonely.

Chapter 19

TO CONCEIVE

Suffrage Loses in New York by 180,000

Abbie thought first of Louise when she saw the headline on the morning after Election Day. What heartbreak her friend must be feeling! When she went on to examine her own emotions, she found she was actually disappointed. Walter pointed out a short article with the headline declaring:

New Suffrage Campaign Begun at 12:20 This Morning

A group of prominent suffragists had issued a statement promptly upon learning of the loss. Walter read aloud Dr. Anna Howard Shaw's declaration. "'This has not been a defeat. We have polled the largest number of votes ever cast for us in the United States. We shall go on and win.'"

"That's a deceptive statement," said Abbie. "It certainly has been a defeat, and I should be devastated if I had spent years of my life on trying to get the vote."

"But look at the optimism," Walter said. "When I read it, I think, yes, these women are determined, and they certainly will go on and win. And I hope they do."

Abbie stroked his arm. "I'm glad you support women, even though I don't feel so strongly about suffrage. Most men are entirely too narrow-minded."

By the time the club met, the following Tuesday, the referendum was old news. Jessie was talking about Mrs. Sanger's return to the U.S., where attitudes had changed during the year she'd been in Europe. Women's magazines were printing articles such as "What Shall We Do About Birth Control?" There was even a National Birth Control League, founded by a suffragist, Mary Ware Dennett.

"Mrs. Sanger actually turned herself in," Jessie reported. "She wants to argue birth control in court and try to overturn the law. Her trial is scheduled for the end of November. We should go and support her."

"Oh, I don't think so," Abbie said, knowing Mrs. Fulton must be on the verge of explosion. "I do think we might write to her and tell how we admire her work."

"And we could write the newspapers too. Oh, let's do that. If the whole club wrote letters, think what an influence we would have."

But the other women were not inclined to join the letter-writing campaign. Only Mrs. Fulton, eager to discourage a more active activism, agreed to write, as long as she could use a pseudonym. Jessie left the meeting early to hurry home and put pen to paper.

The night the condom broke, Abbie didn't panic. Even though it was her fertile time of the month, she had prepared for this possibility by buying a supply of potassium permanganate for douching. As soon as Walter rolled away, and she felt the moisture oozing down her leg, she jumped up from their bed of love, found and filled the rubber bag, and took it to the water closet. When she returned, Walter was sulking over her abrupt departure, and his lack of sympathy made her furious.

When her menses did not arrive on time, she cast around for a reason. Her system was disrupted by lack of sleep, with both of the twins teething. As soon as one began to recover, the other would start, and one or both woke her several times a night. She couldn't send Walter in to them, as he had to be at work early each morning. When her menses were two weeks late, the nighttime awakenings left her even more sleepless, as worry about pregnancy flooded her thoughts.

When she was three weeks late, she told Walter. He was delighted by the prospect of another child. Abbie tried to believe she would adapt, but when a crying baby woke her for the third time in the night, eliciting violent urges, panic set in. She countered it by telling herself she was too sensible to give in to anxiety. In the daytime, the children's demands kept her too busy to dwell on her worries, but at four in the morning, they rose up and consumed her.

Morning sickness set in, worse than before. She couldn't keep down food or drink, except for dry crackers in the morning and occasional sips of soda water. As the twins' first birthday approached, they both began to walk, unsteadily, heedlessly, and headlong. It seemed whenever she withdrew to sit still for a moment, she would soon hear a crash and a wail. She moved all the furniture to the edges of the rooms, but still the boys found ways to hurt themselves. Ben cracked his head on the kitchen sink and cried for an hour, making her worry he had a concussion. Sam, who learned to climb onto the bookshelves, fell and knocked over a lamp chimney that shattered under his elbow. Dr. Shirmer came and gave him five stitches.

Ivy had always been protective of the boys, but she turned against them when they became mobile enough to seek out her dolls. Ben tore off Dolly's arm, and Ivy was hysterical until Abbie sewed the limb back on. She really couldn't blame Ivy for defending herself, but she couldn't allow her to push and slap the boys. Making her sit in the corner as punishment broke Abbie's heart.

With Jessie now employed full-time at the settlement house, Abbie hired Sally, a neighbor girl, to come by for two hours each afternoon. She was not good with Ivy, who developed a disagreeable habit of sticking out her tongue when the girl crossed her. Then Ivy began to do the same to everyone. The day Abbie fired Sally, Walter came home from work to find the three children running around the parlor, shouting, and his wife curled up in bed, crying.

Before he could ask after her, Ivy came into the bedroom to say the children were hungry. He made them bread and butter and then went back to stroke Abbie's hair. "What's wrong, darling?"

"I don't want another baby."

"Did you have a trying day?"

"I can't take care of three children. How am I going to take care of four? And what if I have twins again?"

"Don't be silly. No one has twins twice in a row, and you're the most capable mother I know."

"They've gone wild. I can't control them."

"You're just tired out. You've been sick, but that will end soon."

"Yes, and then the baby will be born. And then I'll be pregnant again, and another baby will be born. And another and another, until I'm old and worn out. All because that lunatic Anthony Comstock made a vicious law. I hate that man."

"Darling, you must calm yourself."

"And I don't want to have this baby."

"Abbie, you don't know what you're saying." She heard a note of alarm in his voice. Her thought ran to visions of him consigning her to a lunatic asylum. No, how ridiculous! But her agitated mind insisted on adding that fear to the list.

"You don't understand," she mumbled.

"I understand you're under a strain, but everything will work out. Now let me make you a cup of tea, and you'll be all better soon."

She pretended to feel comforted. He went off to the kitchen, and she tried to think of someone else to confide in. The person she was closest to besides Walter was Jessie, but Abbie couldn't burden a young person with these torments. Although the other clubwomen were good at solving practical problems, she had never brought them deep emotional pain, which she had reserved for Walter. And now he was failing her.

She thought of seeking an abortion doctor. Even if she had known how to find one, the operation was too dangerous. She couldn't risk leaving her children motherless. If there was a way out of her dilemma, she couldn't find it.

One morning, she felt too sick to move. Walter had gone off to work before the children awoke. Abbie heard them stirring. Ivy ran into the bedroom and burrowed under the covers with her. The boys could not yet climb out of their crib. Their mother lay in bed and let them cry.

Chapter 20

INEZ MILHOLLAND

Y ou give your lifeblood to the Copper Queen, working eight hours a day, six days a week, and what do you get in return?" shouted Rose Winslow. "Five dollars a day and a run-down shack. Women, the bearers of children, know what it is to give our lifeblood and to receive a pittance in return. In the East, though, it's even worse. The women who slave in the factories work twelve hours a day, make only three dollars and fifty cents, and live in crowded tenements, eight to a room."

Miss Winslow was pint-sized but had a clear, bell-like voice. She wore a sleeveless frock over a white blouse, cleaner than the miners' clothing but equally simple. They sensed her kinship with them, which increased as soon as she spoke of her past. "I was born Ruza Wenclawska in Poland and came to the U.S. as a baby. My father was a coal miner in Pennsylvania. When I was eleven, I began working as a mill girl, making stockings in a factory in Pittsburgh. At nineteen, I contracted tuberculosis, and I couldn't work for two years. I am one of the thousands of women who work in the sweated trades, who give their lives to build up tremendous industries in this country, and at the end of the years of work, our reward is the tuberculosis sanatorium or the street."

The miners nodded, murmurs circling through the crowd of men who sat on stumps or stood, all of them clustered in the center of the camp. Rough huts surrounded them, overshadowed by a tower with the words "Copper Queen Mining Co." lettered on the side. Most of the gaunt men had mustaches, and all wore dirt-smudged, sweaty, rumpled pants and jackets. One of them called out something Louise couldn't understand. Miss Winslow answered in Polish. A group of men applauded, while the Finns and Lithuanians whispered to each other. She went back to English, and all the men fell silent.

"Eastern women are merely asking for a chance to help themselves. You can support them by voting against the Democrats, who have failed over and over to grant the vote to women."

"But I thought the Democrats are more for suffrage than the Republicans," said a man with a Finnish accent."

"It's true," replied Miss Winslow. "But what good is the vote of some men if they don't convince a majority of their party to vote for suffrage? And President Wilson refuses to support a national amendment. He says it should be up to the states. The Republican presidential candidate, Charles Evans Hughes, has spoken in favor of the amendment. Even if he loses, your votes will show the Democrats they have to take woman suffrage seriously."

It was 6:30 when the men stopped shaking Miss Winslow's hand and let her go. Damaris pulled the Model T up to the edge of the crowd, and Louise climbed in front, Miss Winslow in back. "You really had them," said Damaris as they bumped their way out of the mining camp to the asphalt road, where they skirted the potholes.

"It always goes best when some of the men are Polish," said Miss Winslow. "And Miss Kelley's speech warmed them up nicely. I'm so exhausted. I'm going to lie down and nap, if the potholes will let me."

To avoid waking her, Louise and Damaris spoke little on the four-hour drive to Tucson. They were weary too, after three weeks on the road, visiting cities, small towns, lumber camps, mining camps, railroad shops. When they addressed a crowd, they often had to jostle for position with Democratic campaigners, bent on recruiting the same workers to vote for Woodrow Wilson. After sleeping on sagging, grimy mattresses in ragged towns for the past week, Louise was looking forward to a night at a hotel in Tucson, with hot running water and a featherbed.

She had been excited about the western tour. Their month in Poughkeepsie, stumping for the New York referendum, had been discouraging. The local branch of the Empire State Coordinating Committee was already in league with the Vassar girls. The women had been trained by Crystal Eastman, the bohemian lawyer from the Heterodoxy Club, and were therefore not impressed with Damaris, despite her Vassar credentials. Even invoking an association with Inez Milholland had failed to open doors. The workers at the harvester factory listened respectfully to Louise, but accounts of her stint as a seamstress were not sufficient to move them.

The two women gave up and joined a group farther north in Troy, where Harriot Blatch's forces had the opportunity to start from scratch, with no existing suffrage organization to compete with. Damaris, bitter from the failure of the Poughkeepsie effort, was terrible company. Louise adapted by concentrating on the development of her own speechmaking skills. The more capable she became, the more she felt conscious of her value to the suffrage movement, as if she were building and flexing new muscles for the arduous work. She felt gratified to be taking action that would benefit her entire gender. And yet, there were moments when she wished she could go to college again and focus on the life of the mind. She escaped from these conflicting emotions by taking occasional trips to Harlem to spend time with Jonathan Harris.

The defeat of the New York referendum was devastating. Mrs. Blatch took it hard and turned away from the state effort. Louise and Damaris followed her to Washington, pinning their hopes on the national amendment. When Alice Paul announced the plan to hold the Democrats accountable by campaigning against them in the states where women could already vote, Louise jumped at the chance to visit the huge open spaces out West. Damaris earned them a role by offering to buy an automobile once they reached Arizona, since Rose Winslow was heading for small towns not accessible by train. Louise was entranced by the pure starkness of the desert, with thin strips of purple mountains lining the horizon, but after many days of driving, the landscape began to lose its appeal, and the fatigue of travel mounted.

The morning after their arrival in Tucson, Miss Winslow said she couldn't get out of bed, much less address the local women's clubs. Louise cabled Miss Paul to report on their success at the Bisbee copper camp and Miss Winslow's state of exhaustion. The reply was unfeeling.

Get Rose on her feet much work to be done.

"I don't think we can force her," Damaris told Louise. "Sometimes I hate Miss Paul."

"She does push herself just as hard. Many times she spends whole nights in her office. She sleeps for a few hours on a pad."

"I don't see why we all have to be just like her."

Instead of trying to prop up Miss Winslow, Louise went to address the clubwomen, who responded warmly. When she returned to the hotel, two messages were waiting. One was her first letter from Jonathan in over a month.

My dear Louise,

I hope the West is thrilling you but not too wild. I miss you and send my fond regards. Forgive me for not writing lately, but you will understand why when I explain.

We are much troubled here by the lynchings in the South, especially the horror at Waco, Texas. Did you hear of it? A black man, upon being convicted of rape and murder, was taken by a crowd, tortured, burned, and hanged, while fifteen thousand people watched. Certainly, if he was rightly convicted (of that we are not sure), he deserved punishment, but not desecration, which all those depraved people watching regarded as entertainment. I am sickened and sorrowed to my depths. I believe President Wilson's permitting of segregation in the government is partly responsible for this barbarism. I encourage you in your opposition to the Demo-

crats in power. They have done a poor job of protecting Negroes.

Mr. Du Bois of the NAACP proposed that I go to the South and use my ability to pass as white, in order to investigate lynchings. The prospect seemed dangerous, and I must confess, my heart was faint, but with you striking out for women, I was inspired to take action for the black race. And of course my appearance and heritage make me uniquely suited for this project. However, Waco was too hot with passion just then. I went to Mississippi, where so many have been lynched this year. My research showed how lax the police and courts have been. Many told me to my face that they regard colored people as undeserving of rights. Upon returning, I reported to Mr. Du Bois, and he is writing an article for his magazine, The Crisis. *He will refer to me by a pseudonym, of course.*

I hope you will burn this letter for my protection and yours. Again, please forgive me for not writing sooner, but you can see that correspondence would have endangered my safety.

Devotedly yours,

Jonathan

Louise was glad he hadn't written to tell her of his errand before he left for Mississippi, as she would have worried about him. At times, she saw him as too comfortable in his money-making ventures, so she admired him for taking on such a daring and righteous mission. But she found herself hoping he wouldn't return to the South and put himself in danger again.

The second communication was another cable from Washington. Two weeks earlier, with several campaigners dropping from exhaustion, Inez Milholland Boissevain had offered to go West on a tour of major cities. Halfway through the schedule, she too was depleted. Miss Paul was ordering Louise to join her and ease the strain by sharing the speaking responsibilities.

"What should I do?" Louise asked Damaris, who was slouched in an armchair in the hotel lobby, simmering with envy. "I don't want to leave you and Miss Winslow." In fact, she liked the idea of traveling by train instead of jouncing over country roads in the Ford, and she was curious about the fabled Mrs. Boissevain. It was flattering to have her speech-making skills recognized. But she also had a sense of loyalty to her two companions.

Damaris, soothed by Louise's protestation of reluctance, exhaled a sigh. "You must go. Inez needs you. We'll be all right."

"But I don't need an introduction," Inez said. "They already know who I am." She was sitting in bed in a hotel room in Ogden, Utah, sipping chamomile tea.

Her sister, Vida, looked exasperated but kept her voice calm. "Still, it adds drama if Miss Kelley recounts your accomplishments and builds up the anticipation with a few suffrage stories. And then you won't have to talk as long, since it will take up part of the time. You must conserve your strength."

"Look at all the converts I've made. It's me they're coming to hear, not some unknown woman." Louise would have been insulted if she hadn't felt overwhelmed by the legendary presence and the signs of severe strain she had already observed. The patrician profile was marred by skin pulled tight over the cheekbones and brownish pouches beneath the eyes. Louise addressed her as Mrs. Boissevain, but in her mind, she always used the name Inez. Its exotic, queenly aura fit the woman precisely.

"Don't worry," said Vida with the barest hint of sarcasm. "No matter who's onstage, you'll still be the star of the show."

"I'm sorry, Miss Kelley." Inez turned her azure eyes to Louise, bathing her in their glow, which was dimmed by fatigue but still held a warmth that spoke of spiritual depth and personal power. "You've traveled far, I expect."

"Only from Tucson. Not so very far, although out West the distances do—"

"I so appreciate your coming. I just . . . my address has been carefully crafted as to timing and emphasis. I simply don't have the strength to alter it. I'm sure you understand."

"I can edit your speech," said Vida. "Your problem is the time spent onstage. It takes so much out of you."

"I'll be all right if I get a day of rest. What did Alice say about canceling tonight's speech?"

"She said Ogden is critical, and she feels canceling would be a disaster."

"All right then, let me nap for a few hours." Inez slid down under the blankets and pulled them over her head.

Vida took Louise next door into the plainly furnished sitting room. Younger than her sister, she was nearly as handsome but more soft-spoken. At a rally in Washington, however, Louise had heard her sing in a well-trained, soaring soprano.

"I'm sorry," Vida said. "She's so overextended."

"She looks ill. She must be working very hard."

"It was insane to schedule fifty speeches in thirty days. And she wasn't well to begin with. In Chicago, the very first week, a doctor said her tonsils are infected, and she should have an operation, but she just asked for medication. I'm sorry for how she treated you. She's really not herself."

"It's all right. I'll go back to Miss Winslow."

"No, please stay with us. We can pay your train fare. It would be so helpful to have another woman along. Inez is stubborn, but maybe she'll give in about your speaking at some point."

"Of course. Whatever I can do to help."

In Sacramento, Inez could barely lift her head from the cushioned seat of the hansom cab on the way to the hall. But when she walked onstage, she became a passionate orator, her voice ringing across the auditorium as she roused the California women to stand against the Democrats. Next came San Francisco, where she packed five speeches into three days, swallowing pills before each appearance. When not in sight of the public, Vida and Louise supported her as she walked, an arm encircling her waist from each side. Although mostly ignored in conversation, Louise cherished each tidbit of attention and excused the rest, knowing the heroic effort Inez was making.

When they reached Los Angeles, after an uncomfortable train ride marked by long delays, Inez was barely conscious. Vida summoned a doctor to the hotel. Inez told him, "Just fix me up," and he prescribed more powerful painkillers.

That night, she stepped onto the stage at Blanchard Hall looking regal as ever in a purple gown with flowing scarves. She addressed a crowd of over five hundred, proclaiming the good fortune of California women to have the vote already, imploring them to help their eastern sisters. "We do not ask you to vote for Charles Evans Hughes, who has made but weak efforts to support woman suffrage. We ask you to vote *against* President Wilson for refusing to endorse a Constitutional amendment for suffrage. If you will use your votes as your voices, we can make the president listen. We must raise our voices in unison. President Wilson, hear our cry!" As her own voice rose to a shout, Inez toppled to the floor.

Vida and Louise rushed out and helped her offstage. "You go out there and talk to them," said Vida, and Louise returned to deliver the speech she had been practicing. Fifteen minutes later, Inez walked shakily back onto the platform, and Louise retired to the wings to watch her finish her address. People asked questions from the audience, and Inez answered gracefully before going to the hotel to collapse.

The next day, Vida cabled Miss Paul, "LA a triumph collected 50 dollars but Inez fainted cancelling rest of tour." The reply was swift.

Calamity not to have her appear only week of campaign left surely she can pull through this.

"Doctor says quite impossible she is seriously ill."

At least come back to Chicago for phone call to suffrage states even if she says only a word or two.

"Inez deeply regrets her inability to continue."

Mrs. Blatch, although she also was not well, took over the last week of the tour. Inez went into the hospital, where she was diagnosed with pernicious anemia. The doctors said she was not strong enough for an operation on her tonsils or even the extraction of several infected teeth. Louise returned to Arizona, determined to keep Miss Winslow from a similar fate.

A week later, President Wilson was reelected by a significantly narrow margin, which even the usually skeptical *New York Times* attributed largely to the suffragists' campaign.

In late November, while still in the hospital, Inez Milholland Boissevain passed away. When Louise heard the news, she wept.

Chapter 21

MARGARET SANGER

It was rare for Abbie to feel conspicuously well-dressed. On this occasion, it was not because she had bought or borrowed anything stylish but because the other women on line were in plain coats, most well-worn, many patched and ragged. They wore shawls over their heads. Abbie pulled her round felt hat with its upturned brim almost down to her eyes and turned up the collar of her three-year-old navy wool coat with its out-of-fashion wide lapels. Luckily, as most of the women in her immediate vicinity had two, three, or four children in tow, they weren't paying her any mind.

Abbie stood on tiptoe, seeking the head of the line. There must still be sixty women ahead of her, she thought, although she had reached the place fairly early in the morning. Most people were speaking Yiddish or Italian, but on arriving, she had passed a woman up ahead and heard her say in English, "It's good we got here just before the clinic opened. Look how many are behind us already."

"I saw notices all over Brownsville," replied her neighbor. "Yesterday they had to turn people away. They've only been open for ten days, and everyone knows they're here."

When news of the clinic had come to the Henry Street Settlement, Jessie notified Abbie. They were following Mrs. Sanger in the papers and had read that her trial over *The Woman Rebel* was dismissed in February, the judge apparently preferring to minimize publicity. Disappointed not to present her case in court, she undertook a nationwide speaking tour, then returned to New York, where she made plans to open a birth control clinic.

Now that Abbie was standing among the residents of Brownsville, out in the borough of Brooklyn, she felt guilty. She already had access to condoms, which were imperfect but useful. Maybe it was selfish to hope she could get a pessary, when these women probably had no method at all. But she needed a reliable means to prevent pregnancy, and she had traveled all the way from the Bronx. Walter had taken the day off from work to watch the children. She wasn't going to leave empty-handed if there was any chance at all of making it through the door.

The line shuffled forward a little at a time. Abbie turned to the woman behind her, one without children underfoot. "Do you think they'll get to us today?"

The reply came in Yiddish. The woman in front of Abbie, having heard her question, said, in heavily accented English, "My cousin came a few days ago. She got here in the afternoon and had to come back the next morning. Then she got in."

"So today seems possible."

"I think so."

"How many children do you have?"

"I got pregnant twelve times, and eight babies lived. I can't go through it again. If I get pregnant one more time, I swear I'm going to smash up a glass and swallow it down."

"I've only got three, but I feel the same."

The day wore on, and Abbie's feet began to ache. She made an agreement with her neighbor, Mrs. Steinman, that they would take turns sitting on a stoop and saving each other's place in line. A man selling potato *Knödel* from a cart came by, and she bought three, eating the boiled doughy pillows hot with mushroom sauce. Most of the other women had brought food along, and Abbie suspected they couldn't afford to buy dumplings. She bought three for Mrs. Steinman, who shared her jar of homemade sauerkraut.

It was late in the afternoon when Abbie finally reached the head of the line. Inside the clinic, she was greeted by a young woman sitting behind a desk. "I'm Fania Mindell. I'm a social worker. Please sit down, and I'll take a medical history."

Miss Mindell charged Abbie ten cents, then asked a list of questions, writing the answers on a chart. "How many pregnancies have you had?"

"Do twins count as one pregnancy or two?"

"One."

"Then I've had three pregnancies."

"How many live births?"

"I had one daughter, then the twins, and then a miscarriage in the third month, earlier this year."

Miss Mindell looked up, hearing the catch in Abbie's voice. "I'm sorry."

"It was for the best. I didn't want more. I need a pessary. Can I get a pessary?"

"Yes, ma'am. Mrs. Sanger will see to it that you get what you need."

After the interview, Abbie was sent to the spartan waiting room. She sat down opposite Mrs. Steinman, two mothers nursing babies, and a weary woman who tried half-heartedly to stop her three children from climbing onto chairs and jumping down. Abbie wondered how many older children were at home, waiting for her return.

She tried not to think about the baby she had lost. What worried her at the moment was the disastrous effect her last pregnancy had had on her marriage. It had taken several weeks for her body to recover from the miscarriage. Even once her strength had returned and her private parts were no longer raw, she still resisted Walter's advances until one day she took pity on his frustration. But his touch did not bring her pleasure. As his hands traveled over her body, an anger welled up that left her limbs stiff and her skin cold.

"What's wrong?" he asked.

"I can't get it out of my mind that the condom might break." She was telling the truth, but she knew there were other factors, which she had no way to discuss with him. He had been so opaque in response to her fear of having another child, she simply didn't trust him.

"I can't function if you're going to be so tense," he said. "It isn't working."

"Well, I can't help it." She turned her back and drifted off to sleep.

He stopped asking her to satisfy him, and a coldness crept into their relationship. They spoke to each other cordially and enjoyed the children together. He continued to bring her a weekly rose and poem, but the poems became shorter and more abstract, with a mournful, yearning undertone that made her feel despair. She pinned her hopes of relief on the pessary. If she weren't so worried about pregnancy, surely she'd be able to relax with him. A little rubber cup seemed to be the key to her happiness.

When there were eight women sitting in the waiting room, an inner door opened, and a patient came out carrying a small cardboard box. A nurse, wearing a white uniform with a winged cap, summoned the eight into the next room. On the white walls, which still smelled slightly of paint, posters showed diagrams of the female reproductive system. Abbie stared at the drawings, contemplating the structure of her own insides.

"I'm Margaret Sanger," said a small woman whose resonant voice contrasted with her fragile appearance. "This is my sister, Ethel Byrne. We're both trained nurses, and we're here to tell you how to keep from having children you don't wish to have."

The lecture was similar to the text of *Family Limitation*, which Abbie had read over and over. She knew from the booklet that a pessary had to be fitted, which would require an examination. After giving birth to three children, she wasn't nervous about the examination, but she was impatient. It had been a long day, and she missed her family.

Mrs. Sanger asked how many women would like to receive pessaries. Only two raised their hands. Mrs. Byrne wrote down their names and handed the paper to her sister, who said, "Please come with me into the examination room, Mrs. Steinman. If you would kindly sit in the waiting room, Mrs. Bergholtz, you'll be next."

Abbie was feeling light-headed. It was almost dinnertime, and she had eaten only the three dumplings since morning. Miss Mindell was talking with the other women, offering copies of a booklet, *What Every Girl Should Know*, for twenty-five cents apiece.

Raised voices from outside made Abbie uneasy. "Hey, what are you doing?" someone shouted. "Get in line!" Through the open door between the waiting and reception rooms, she saw a stocky, red-haired woman in a thick wool coat barge in, followed by three men in black suits.

Miss Mindell stood up. "I recognize you," she said to the woman. "You were here yesterday."

"That's right, and you're under arrest for giving out obscene information."

The social worker did not look surprised. The red-haired woman marched through to the next room, while one of the men opened the drawers of a filing cabinet. "You can't look at the patient files," Miss Mindell said. "They're confidential."

"You're breaking the law," said the man. "These belong to the government now."

The other men were writing down the names of the patients in the waiting room. Most of the women were crying, which made the babes in arms scream. Abbie was trying to stay calm. She hadn't done anything wrong, and she wasn't going to let these men intimidate her.

"Name, please," one of them said to her.

"What is the charge?"

"You're not being charged. We just want your name."

"I don't believe I'm required to give my name if I'm not being charged."

He shrugged and moved on.

Mrs. Steinman emerged from the inner room, carrying one of the little cardboard boxes. Abbie wanted to grab it from her hand. Mrs. Sanger walked in, shouting, "Ladies, don't be distressed. You have not broken any law, and you'll be home quite soon. Please calm down." She addressed the men. "If you insist on arresting the three of us, go ahead, but you must let these women go."

It occurred to Abbie that Mrs. Sanger had known all along she was going to be arrested, which would give her the chance to challenge the law in court. But what about her innocent, frightened clients?

Two policemen came into the clinic. A pair of black patrol wagons had pulled up outside, with a crowd of curious men and women looking on. "Into the wagons with you," said a man in black to the shawled women in the waiting room. Although Mrs. Sanger's words had quieted her patients, they began to cry again. She argued with the man, while the policemen herded the eight women outside and helped them into the police vehicles. Abbie mounted the two steps to the shadowed interior of a van and sat down on one of the cold steel benches. The door of the wagon slammed. Light filtered through a mesh partition separating the chamber from the vehicle's cab.

"It will be all right," she told the three sobbing women confined with her. "I'm sure Mrs. Sanger will not let them hold us." But what if they had to go to jail for the night? No, she was sure such a resourceful woman would get them released. She decided both Mrs. Sanger and her patients were doing a service for all women if this outrage might influence public opinion.

At last a policeman opened the door and told them they could go. As Abbie was stepping down, she saw Mrs. Sanger and Miss Mindell standing with one of the men in black.

"Get in the wagon, you two," he said.

"Absolutely not," Mrs. Sanger replied. "I will not be ordered about by brutes who have terrorized my clients and stolen their confidential records. Which way is the station house?"

The man pointed south. "About a mile." She turned and marched off, two policemen trailing her.

Abbie hastened toward the streetcar, anxious to get home to her family. She sensed she had witnessed a historic event, but she was disappointed to leave without a pessary.

Chapter 22

JESSIE

Mrs. Fulton slapped the *New York Times* down on Abbie's dining-room table and pointed to a headline.

Are Suffragists Menacing Wilson's Life? Antis Say Picketing of White House is an Invitation to the Assassin.

"It's traitorous," Mrs. Fulton said. "And while we're on the brink of war."

"Picketing only harms the suffrage cause," Abbie agreed. "It makes people angry." She read down the column to a quote from Ruth Kimball Gardiner of the National Association Opposed to Woman Suffrage.

It is impossible to follow the mental processes of the women who devised the picket idea. As an argument it ranks with the small boy's thrusting out his tongue. As a demonstration of fitness for the vote it is idiotic.

Abbie found the antis shrill and self-righteous, but she had to agree with this woman's view of the picketing.

"Poor President Wilson," Mrs. Fulton said, "with all this war pressure, and now he has those women standing at his doorstep, whining and trying to draw the country's attention."

Abbie hoped Louise had not joined the pickets. "I can understand wanting to change the law," she said, "but picketing is unpatriotic. Some people believe the suffs are being paid by the Germans, just to undermine Mr. Wilson and cloud his judgment." She glanced across the room at the children, who were sitting at a low table with pencils and paper. Ivy, now four, had learned to draw stick figures and was trying to instruct her two-year-old brothers.

"I didn't want to say anything," Mrs. Fulton said, her voice lowered, "your husband being German, but I've heard the same."

"The anti-German sentiment is absolutely feverish. Mr. Schmidt at Walter's office arrived at work with a broken arm last week, and they had to take him to a hospital. A gang of young hoodlums beat him outside his home in Canarsie. We've even discussed changing our name from Bergholtz to Burke, but my brother-in-law already has a career in education. If one family member changes, the rest would too, and he fears it would look dishonest."

"Has anyone in your family been attacked?"

"No, but the butcher gives me a hostile look these days and I hear him say 'Kraut' under his breath. I've considered switching to the German butcher, but his cuts are not nearly as good."

"I'm so sorry, my dear. We live in frightening times. About these suffs . . ." She took a sip of tea, and looked back at the headline. Abbie waited, suspecting Mrs. Fulton was getting around to the real point of her visit. The words burst out in an angry stream. "Jessie is entirely in favor of them. I don't know what to do. I'm afraid she's turning into a radical. If I say a word about my own opinion, she . . . she attacks me. She argues with me. Our house is no longer the peaceful haven it was."

"Perhaps you should make a rule, just like in the club, not to discuss suffrage."

"I've tried, but she waves the paper at me and starts going on about 'those brave women, standing up for us all.' And I can't keep my mouth closed. It just riles me."

Sam squawked, and Abbie looked over. He was pushing Ivy away, but instead of battling with her brother, she laid her pencil down and kissed his cheek. Once the boys had become steady on their feet, their relationship with Ivy had righted itself as well. Abbie smiled, then turned back to Mrs. Fulton. "Jessie's growing up. You've kept her close, for good reason, and she's trying to break away. I had to do the same with my mother, eventually."

"But it frightens me. What if she decides to join them and starts marching in parades and handing out bills and such? I just couldn't . . . Will you help me, please? Take her under your wing and help her see how wrong-headed all this suffrage nonsense is?"

"I don't think . . . I'm not sure she'll listen to me." Abbie was surprised Mrs. Fulton was asking her for help, since it was her own papers on social problems that had inspired Jessie's interest in politics. But Mrs. Fulton had her reasons.

"She respects you. She admires your reform interests, which are much more sensible than what the suffragettes are up to. I do think she'll listen, and you might be able to rein her in. Young people are so idealistic these days, and they need to hear common sense from someone they trust."

"Well, of course I'll try. But please don't hold it against me if I fail."

"I have every confidence in you, Mrs. Bergholtz. Thank you so very much."

A few Sundays later, it was Jessie who appeared at Abbie's door with a handful of newspapers. "Did you see? They're force-feeding Ethel Byrne. That poor, brave woman."

Jessie and Abbie had both been following the trial of Mrs. Sanger's sister for disseminating birth control information at the Brownsville clinic. As soon as the woman was sentenced to thirty days at the workhouse on Blackwell Island, Mrs. Byrne announced she was going on a hunger strike and wouldn't even drink water. The Commissioner of Corrections said prisoners who threatened hunger strikes always gave in after a day or two, but Mrs. Byrne would be monitored by a doctor and forcibly fed if her health appeared to decline. Within less than a week, that time had come.

"It says she didn't resist, and they put a tube down her throat with milk, eggs, and brandy," Jessie said. "Mrs. Sanger's trial is tomorrow, and she says she'll go on hunger strike too if she's put in prison."

Abbie read down the page. "Mrs. Byrne went into a coma, although she's out of it now."

"Mrs. Sanger said it was a coma, but the commissioner said that's not true. If Mrs. Sanger wasn't there, how would she know?"

"Maybe Mrs. Byrne wrote her a letter when she came out of the coma? It doesn't say."

Jessie shook her head. "Someone is lying, either Mrs. Sanger or the commissioner. I don't like it when people lie. How do you know the truth?"

"That's the problem. The newspapers report all sorts of things, and you can't really know."

"The commissioner said he wasn't going to let the newspapers report on her condition, but you know what? There's been an article every day, and they quote Mrs. Byrne a lot." Jessie unfolded another paper. "She said eight thousand women have died in New York from illegal operations, and so . . . Here it is. 'It does not make much difference whether I starve or not, so long as my plight calls attention to the archaic laws which would prevent our telling the truth about the facts of life.' She's so noble. Do you know she's the first woman prisoner in the country to be forcibly fed?"

Abbie also admired Mrs. Byrne, but this sort of activism was dangerously akin to what the suffragettes were heading towards, and she had promised to discourage Jessie's interest in that direction. "As you say, dear, even good people sometimes tell lies. Politics can be a nasty business."

Jessie looked puzzled. "Is this what you call politics? I thought politics was getting elected and going to Congress and such. This is just two women standing up for what they believe."

"And they are admirable, too. But they're trying to get the law changed, so I would call that politics."

"Oh. Well then, politics isn't all bad, is it?"

Abbie looked back at one of the articles, groping for direction. "Mrs. Byrne isn't putting up any resistance to the tube being put down her throat. In a way, she's giving in to them."

"But if she resisted, they would strap her down and put the tube down her nose, which is terribly painful. That's what they did to the suffs in England. I don't blame her for not wanting it."

Abbie was stumped. The education of Jessie wasn't quite going the way she'd hoped.

After serving ten days of her sentence, Mrs. Byrne was pardoned by the governor and released, on the condition that she stop giving out birth control information, which her sister promised on her behalf. Then Mrs. Sanger was convicted and also given a thirty-day sentence. She decided not to undertake a hunger strike but instead to study conditions in prison.

Jessie was dismayed. "I thought she was so brave, and she went back on her word."

"Yes," said Abbie. "Rather cowardly of her."

"Although I suppose prison reform is important too. Conditions at the workhouse are appalling. Maybe she decided Mrs. Byrne had gotten enough publicity for birth control, and it would just annoy the public to keep reading about it."

"Still, it was rash of her to say earlier—"

"Then again, at Mrs. Sanger's trial, they were going to let her off if she promised not to break the law again, and she said she'd rather go to jail."

"That's true."

"No one is perfect. I still think she's wonderful."

Chapter 23

THE CATSKILLS

D olly, be careful, or you'll fall in and drownd," Ivy said. She was reaching her cloth doll up to peer over the ship's rail at the Hudson River rushing past.

"Ivy, bring her down," Jessie urged. "There's no way to get her back if she falls."

The impudent Dolly continued to gaze down at the water, the little gingham dress Abbie had sewed for her whipping in the wind.

A stocky matron in a blue mackintosh was standing next to them at the rail. She bowed her head and told Ivy, "I think the dolly needs a spanking."

Ivy stepped back and hugged the doll to her chest, frowning at the woman, who chuckled. Pulling Jessie down so she could whisper in her ear, Ivy asked, "What's a 'panking?"

"Something you've never had and never will, because you don't need it," Jessie answered.

Abbie tilted her head back to bathe her face in the sun, its heat conquered at last by the river breeze. She had been melting all summer, soggy with sweat and exhausted from keeping up with two spirited three-year-olds. Ivy's sensitive skin broke out in a heat rash every few days, making her cranky and uncooperative.

It had been Walter's idea, now that they had saved up some money, to go to the Catskills for a week. Summer in the city was not only uncomfortable but unsanitary. Despite the humidity, the heat dried out the horse droppings on the roads. The street cleaners couldn't scoop up the manure that fell between the cobblestones, and the resultant dust blew through the air, clogging nostrils and begriming hair. In addition, tuberculosis was rampant. Abbie went about with a stack of hankies in her purse in case she had to touch handrails. On streetcars and subways, the upright poles were polished bright by the handkerchiefs of the riders. She wished her family could spend the whole summer in the country, but hopefully this one week would fortify her system and help her endure the city heat till the end of August.

Like most of the husbands, Walter would be working until he took the train up to join his wife and children on Friday night. Jessie had taken the week off to help out on the trip and get her first taste of the mountains. She was looking forward to a vacation from her mother, who had gotten it fixed in her head that Jessie must get married. She kept trying to match her daughter up with dull, responsible suitors. In fact, Mrs. Fulton was pleased about the trip. "See if you can introduce her to a respectable young fellow," she told Abbie. "Maybe on the ship, or at the hotel." The last thing Abbie wanted to worry about was matchmaking, but she said she would try.

Just above Poughkeepsie, Ivy shouted, "Look, Mama, another big boat!" She jumped up and down, pointing at the "down boat" about to pass in the opposite direction. The boys covered their ears as the deep-toned horns of the two ships bellowed their salute. Sam tugged at Abbie's skirt. "I'm hungry."

They left the view of rippling green hills and dazzling water to search for the cafeteria. Down stairs and up stairs they roamed, past the ladies' lounge and the gentlemen's saloon, a writing room, a news-stand, a barber shop, more lounges. In one room, a band played ragtime, and in another, a chamber ensemble was performing a piece Abbie recognized as a Debussy sonata. By the time they found the cafeteria, the children were whining. Abbie bought hot dogs for the five of them, but the boys barely ate theirs. "It's past time for their nap," Jessie pointed out. When she and Abbie had finished the remains of the children's meals, they went to look for a quiet lounge.

On the east side of the ship, out of the direct sun but with a breeze swirling through the open windows, Abbie settled the boys down on upholstered benches along one wall. Jessie squeezed Ivy next to her in an armchair and began to read aloud from Rudyard Kipling's *Just So Stories*. Sam fell asleep instantly, but Ben began to fuss. Not wanting to disturb the other passengers, Abbie carried him around the lounge, hoping the movement would lull him to sleep. Some people were reading, others conversed, and a few square tables were surrounded by people playing cards.

As she reached the opposite end of the room, she noticed a couple gazing at a chess board. The man had curly hair and heavy eyebrows, and the woman . . . At that moment, the woman looked up and said, "Abbie?"

"Louise!"

Ben moaned, a sign that he was falling asleep. "I have to lay him down," Abbie whispered. "We're at the other end of the lounge."

"I'll come find you in a moment."

As Abbie carried Ben away, she wondered about Louise's relationship with the man, whether they were companions or had just met on the boat. He was stylishly dressed, as slim and elegant as she was.

Having exercised the motherly art of putting a sleeping child down without waking him, she turned to wondering why Louise was riding on a Dayliner heading toward Albany. It was three years since their last meeting. They had exchanged a few letters after Louise sent her Mrs. Sanger's newspaper, and Abbie had written her about the twins. The last she'd heard, over a year ago, Louise was about to travel West with the suffs. Surely she would have written if she'd decided to marry.

"Oh, they're darling! Two perfect little boys." Abbie looked up, and affection flooded her heart. How sad that she and Louise had fallen out. They had been so close.

"Miss Kelley?"

"Why, Miss Fulton! What a surprise! And this used to be little Ivy, who has grown into a great big girl."

Ivy peered up at Louise, then hid her face in Jessie's shoulder.

"Jessie has been helping me with the children," Abbie said. "We're on our way to the Catskills. The city has been so beastly this summer. What about you?"

Louise sat down. She looked radiantly attractive, despite dark smudges beneath her eyes. "I've been picketing in Washington with my employer, Miss Oakley. It's tiring and rather boring most of the time, and of course the heat is just awful. We decided to take a break and come up to New York. She's gone with her family to Newport for a few days, so I thought I'd see the Catskills with my friend, Mr. Harris."

"Where are you staying?"

"We're booked at the Glenview in Round Top."

"Oh, we're in Round Top too, at the Winter Clove House. You must come visit us."

"I certainly will."

The long wagon ride from the dock at Catskill brought them to their destination in the dark. The next morning, Abbie stepped outside into pure glory. The grass wetted her feet with freshness, and the sun cast crisp shapes of shade and gilded light upon the leaves. The air braced her entire being and swung open the gates of her heart. As Abbie watched her children bound across the lawn, she saw their jubilant natures in full expression. In a rare burst of spiritual feeling, she thanked God for the perfection of the morning, and then she added thanks to Walter for sending her to this place of refreshment.

The rest of the day was more challenging. Accustomed to her routine of housework, childcare, and club papers, Abbie felt restless after she had spent ten minutes rocking in a porch chair, gazing at the rounded peaks in the distance. Meals in the dining-room gave structure to the day, while socializing and games of rummy or Flinch or croquet occupied her mind, but an inner restlessness kept her from fully relaxing. With her mind unattached to an activity, watching the children play often led to a welling up of grief over the baby she had lost, a feeling hard to acknowledge when she was also so relieved. Still, in those moments, she touched an emptiness in her life, as her tongue might explore the space where a tooth had been pulled. She decided the most therapeutic response would be to bond with the natural world, although she didn't quite know how. Walking in the woods would have been ideal, but her long skirts continually caught on twigs and brush each time she ventured down the paths.

When she saw Louise come striding up the road in knickerbockers and knee-high stockings, Abbie wished she'd bought a hiking outfit for herself. Three days into the vacation, Louise looked as if she'd been roaming the mountains, her cheeks ruddy, her gait buoyant. She reached the shade of the elm where Abbie was seated in a lawn chair, alternately trying to read a novel by Maria Thompson Daviess and watching the children bounce balls across the tennis court with Jessie. Louise flung herself down with the awkward grace of a deer, casually arranging her long limbs on the grass. "I never knew a place could be so spectacular," she said. "I wish I could live in the country."

"I adore it here," Abbie said. "But eventually I think I would miss all there is to do in the city."

They had years to catch up on, but they began to feel their way back together with small talk, comparing notes on their respective hotels. Jessie brought the children around the tennis court fence. The boys chased Ivy in circles on the lawn, the three of them laughing and tumbling to the ground, then picking themselves up to run again. Jessie, sitting down next to Louise, bubbled over with questions.

"Did you know that famous suff who died?"

"What a tragedy! In fact, I was touring with Inez when she collapsed."

"You were? Tell me, what's it like picketing the White House?"

"At first, it was boring. And cold, because we started in January. Sometimes women would bring us hot bricks to stand on. One suff sent us a big muskrat fur coat that we took turns wearing. But once the country joined the war, it became frightening."

"Why? What happened?"

"People passing by grabbed the banners and tore them up and shouted that we were traitors. Some even pushed and kicked us." Abbie was curious about the subject, but Jessie's interest worried her. Thank goodness Louise was emphasizing the unpleasantness. Abbie was shocked when Louise said, "Finally the police started arresting us."

"But picketing is legal, isn't it?" asked Jessie.

"The police answer to the president, and he doesn't want us protesting in front of his house. They charged us with obstructing the sidewalk, or rather, causing an obstruction. At first, the cases were dismissed. They just wanted to scare us away. But two weeks ago, a few of us were hauled in and given a choice between paying $25 or going to jail for three days."

"So you paid the fine?" Abbie asked.

"No one would notice if we paid a fine. But going to jail—that made the newspapers."

"You were in jail?" Jessie exclaimed.

"I'm glad I missed those newspapers," said Abbie. "Honestly, Louise, I should be embarrassed if the papers reported I had gone to jail." Being so unusually forthright caused her a little shiver of pleasure. After all, Louise used to criticize her, so why shouldn't she criticize Louise right back?

"But I'm not a criminal. I'm standing up for what's right. I have nothing to be ashamed of, and publicity helps our cause."

"Was jail awful?" Jessie asked.

"No, not so bad. The beds were hard, but the food was edible. The other prisoners were mostly black women, and they sang a hymn with us, and we talked to them about suffrage. They let us out after two days."

"Will the picketing stop now?"

"Oh, no. Most of the women who were arrested went right back out with their banners a few days later. But my employer was upset and didn't want to risk getting arrested again, so here I am."

"Now that's a sensible woman," Abbie said.

"I do admire you all," Jessie said.

"Do you consider yourself a suffragist, Miss Fulton?" At Louise's question, Abbie's fingers tightened around the book in her lap.

"Of course, I'm in favor of getting the vote, but I've never . . . I mean, I don't parade and such."

"What about you, Abbie? Have you changed your mind about suffrage?"

Abbie looked out across the sweep of lawn, thinking she'd better choose her words carefully in front of Jessie. "I am coming more and more to the idea that it would be best for women to have the vote. What woman who understands the benefits of birth control would not vote to get rid of those awful Comstock laws?" Her voice unexpectedly spiked in volume, as if of its own accord. "Men don't really care. They would have us stuck at home, bearing child after child, regardless of what we want. They don't understand us in the least, and I fear they never will, even the kindest of them." She paused, surprised by her own passion.

"Well said," Louise remarked.

"But . . . I don't feel that picketing under the president's nose, especially in the midst of a war, is the best way to achieve the vote. It only angers people. Surely there are other ways to apply pressure to Congress."

"There are, but they haven't worked. We talk continually to congressmen. Miss Paul even takes delegations to the president, and he always dodges her requests. We've been talking for seventy years. Maybe if we keep doing it for another seventy years, they'll come around, but I, for one, don't want to wait that long. I have a life to live *now*, and I'm not going to let men stop me from living it."

Jessie's eyes were bright with excitement, and Abbie decided the conversation had gone far enough. "I would like to show Louise the waterfall," she said. "Jessie, why don't you take the children up to the room and see if you can get them to nap? They were up so early this morning."

Jessie gathered the children, and Abbie led Louise up the sunny slope behind the hotel. At the crest stood a summerhouse, as the small, rough-hewn gazebo was called. They stepped inside, and Abbie pointed out the many names carved into the benches, most of them representing couples.

"This must be a favorite spot for courting," said Louise.

"And spooning, after dark, I expect."

"The Catskills are so romantic."

"I notice you're wearing a wedding ring."

Louise glanced at her hand. "It's just for the hotel. At the Glenview, I'm Mrs. Harris."

"So you're lovers?" Abbie had been wondering, but still she was stunned.

"Yes."

"Is it . . . Has your divorce not—"

"It came through a few months ago."

"But don't you want to marry? Don't you love Mr. Harris?"

"I love him, but I want my freedom."

"But you're so modern. Couldn't you marry and keep working at suffrage? If you're working, you could hire a housekeeper."

"Marriage means living together, being tied to another person. I'm not ready for that."

"Do you mean . . . you're promiscuous?"

"No, I haven't been, but I may want another lover at some point. I'm sorry to shock you. But I've met women who believe in free love, and they seem . . . I don't know . . . free . . . fully alive. I may marry at some point, when I'm ready to stay in one place."

"And what about Mr. Harris? Does he have other lovers?"

"I suppose. I don't ask. He can do as he likes."

Abbie shook her head. "It's a strange way to live, but if you're happy . . ."

"I would've brought him to meet you, but I didn't know how you'd feel about us not being married."

"Well, since you care for each other . . . I'd be happy to meet him if he's a good man." But Abbie wondered what he would he think of her, a boring housewife.

They left the summerhouse and descended into the woods at the back of the hill. Beneath the tall pines, there was no underbrush to catch at Abbie's skirt, but she had to bunch the cloth in her hands to keep from tripping on the hem when the path angled upward toward the waterfall.

"I would like to tell you something," Abbie said. "I don't want to impose on you, but there's no one else I've been able to tell, and . . . I've been longing to talk to someone about it."

"I'm touched that you trust me, even though we've had our differences."

"Being so modern, I think . . . I just know you would understand."

"I'd be glad to listen."

They reached the waterfall. Its frothing water crashed into a deep green pool, where it settled before trickling down a rocky channel. Abbie stopped where she could see her reflection trembling in the water at her feet. Louise stood beside her and gazed out at the fall.

"I became pregnant last winter," said Abbie, "even though we had . . . we were using prevention."

"Condoms?"

"Yes."

"When they break, it's terrifying. Luckily it doesn't happen often." Abbie was startled by the level of worldliness Louise's words suggested, but it was calming to hear them said aloud so matter-of-factly.

"I became very sick, and I didn't want another child. I told myself four wasn't so many, but I simply couldn't adjust to the idea. I didn't see how I could take care of them all without . . . losing myself, and neglecting some of them. I even thought of trying to have . . . to get rid of it, but I was afraid of the danger. And of course it would have been wrong."

"Yes, it's quite dangerous."

"I became miserable and angry that I had to have this child. For days, while I was sick, I could think of nothing else. And then in the third month, I miscarried. I should have been glad, but instead I'm haunted by remorse and grief. I believe my hostility killed my child." Abbie's eyes filled with tears.

Louise faced her and took her hands. "You have the heart of a mother. Of course it's broken."

"But what kind of mother kills her own child?"

Louise's strong fingers squeezed Abbie's hands. "You did not kill that child. You were honest about what kind of life it could expect. You did not hold out false hope. I think . . . I believe the child understood, and out of mercy to you and itself, it left."

Abbie leaned her head on Louise's shoulder and sobbed until her heart was cleansed.

That night it rained, a deluge of drumming water. The next morning was the most spectacular one yet, sunny and brilliant, with the freshness of a just-picked peach. Lured by the forest, Abbie borrowed knickers from another guest and went for a short hike to try them out. Walter was due to arrive that evening, and she thought they might take a longer hike together on Saturday. She returned from a glorious communion with the woods to find Jessie and Louise talking near the barn. The children, arms hanging over a fence rail, watched the three dairy cows graze with their calves.

"You look ducky in knickers," Louise said. She was wind-blown and flushed from her walk up the road, and Abbie for once felt able to match her vigor. "I came to let you know I got a letter from my employer.

She's decided to quit picketing altogether and work in Albany to promote the next state referendum. We'll be working with the Woman Suffrage Party. They're much more tame than Alice Paul's bunch."

"Ah, I'm so glad. You'll be safe there."

"Safe and bored. But Miss Oakley has been good to me. Anyway, I must go and pack my bags. I'm leaving this afternoon."

"Let me walk you to the road. I'll be right back, Jessie." They headed down the long drive.

"Do you like the knickers?" Louise asked.

"I like how they feel. They're so liberating. I suppose I will get used to being seen in them."

"More and more women are wearing them for hiking. Soon they'll be commonplace."

"Louise, I want to thank you for being so understanding yesterday and also for . . . for telling me things, in the past, that . . . made me look into . . . issues. I actually wrote papers for the club on child labor and birth control. It's been good for me to know more about the world."

"That's kind of you to say."

"I suppose you don't think much of me for being just a housewife and mother."

"That's not so. You're doing what the club set you out to do—educate children who will make the world better. Look what a lively little girl you have. You don't make her act prim and proper. Your boys will grow up with respect for women and all they can do."

"Thank you for saying that."

They reached the road and stopped to embrace. "I'm glad we're friends again," said Louise. "Write to me in

Albany. I gave Jessie my address so she can write to me too. Take care of yourself."

Abbie watched her stride away, dreading what Mrs. Fulton would say when she found out Jessie was corresponding with Louise, a dyed-in-the-wool suffragette.

Chapter 24

TO LOBBY

I want to start a school for boys, right next door to the Juvenile Hall in Brooklyn. I believe the best way to reform wayward children is education." Nell Bergholtz, propelled by her enthusiasm, stood up from the sofa and paced the room, hands waving. "We treat them like criminals, when it's clear that growing up in poverty is the real cause of their problems, and it's not their fault they've been driven to criminal acts. Many of them are there merely because they've stolen a piece of fruit or a handful of nuts, out of hunger. If we teach them skills to make a living, they won't have to steal."

"Nell has been studying reformatory schools in Yonkers and White Plains," said Walter's brother Joe, who was now principal of a high school in Brooklyn. He looked distinguished, with his graying hair and a new tweed suit.

"I joined an education club, and the research was one of my projects," Nell went on. "Schools for wayward boys have had significant success in Westchester County."

"That's marvelous," Walter said. "Would you like more soda water, Joe?"

"But how do you go about starting a school?" Abbie asked. "It sounds like a huge project."

"The Froebel Club is connected with a school based on the theories of Friedrich Froebel, a German educator with innovative ideas. The parents and teachers will help me, and Joseph is our advisor."

"That's very enterprising, Nell. And I think it's wonderful Joe is being so encouraging. Some husbands wouldn't be."

"I've always felt women are capable of great accomplishments," said Joe, "but now even more so, since we've become Christian Scientists. You know, our founder was a woman, Mary Baker Eddy."

"Oh yes, the healer."

"It's incredible, all she's accomplished for the world, and for our family. We haven't used medicine, for ourselves or the children, for over a year now. We rely entirely on metaphysical healing."

"Joe has even given up tobacco and strong drink," Nell said.

"I struggled for years with those vile habits. Then our church needed funds for renovation, and I had nothing to contribute. I thought, if I could just stop smoking and drinking, I'd have a bit of extra money to donate. And with that high objective, all my desire fell away."

"How remarkable!" Abbie said. "Walter gave up his pipe when Ivy was born. It seemed the smoke was making her cough."

"But it wasn't easy," said Walter. "I struggled over it for months."

"Still, love is a powerful motivation," Nell said. "And I find love is what's pushing me to pursue this project.

Love for all children, and those boys in Juvenile Hall need love as much as anyone."

"Would you like more cookies?" Abbie held out the plate. She wondered why Nell had come to tell them about her project. Did she have a favor to ask? She must know they couldn't afford to contribute funds.

"Money is what we need next. We've found a sponsor, but he can only pay for part of the project. The state has increased its funding for education. I'm going to Albany to talk to the Education Committee and ask them to add a budget item for my school."

"That's very bold."

"And I thought . . . perhaps you would like to come with me, Abbie."

"I?" She was flustered. "What would . . . Aren't there people in your club who could go with you?"

"The school year just started. The teachers are all working, and the parents are helping out with school projects. They're all very involved, in the Froebel tradition. But your children could spare you for a couple of days, couldn't they? We have a woman who comes in for Hazel in the daytime while Charlie's at school, and your three could stay at our place."

"Oh, I don't know. They've never been apart from me overnight."

"It would do them good, give them a bit of independence. Walter can spend the night as well."

"But I wouldn't . . . Do you really think I'd be any help to you?"

"You've been writing on social issues, and I saw from the Federation letterhead that you're now the borough chairman for the Bronx clubs. Going to Albany is the next step for you. It's important to write papers, but so is taking action."

"Abbie was elected president of her club in May," Walter said.

"See, that's just what I mean. You're ready. I'll get us train tickets for a week from Wednesday."

The chairman of the Education Committee looked like a character out of Dickens. The strands of hair combed across his bald dome had been dyed a bluish black, and his small eyes peered out from beneath bushy gray brows. The bulbous nose was lined with the delicate, winding purple veins of a drinker. The sharp central notch of his fleshy upper lip gave his mouth a sensuous cast, in contrast to the onyx eyes.

Abbie quailed when she first saw him, but Nell seemed not a bit fazed. "Senator Beale, we come to you with a worthy project, and we pray your patience while we present a few facts that will attest that worth."

The five other men sat in rather indolent postures, leaning as if tired from a night's exertions, of what kind Abbie forbore to imagine. Senator Beale, however, appeared to be paying the keenest attention as Nell set out the data she had collected on the two Westchester schools, which had reduced recidivism of its students by forty-six percent. Seventy-one percent of the graduates had found jobs within six months of leaving the reformatory. After presenting graphs, charts, and quotations from students and administrators, she went on to describe the building to be purchased for the Brooklyn school. She outlined staffing needs, a breakdown of costs, fundraising plans, and a tentative schedule for renovation. "I hope you will see fit, Senator, to include funding in the state budget for a portion of what it will require to create and maintain this school, which will be of immense benefit to the children in question and to society."

Senator Beale grunted and cast his eyes around the room, landing on Abbie. "And what is your role in this project, my dear?" he asked.

"I . . . well, I'm here to help out in whatever way I can." His leering stare made her uncomfortable.

He glanced back at Nell. "And what are your qualifications for administering the creation of a school, Mrs. Bergholtz?" Then he looked again at Abbie, confusing her, since they were both Mrs. Bergholtz.

"I have served on a board of education for three years," Nell said. "My husband is a high school principal. He discusses his work with me daily, so I am deeply familiar with educational issues. I have belonged to three women's clubs and have been president of one. In all of them, I have researched and written papers on the needs of children and the conditions at educational facilities in New York City. And I have two children of my own."

"But no formal training in education, no teaching experience?" He continued to stare at Abbie.

"No, but I managed the office of an insurance broker before my marriage, so I have administrative skills."

"Insurance and education are not so very similar, Mrs. Bergholtz." Abbie tried not to squirm under his squinting gaze. She looked at the wall, where a painting of a former governor presided solemnly over the room. "You women would do better to spend your time caring for your own children rather than asking us to invest taxpayer money on the fate of young thieves and reprobates."

Nell drew a packet from her portfolio. "I have here letters from thirty-five people, educators and prominent Brooklyn residents, urging you to support a school for wayward boys. They believe the investment is entirely worthwhile, as a means of helping the boys become responsible members of society."

Beale took the sheaf of letters and flipped through them, looking at the signatures. "Most of these people are women. I don't particularly care about their opinion, to be honest. Too soft-hearted and easily swayed. What do you gentlemen think?" He surveyed his colleagues, who straightened their spines for a moment to nod or mutter their agreement. "All right, then. We have other matters to discuss now."

"Well, I hope you don't mind if I leave this material with you for reference," said Nell. "We will contact you with further information as our project develops, just in case there's some change."

"Thank you, ladies. Have a pleasant trip back to Brooklyn." Abbie felt his eyes still upon her as she and Nell left the room.

Their steps echoed on the marble floor of the hallway. They waited until they were well away from the door to speak their minds. "What a repulsive man!" said Abbie.

"I was told I would face resistance," Nell said, "but I didn't expect the senator to be a lecherous boor. I apologize for subjecting you to his leering."

"But I've learned so much. This experience has really opened my eyes, Nell."

"He doesn't care about women because we can't vote. That's what he really meant."

"That's surely true, but he also despises women. And this is the type our men elect to office."

"It almost makes me want to put on a yellow sash and shout from a soap box."

"You?" Abbie took Nell's arm. "I bet you'd be good at it, too."

Two weeks later a note came from Louise, stating that she was leaving Albany immediately and asking if Abbie could put her up for a night. When Louise arrived, on a Sunday afternoon, Jessie was seated on the parlor floor, helping the twins make piles of blocks in order to knock them down. Ivy had gone to play with a neighbor child.

"I'm so glad to get away from those strait-laced women," Louise said, plopping onto the sofa. "Albany is so dull."

"You're quitting your job with Miss Oakley?" asked Jessie.

"She's taken a lover, one of Mrs. Catt's lieutenants, and the woman is jealous of me."

"What? A woman?" Abbie was taken aback, not least by Louise's casualness.

"She's moved in with us, and it's clear I'm not welcome any more."

"But you've been with Miss Oakley so long."

"It's time for me to go back to Washington. A lot of the women I was picketing with are now in prison, and my conscience is saying I ought to be with them."

"Oh, you mustn't," Abbie said. "Isn't there anything else you can do for suffrage?"

"It's the right thing to do. We have to keep up the pressure on old Woody."

"Who's Woody?"

"Woodrow Wilson. I'm taking an eight o'clock train tomorrow morning."

"I'm going with you," said Jessie.

Abbie gasped. She had been expecting and fearing such a moment for weeks, even while assuring Mrs. Fulton her daughter was far too sensible to fall in with the suffs. A response came by reflex, with an unfortunate parental tone. "Oh, no. Put that thought right out of your mind. You're too young."

"I'm twenty-four. I'm quite old enough to make my own decisions."

"But your mother will blame me."

"It's nothing to do with you."

"Picketing is not a game," Louise said, leaning forward, elbows on her knees. "It's not romantic, and it's not fun. Sometimes we stand for hours in the pouring rain. Men, and sometimes women, call us foul names and knock us down. These days lots of pickets are getting arrested."

"I'm prepared to go to prison, and I don't expect it to be fun."

"From what I hear, the latest ones arrested have been sent to a workhouse that's nothing like the cell I was in for two days. It's a horrible, disgusting place, and the women are treated most inhumanely."

Jessie scrambled to her feet. "It doesn't matter to me. I'm going."

"I can't be responsible for you. It's not that you're young, it's that you've never done anything remotely like it. I was toughened up by speaking on the street and then—"

"I work with the poorest of the poor." Jessie's eyes were shooting sparks. "I sit with women whose babies have died of filth and sickness. I'm not an innocent. And I want to do something for all women, not just those few I work with."

The twins stopped their building and demolition to stare up at her.

"Are you sure?" Louise asked.

"I've been thinking of it for a long time, and now I've decided. If you won't take me, I'll go by myself. But if you're worried about my mother, I'm sure she would rather I didn't go alone." Jessie had her fists curled, her feet planted apart like a pugilist.

Louise studied her face, but Jessie's gaze did not falter. "All right then," Louise said.

"No!" said Abbie. "Mrs. Fulton will never forgive me."

Louise's scornful glance made her shrink back. "Keep yourself out of this, Abbie. It's Jessie's decision."

"I'm going home to pack," Jessie said. "Abbie, I'll come say good-bye to you in the morning." There was a wounding coldness to her voice. The door slammed behind her.

Ben came and draped himself over Abbie's lap. She stroked his hair, thinking how she'd feel if he went off to Washington some day, or even off to war.

"Am I sleeping on the couch?" Louise asked.

"No, there's a bed in the sewing room. But wait a moment." Abbie jumped up and went to the bedroom. She returned with twenty dollars, nearly a month's rent. "It's for Jessie. I hope you will hold it for her until she needs it. I don't know what else I can do."

Chapter 25

TO PICKET

Alice Paul could have designed Broadway shows, thought Louise, who was bringing up the end of the line. She watched the row of purple, white, and gold banners making their way down Madison Place after leaving the National Woman's Party headquarters. The dark branches of the sidewalk trees released golden leaves that floated down, tasteful accents matching the gold of the banners. The somber women looked straight ahead as they marched the short block past Lafayette Square to the White House. The banners, like tricolor sails of a ship, billowed bright against the ironwork of the fencing. The women spread out on either side of the gate, and two lettered banners were hoisted among them. Jessie had asked for the honor of holding the one that read, "HOW LONG MUST WOMEN WAIT FOR LIBERTY?", reported to be the final words of Inez Boissevain, who had since been celebrated as a martyr to the suffrage cause.

There were three four-hour shifts each day, from eight in the morning to eight at night. The women never knew when the police would decide to swoop down on them, but Louise had learned to gauge the

266

mood of the crowd and the police. If she sensed either group growing agitated, she suggested taking the next day off, and twice in October she and Jessie missed getting arrested. Despite Jessie's protestations of worldliness, Louise felt protective and thought it wise to give her time to adjust to the rigors of suffrage life before heading off to jail.

Jessie was blossoming, invigorated by the novelty of visiting Washington, of picketing, of camaraderie with bold women. Upon returning from the silent picket line, they sat at the Cameron House headquarters, drinking tea in a group of women who chatted, joked, cursed, and read news articles aloud, with discussion following. Each evening, Louise and Jessie retreated to the little room they shared at a boarding-house catering to suffs. They weren't getting paid, but they both had money saved up from working, and Louise put Abbie's donation towards Jessie's meals.

Miss Paul had been in the hospital for a month that summer with a suspected case of Bright's disease, an often fatal kidney ailment. Having been misdiagnosed, she emerged intact though weak. Her lieutenants kept her off the picket line for a few weeks, insisting she recover her strength. She appeared in front of the White House in September, bearing a banner that compared President Wilson to Kaiser Wilhelm for claiming to fight for freedom while refusing to give women the freedom to vote. She was knocked down three times, and a sailor dragged her across the street, trying to tear off her tricolor sash. The police seized 148 of the silk and linen banners, and six women were arrested. To the suffs' relief, Miss Paul was not among them. On October 6, however, she was finally arrested and received a suspended sentence. It seemed to Louise they were all holding their breath, knowing their leader would make her way into prison at some point.

On October 20, Louise and Jessie went out on the morning shift. They wore rubber coats against a fine drizzle that set the banners off with a soft gray aura. One of the signs quoted the president's speech about entering the war: "THE TIME HAS COME TO CONQUER OR SUBMIT. FOR US THERE CAN BE BUT ONE CHOICE—WE HAVE MADE IT." One passerby called out, "Keep at it, girls!" Another, an old man with a crutch, told them, "You'll make it, I'm sure." Then a sailor spit on the banner, prompting Jessie to shout, strictly against the rules, "You know, those are the president's words you're spitting on." He stopped and gave her a push that made her stagger back, while a policeman pointedly looked the other way. The sailor spit on her shoes and walked off. Louise, worried, examined Jessie's face and saw her swallow her shock and anger, compose herself, and step back into the line.

The gates opened, and a long black automobile slid through, carrying President Wilson to his daily round of golf. Some days, he tipped his hat at the pickets, while his wife sat beside him, glaring at them. Today, both of the Wilsons looked straight ahead as they rode past. The gates closed behind the automobile.

At noon, the next shift of women came marching down Madison at their usual slow, solemn pace. "That's Miss Paul at the front," murmured Jessie. The thin, pale face wore the look of a warrior.

"You're right," said Louise. She had an intuition it was Miss Paul's day to be arrested.

"Should we stay?" Jessie asked.

"No, I don't think so. We're scheduled to go back."

They handed over their banners to the newcomers and returned to headquarters. An hour later, they were in the midst of tea and sandwiches, when a woman ran in, shouting, "They've arrested Miss Paul and Miss Spencer!"

"Oh, no!" Jessie said.

"It's what she wants," Louise reassured her. "It'll make the papers for sure, with a big headline just because it's Miss Paul."

"I feel bad, though. She's in there, and we're out here. Oh, why can't we get arrested?"

Alice Paul was given seven months in the District jail, the longest sentence yet. "The judge is making an example of her," said Dora Lewis, who took charge in Miss Paul's absence. "She's going to insist on being treated as a political prisoner, which would mean visitation rights and keeping her own clothes and being allowed to read and write."

"Do you think it will be granted?" asked Jessie.

"No. She may go on hunger strike in protest."

"But she was in the hospital not so long ago. She might die."

"Wilson can't afford to let her die. The publicity would destroy him. They'll either let her out or forcibly feed her."

"I don't see how they could stick a tube down the nose of that gentle little woman."

Mrs. Lewis snorted. "Oh, yes, gentle like a tiger."

At Cameron House, anyone planning to picket was given a thorough warning on the experience of past pickets and what might happen to those arrested in the future. Miss Paul wanted only committed women on the line, who were strong enough to deal with the consequences and couldn't complain they didn't know what was coming. Women were told they might be sent to the District jail, where they would find maggots in the food and reeking toilets inside the cells. Hunger strike was presented as an option for those arrested. Pinned to the office wall was a copy of an article from *New York World Magazine* by journalist Djuna Barnes, who had voluntarily submitted to force-feeding, just to see what it was like. Jessie read the article over and over, once reading passages aloud to Louise.

Unbidden visions of remote horrors danced madly through my mind. There arose the hideous thought of being gripped in the tentacles of some monster devil fish in the depths of a tropic sea, as the liquid slowly sensed its way along innumerable endless passages . . . .

I had lapsed into a physical mechanism without power to oppose or resent the outrage to my will.

Jessie was awed by the audacity of a woman who had done nothing to merit punishment and yet subjected herself to excruciating pain just to report on the experience other women had gone through. Louise didn't know what to make of Jessie's interest. Was it a fantasy of personal heroism or a morbid focus on suffering? At some point, Jessie would surely be tested. Louise just hoped to be at her side to shepherd her through.

Suffs released from the District jail reported that Miss Paul had thrown, and incited other prisoners to throw, objects—tin cups, light bulbs, even her accurately tossed volume of Browning's poetry—in an effort to break the closed windows high up on the walls of the airless cells. As a result, she had been placed in solitary confinement. Then Miss Paul and Rose Winslow, the scrappy Polish-American labor organizer, ended up in the hospital wing because they were so weak from lack of exercise and from eating the wormy pork and greasy broth that passed for food.

On November 6, largely thanks to the doggedness of Carrie Catt and her foot soldiers, the woman suffrage referendum passed in New York, the first eastern state to add its women to the ranks of female voters. The milestone had come despite predictions that the picketing would turn the state's voters against suffrage. The rejoicing at Cameron House was muted by the knowledge that Miss Paul was waning in strength.

Meanwhile, women from eleven states traveled to Washington to protest her incarceration. Dora Lewis called a meeting at Cameron House. "Before Miss Paul was arrested," she explained, "she told me we'd have to stop the picketing soon because it was becoming stale news. Her idea was to have one final demonstration with a mass of people that would clog the justice system. With the visitors from the states, we have a sufficient number. How many women here are prepared to picket tomorrow and get arrested?"

"It's our last chance," Jessie whispered to Louise. "This time, we have to stay out until the police grab us, no matter what."

"Yes, you're right. We'll do it."

Their hands went up, along with thirty-nine others.

Someone suggested going to the jail and standing under Miss Paul's window. A cleaning woman had been smuggling information out, so they knew where her room was and that she had started a hunger strike. In a dank courtyard, permeated with smells of mold and soot, the women stood on rubble-strewn dirt. Each one shouted up her name and the state she had come from. Mrs. Lewis called out the information that the National Women's Party had received a flood of donations, and the forty-one women now in the courtyard would be protesting tomorrow.

"I'm being forcibly fed three times a day," Miss Paul called down. "It's worse than in England. There it was only twice a day."

"She's so noble," Jessie sighed. "I know I could never be like her."

"No one could," Louise replied.

"Hey, you!" came a shout, and a squad of guards hustled the women back out to the street.

The government workers were going home for lunch, women and men in their fall coats pouring along the sidewalk outside the White House gates, many of them saluting the pickets as they went by. Two patrol wagons pulled up. The policemen seized the banners and herded the fifteen women into the vans, while the spectators applauded, as they often did during arrests. Louise wasn't sure how many were clapping for the police and how many for the suffs, but today the mood seemed sympathetic to the pickets. Jessie was the last to climb into the wagon, and as she was sitting down on the bench, they heard the spectators saying, "Look! More of them!"

"The second group is coming," Jessie said, peeking out the door. "Mrs. Lewis was sending ten, I think." Soon five more women were added to their wagon, and the back door closed. Another wagon would have to be sent for the other five. The police had no idea three more groups were waiting to head out to the White House.

The women spent the night on mats on the floor of the District House of Detention. The next day in court, several who had been arrested repeatedly were given sentences of anywhere from sixty days to six months. Louise and Jessie each got fifteen days. Off they went to Occoquan Workhouse and what came to be known as the Night of Terror.

"We refuse to give our names to anyone but the workhouse superintendent," said Dora Lewis, appointed by the prisoners to speak for them. She was a widow in her fifties, bold, articulate, and a natural leader.

"Superintendent Whittaker is out," Minnie Herndon, the matron, said, her consonants crisp and forceful. "You'll have to sit here all night. He may not be back for two or three days."

"We will await his return," Mrs. Lewis replied.

The room was stuffy and brightly lit. The women sat in chairs lined up in rows, facing the matron's desk. She read out their names in a roll call but received not a single reply.

"You'd better answer up, or it'll be the worse for you," said a male guard, one of five lounging against the wall.

The man next to him strolled to the back of the room, where Lucy Burns, a redheaded fireball who had been arrested numerous times, sat with her eyes closed. "I'll handle you so you'll be sorry," the man said, leaning over her. She did not open her eyes.

The women had been told to expect threats of violence from the prison staff, but past experience had showed they were generally bluffing. Louise tried to keep calm, inspired by Miss Burns and Mrs. Lewis, knowing she had to be a model for Jessie, who was trembling next to her. She wanted to hold Jessie's hand but didn't want to attract the guards' attention. A cluster of men stood in the hallway, peering through the office windows.

A woman asked for a glass of water, and Mrs. Herndon refused. She did allow three prisoners to use a water closet out in the hall, then changed her mind when Miss Burns asked.

Several hours went by, and some of the women stretched out on the floor to rest. Louise thought it looked none too clean, so she stayed in her seat, wondering how long she could endure the growing discomfort in her bladder.

The door opened, and a big man in a long black coat stepped to the front of the room, where he stood with his arms folded. The number of guards in the hallway had increased. Mrs. Herndon jumped up. "They refuse to give their names, Mr. Whittaker. I've been waiting for you."

The women on the floor sat up. Mrs. Lewis rose to her feet and said, in a ringing voice, "We demand to be treated as political pris—"

"You shut up," Whittaker barked. "I have men here glad to handle you. Seize her!" Two men grabbed Mrs. Lewis by the arms and dragged her out of the room. "And seize her! And her!" Men hauled away Paula Jakobi, a playwright Louise recognized from Heterodoxy meetings, and slender little Dorothy Day. Miss Burns shouted as her arms were twisted behind her.

Delicate, white-haired Mary Nolan, cried out, "I'll come with you. Don't drag me. I have a lame foot." The men ignored her, but luckily Mrs. Nolan's feet left the ground as they hustled her out. Whittaker still stood in the front of the room, shouting orders.

More guards stomped in, hurling aside chairs that had been emptied. Louise was jerked up from her seat. She smelled stale tobacco breath as two men pulled her toward the door. "Don't resist," she called to Jessie. "There's no need to get hurt."

Outside, the fresh air rushing into her lungs was so welcome, Louise barely noticed the November cold. The darkness was complete except for a light in front of a low building across the yard. Half-walking, half-dragged, Louise scuffed her boots across the hard ground until she was propelled through a door and down a long central aisle between two rows of cells. The odor of sour bedding and dirty toilets made her want to vomit.

The two men tossed her into a cell, and she skidded across the floor, bruising her shoulder. Jessie and another girl were thrown in after her but landed on the narrow bed. Across the passageway, Miss Day was crying out for help, and Miss Jakobi, struggling with two guards, was trying to get to her. Five men grappled with Miss Burns, who resisted every step. They heaved her into a cell and slammed the door.

At last, boots shuffled away, and relative quiet prevailed. Women wept, groaned, and conversed in low voices. Louise picked herself up and sat gingerly on the bed, holding her shoulder. "Are you all right?" she asked the two girls. Sadie Cutler introduced herself and said she was frightened but unhurt.

"I'm fine," said Jessie. "But what about your shoulder?"

"It'll be all right. Nothing's broken."

"Who's here?" a clear voice rang out. "Miss Lincoln, are you here?"

"Yes," came a reply from down the aisle.

"It's Miss Burns," Jessie said. "Isn't she marvelous? She's not afraid of anything."

The resonant voice continued to shout a roll call. A guard yelled at Miss Burns to shut up. "Where is Mrs. Lewis?" she demanded.

"They've just thrown her in here," someone replied. "She's unconscious."

"If any of you say one more word," a guard threatened, "we'll put you in straitjackets."

Miss Burns went on calling the roll. Two guards handcuffed her wrists to the cell door above her head. Julia Emory, in the cell opposite, raised her hands in the same position and stood there in silent solidarity.

"I'm so cold," Jessie said, keeping her voice low. "And it stinks in here."

The cell had no window and no light. By the corridor lamp, Louise made out an open toilet in the corner, which she gratefully made use of. But there was no handle to flush it. "I was told we have to ask the guards to flush the toilet from outside," she explained to her cellmates.

"Those bullies who dragged us in here?" Miss Cutler said. "I hope never to speak to them in my life."

"Where do we all sleep?" asked Jessie. The flimsy bed and the narrow mattress on the floor were each covered with one gritty blanket.

"I suppose we'll have to take turns sleeping," Louise said. "Or try to jam two of us on the mattress."

"We're friends, so we can take the mattress," Jessie decided. "Miss Cutler, you take the bed."

Exhausted, using their arms for pillows, the three of them managed to fall asleep.

A metal cup clanging against the bars jarred Louise to consciousness, her next sensations being intense thirst and the soreness of her shoulder. She sat up, back and limbs aching from the hard floor. "My mouth's like cotton," Jessie said. Having slept half off the mattress, she rolled onto the floor and then exclaimed, "My God, the filth!" She stood up and brushed her skirt off in the corner, raising a cloud of dust.

"I'm starving," Miss Cutler said. "We haven't eaten since yesterday noon."

"I need a wash." Jessie regarded her grimy hands.

"All right, everyone this way," said a wardress, unlocking the cells one after another. "Mr. Whittaker wants to see you."

They shuffled down the corridor and were allowed to stop at the door, where a large basin of water stood. They took turns dipping a single cup into the bucket to drink, sharing germs freely. Out in the anemic morning light, a lone raven rode the wind against the mottled gray and purple sky. Beyond the fenced yard, crop fields stretched out to a row of trees waving bare branches, snaky and black. A hoarse cry echoed over the yard, and the raven wheeled off.

In the room where the women had sat the day before, the superintendent was waiting. He looked over the rows of anxious faces and pointed to Miss Jakobi, who was on her second visit to Occoquan. "Will you obey prison regulations and do as you're told?"

"No," she replied. "I will not wear the prison uniform, and I demand to be given the rights of political prisoners, as we have been—"

"Then you'll go to the *male* hospital and be in solitary confinement. Do you change your mind?" "No."

Whittaker gestured to a guard, who grasped her by the arm and led her away. Wardresses herded the rest of the women into another room. The matron came in with three black female prisoners pushing carts piled with clothing. "All right, take off your clothes and put these on," commanded Mrs. Herndon. Louise picked up one of the heavy chemises, made of unbleached muslin the texture of sandpaper. Another cart held drawers of the same material and petticoats of cotton ticking, such as ordinarily was used to cover mattresses. On top, the women were to wear heavy, shapeless gray cotton dresses and dark blue aprons. There were not enough of the thick, clumsy stockings to go around, nor of shoes, which came in two sizes, large and small. Louise was not among those who were allowed to keep their own shoes and stockings due to the shortage. She tried to hide herself as she changed, aware of the watching matron, female guards, and Negro prisoners.

All possessions were taken away with their clothing. Each woman was given a small rough towel that was supposed to be folded and tucked into the apron. They returned to their cells, still hungry and unwashed. At noon, bowls of thin, greasy pea soup arrived. Some of the women had declared their intention to undertake a hunger strike from the start, but Louise had resolved to eat in the hope that Jessie would eat and keep up her strength. Miss Cutler took a look at the grayish soup and said, "I'd rather starve than eat that."

Louise dipped a spoon into the bowl and conveyed a chunk of pork to her mouth, along with the cloudy broth. She chewed and swallowed, trying not to make a face. "Salty," she said. When she looked back down, a worm had floated to the surface. She picked it out and threw it in the toilet, then forced herself to take another spoonful and then another.

"It smells even worse than it looks," said Jessie. "I'm joining the hunger strike." Louise was torn. Should she eat, just to make sure she had the strength to look after Jessie? Or was it more important to support her friend by fasting as well? She ate half the bowl of soup before giving in to disgust.

In the evening, toast and hot milk were brought, and although they smelled alluring, Louise had no appetite. Her cellmates refused to take even a taste. That night, intestinal cramps woke Louise repeatedly to sit for long periods of time on the toilet, adding to the ever-present stench. She could see the plate of toast still waiting at the door of the cell in a semicircle of light. A rat was nibbling the crust.

During the daytime, the prisoners sang hymns or made up satirical lyrics to popular tunes, ridiculing President Wilson and joking about the conditions in the prison. In the evening, the pious Helen Bayles, a suff from Maryland, said prayers in a loud voice that all could hear, including the "regular" prisoners housed at the end of the corridor.

"Dear Lord and Father of us all," intoned Miss Bayles on the second evening. "Forgive the matron and trusties for their callous behavior. Forgive Mrs. Herndon for feeding us worms and the most disgusting rotten vegetables sent down from Washington, while the squashes grown on the workhouse land pass by on wagons to be sold elsewhere. Forgive the wardresses for forcing us to shower in front of complete strangers. Forgive Mr. Whittaker for directing men to twist our arms. But if divine justice deems punishment the fit consequence for these tormentors, see to it that they reside in the hottest circle of hell until they repent of their sins. And then, dear God, feel free to keep them there forever, according to thy will. Amen."

The "regulars" laughed harder and longer than the suffs. The matron was incensed.

Much effort went into trying to pass notes among the cells. A few women had hidden pencil stubs and scraps of paper in their cuffs, to be secretly transferred to the prison clothing upon changing. The water pipes running along the backs of the cells had a tiny bit of space around them where they penetrated the walls, just enough room for a slip of paper.

On the third day, after fried chicken and salad had been brought in to tempt the women on hunger strike, Jessie heard a tapping at the pipe. She went to the wall, gave an answering tap, and held out her hand to catch the morsel of paper that came sliding through. "It's from Miss Burns. It says, 'They think there is nothing in our souls above fried chicken.'" They all felt heartened by her mettle. Jessie went to the other side of the cell to pass the paper onward along the pipe.

The effects of the pea soup seemed to have passed, but Louise felt weakened by the loss of fluids. She was feverish and dizzy, and her skin felt painfully dry, on top of the irritation caused by the coarse clothing. Miss Cutler complained of nausea, while Jessie, although limp with weakness, seemed not to be severely affected by fasting.

That evening, Louise and Jessie were each made to trade places with another suff. "But I must stay with Miss Fulton," Louise protested. "I have to look after her." The guard escorting her snickered and shoved her into a nearby cell, where she sat on the bed, shaking with anxiety. Her new cellmates did their best to comfort her. "Why did they make us move?" she asked.

"It's a way to disorient and upset us," said one of them. "But we're all in it together. Whoever's with your friend will take care of her."

Louise's distress earned her the bed for the night, which made her feel guilty, so she tried to pull herself together. The dizziness had been replaced by a sense of floating, as if her mind had partially detached from her body. The only mercy she found in fasting, besides not having to eat the prison food, was the tendency for sleep to overcome her for much of the day as well as the night.

One morning, when she'd lost track of the passing days, a doctor came into the cell. He barely glanced at the other two women, who were not on hunger strike, but he sat down to take Louise's pulse. That afternoon, she was summoned to Whittaker's office. The wardress who came to fetch her kept tugging at her upper arm, trying to speed her up. The oversized prison shoes felt made of iron as she struggled to lift them on the walk down the corridor and across the yard.

Whittaker greeted her with a broad smile and invited her to sit down. He perched on the edge of his desk, making her shrink back in the chair. "It looks as though your hunger strike has been difficult and painful," he said in a genial voice. "The doctor is worried about your health."

She wanted to say something about the pea soup being the cause of her ill health, but the words refused to take shape on her lips. He put a hand on her shoulder, which made her flinch away. He stood up and walked around to sit behind his desk. "Please tell Mrs. Herndon to come in," he told the wardress. Each time he smiled, Louise focused on the crooked brown teeth in the front of his mouth. When his lips closed, she missed the sense of focus they had given her.

"Where are you from, Miss Kelley?"

She didn't recall giving her name. How had he learned it? She concentrated on the question, thinking it ought to be easy to answer. The two words made their way from her blurred thought to the thick tongue, which was reluctant to move, but she forced it to spit out "New York."

"You're a long way from home. I suppose you miss your people there. Maybe you have a beau, a lover?" The way he said the word "lover," drawing out the letter "l," made her shiver. "You are, I suspect, an attractive woman when you're healthy. I would hate to see your health so ruined that your fellow doesn't want you back. Wouldn't that be a shame?"

She shook her head, trying to clear it. Why was he talking about her beau? The matron arrived, carrying a plate of fried eggs and toast. She held the plate in front of Louise, who almost gagged from the smell. The two yellow eyes staring up at her from the plate made her understand, finally, what Whittaker wanted. Rage funneled its way up from deep in her shrunken belly. The brown teeth, so expectant of cooperation, were showing again. She raised both hands from her lap and struck the bottom of the plate. It flew across the desk and splattered egg yolk across Whittaker's shirt. He swore, batting at his chest. "You are insane! Mrs. Herndon, take this maniac back to her cell. Just you wait, Miss Kelley. The doctor will be on his way quite soon with a straitjacket."

The matron hustled her out, and Louise heard herself laughing. Maybe she *was* going insane. But once she was back in her cell, the superintendent's threat ballooned in her mind. She was terrified of being confined in a straitjacket, unable to move. How long would he leave her bound up? She curled up on the bed and wept silently, unable to form the words that would tell her worried cellmates what had happened.

No doctor arrived that night. She insisted on taking the mattress on the floor but continued to cry intermittently, helpless to stop, wondering when the straitjacket would come.

The next morning, the doctor walked in with two other men. They took her to a white room and strapped her to a chair while she struggled in panic. When the doctor produced a long rubber tube, she calmed down. It's all right, she thought, they're going to forcibly feed me, and I can survive that.

Miss Burns always fought the procedure, clamping her mouth shut so they had to shove a smaller tube down her nose. Miss Paul did the same. But Louise didn't see any purpose in struggling. She opened her mouth and let the doctor insert the tube. As it slid down her throat, grating against the soft tissue, she gasped, feeling she was going to suffocate. Unable to draw breath around the tube, she began to choke. Her teeth clenched down on the tube. "Oh, stop that now," the doctor said, but her jaw refused to open. Her whole body was shaking, muscles in spasm, as she struggled for breath. "All right then, we'll have to go through the nose. Hold her head still," he said to the two men. He let go of the tube and picked up a narrower one. Her mind swarmed with thoughts of drowning, dying, release.

The tube went up her nostril, and she felt blood trickle over her lips. Furrows of pain dug through her face and followed the tube arcing over and down into her throat. The two men pressed their fingers deeper into her temples and the back of her head. The doctor held up a funnel and began to pour the milk. The liquid slid down the tube and leaked its cold through all the crevices of her throat and head, provoking a repeated throb that echoed in the frantic racing of her heartbeat. The milk took forever to wind its way into the depths of her body, chill and punishing. She couldn't halt the stuttering cry that came through her mouth, as the jaw finally let go. Inkblots of darkness appeared and spread. She gave in to nothingness.

Chapter 26

WASHINGTON, DC

The main hall of Washington's Union Station teemed with people walking in every direction, frowning or smiling or bland-faced, bent on departure or arrival, miraculously avoiding collisions. But at the eastern end of the station, the last train platform was almost vacant. Wind swept in from the south, scooped up a stray sheet of paper, and flattened it against Abbie's cheek. Mrs. Fulton looked yet again at the clock with the broken glass face, mounted on a fluted iron column on the platform. "Maybe it's slow. I'm sure we've been here more than an hour."

"Don't forget, we got here early," said Mrs. Cutler. "Even though the trains are always late, it never hurts to be early for the one time the train will be early. You only get one chance a day."

"Do you come every day?" asked Abbie.

"No. It's my third time in a week."

"And the other two times, you got news of your daughter, right?"

"Oh, yes. All the prisoners know about the suffs. The guards gossip about them all day long. The last time, I met two pickets who were released because they'd been arrested earlier than Sadie. They had actually spoken with her."

"And what was the news? How is she?"

"The food's horrid, but they say she's all right. That Miss Burns, the wild one, though. She got her clothes taken away 'cause she wouldn't wear a prison dress, so she had to lie wrapped in a blanket. My Sadie would never do anything like that."

"We already read about Miss Burns and the blanket in the *New York Times*," said Mrs. Fulton, starting to pace the platform. "Why she didn't just wear the prison uniform, I don't understand. And why doesn't this train run on time? If there's only one a day, they ought to be able to get it right."

"I hear something," Abbie said. They faced south, squinting down the tracks. The faint rumbling grew louder, and a plume of smoke appeared. A few minutes later, the train roared down upon them and halted with a long shrieking of brakes. The conductor poked his mustachioed face out and jumped down. Two women followed, one black and one white, both dressed in threadbare coats and ill-fitting shoes with no stockings. An engineer climbed out of the cab of the locomotive and trailed the conductor into the station.

Mrs. Cutler went straight to the women. "Have you heard anything about Sadie Cutler? She's one of the suffs arrested eight days ago."

"Sadie," drawled the white woman. "Lemme see. Ain't she the one went to the sick wing with a bad case of the trots?"

"Naw," the black woman said, as Mrs. Cutler went pale. "That's Sallie. She ain't a suff. I ain't heard a thing about Sadie."

"What about Jessie Fulton?" Mrs. Fulton grabbed the white woman's sleeve. "She's quite young, probably the youngest there."

"Uh-uh. Dorothy Day is the youngest. She's only twenty-one. The guards like her best 'cause she asks about their children."

"But what about Jessie? Have you heard anything?"

"No. You?"

The black woman shook her head. "I did hear, though, a whole bunch of 'em is gone on hunger strike."

"Oh, no," Mrs. Fulton moaned. Abbie put an arm around her shoulder.

"Don't worry, lady, they won't let no suffs die. They don't care a pin about me, but then I won't never get in the papers for stealing apples."

"Them suffs may be crazy, but they's tougher than you think," said the white woman. "Don't you worry, your girl's gonna be okay. Even if they shove a tube down her nose, it might hurt some, but she's gonna be fine."

"Maybe we should just go there." The bed springs creaked as Mrs. Fulton bent over to unlace her boots. "Forget about asking permission, just take the train and bang on the door of the workhouse until they let us in."

"Alice Paul's mother and sister went to the District jail to see her, and even they couldn't get in." Abbie lay back on the other bed, too tired to take off her boots. "Miss Morey went to Occoquan with that lawyer, O'Brien, and they let him in but not her. I still think we should go to the National Woman's Party office and ask what they've heard."

"No. I am furious at those fanatics, and I want nothing to do with them. Mrs. Cutler said they were rude to her, and that's why she didn't go back. Thank goodness she didn't give up on the Bureau of Prisons, or we wouldn't have met her. Not that they've been any help."

"Well, they did tell us her sentence was only fifteen days."

"A lot more than Louise told us."

"She wrote us before they were even arrested. They're not allowed to write from jail."

Mrs. Fulton took out the note Louise had sent Abbie and read it for the hundredth time.

Just to let you know, we are likely to be arrested tomorrow and will land in court. Will write again if we don't get a sentence. Otherwise we are in the jug. Jessie is in high spirits. Don't worry, I am sticking close by her side and will look after her whatever happens.

"No apologies. No regrets," muttered Mrs. Fulton. "I wish I'd never let that woman into the club."

Abbie said nothing. She preferred the anger directed at Louise rather than herself. Since agreeing to accompany Mrs. Fulton to Washington, she had been the target of no more diatribes. She had almost offered to pay the entire hotel bill but decided she didn't feel *that* guilty. After all, she had done her best to steer her protégée away from the suffs. But Louise had come along just when Jessie's curiosity about suffrage was growing. Still, Abbie felt sorry for Mrs. Fulton. She was concerned herself, but she had watched Jessie become a capable young woman, and she was confident Louise's protection would pull her through without too many scars. She would probably end up stronger and wiser. But a mother couldn't help worrying.

Mrs. Fulton unfastened her skirt, unlaced her corset, and announced, "I'm taking a nap."

Abbie closed her eyes, thinking of the children. Nell and Joe had agreed to take them again, since they'd had a successful visit during the trip to Albany. But that stay had been only one night, and who knew how long this adventure would last? After three days apart, she missed them profoundly. If she had to stay until Jessie's release, she wouldn't get home for another week. She opened her eyes. "What will we do," she asked Mrs. Fulton, "if she gets out and then goes right back to picketing? That's what they do, you know."

There was no answer from the other bed, and the regular breathing suggested the nap had begun. If Mrs. Fulton insisted on staying another week, perhaps she could be persuaded to visit the Capitol rotunda and the Smithsonian. The children would love to hear about the taxidermy exhibits at the Arts and Industries Museum. If only Walter could have come with her, Abbie might have gleaned the pleasure of his company from this trying trip. As his physical urges weakened over time, their relationship was moving into a new kind of strength. The children kept them close to each other.

When Mrs. Fulton's snoring woke her, it was not yet dinnertime. She wrote a note saying she was going out for a walk, spruced herself up, and headed for the street.

The hotel was just off Pennsylvania Avenue, on the edge of a seedy district of bars and tenements. Abbie hastened away from the bars and turned down the avenue toward the White House. The street seemed wider than just about any in New York, but the buildings along it were in poorer condition, many of them with sagging awnings and broken or boarded-up windows. At Sixth Street, however, stood the august Metropolitan Hotel. What would it be like to stay there, instead of the shabby little room at the absurdly named Hotel Maximus?

The avenue was brimming with wagons, streetcars, and honking automobiles. Pedestrians walked briskly in the autumn chill, women stopping to squeeze the fruit at produce stands set up on street corners. Abbie followed the avenue all the way to the White House. No pickets were in evidence outside the iron gates. She clutched two of the fence bars and stared through at the stately building. What was President Wilson doing today? Did he give any thought to the women in prison?

"Move on, please," said a policeman, and she hurried along, throwing glances past the fence. No doubt the pickets had made the police jittery. A block north, opposite Lafayette Park, she found the brick building with the words "Congressional Union for Woman Suffrage," the former name of the Woman's Party, lettered above the rounded bay entrance. Inside, she asked a bespectacled woman at the front desk if she had any information on the prisoners, especially Miss Kelley and Miss Fulton.

"Not specifically," said the woman. "But our attorney, Mr. O'Brien, has brought a suit against the government for sending the women to Occoquan. Technically, since they were arrested in the District of Columbia, they should have been put in the District jail. Not that the conditions there are much better, but it's always good to force the government to admit they made a mistake."

"When will the case be brought to court?"

"It was scheduled for November twenty-seventh, but many of the women are on hunger strike, and Mr. O'Brien fears for their health, so he got it moved up to the twenty-third."

"You don't know which ones are on hunger strike?"

"No, I'm sorry."

"Where is the courthouse?"

The woman wrote out the address and then added, "We had a gentleman here yesterday inquiring about Miss Kelley. A Jonathan Harris."

"He's a friend of hers. I didn't know he was in town."

"He left an address in case we had more information." She pulled open a drawer. "Here it is. The Metropolitan Hotel."

Perhaps it wasn't quite proper for a woman alone to visit a gentleman at his hotel, but Abbie couldn't resist the excuse to go inside the Metropolitan. There was a chance Mr. Harris would have more information on Louise. The lobby was less opulent than she had hoped, but she gaped for a few minutes in the carpeted hush, noting the marble pillars and extravagant potted foliage. Then she marched to the desk, trying to pretend she owned the place, and gave the clerk Mr. Harris's name. All the guest rooms had telephones, so ten minutes later, she was sitting in a leather armchair in the lounge, introducing herself to the urbane Mr. Harris. He was wearing a suit and tie but was in need of a shave.

"May I buy you a drink?" he asked.

"No, thank you."

"I hope you don't mind if I—"

"Of course, go ahead."

He waved over a waiter. "I'll have a whiskey and . . . no, wait, make that a cup of tea. Are you sure you won't have tea, Mrs. Bergholtz?"

"All right." She wondered if he were being tactful or simply trying to get on her good side.

"I had hoped to meet you in the Catskills," he said, "but Miss Kelley left so abruptly, I didn't get the chance. She spoke fondly of you."

"How kind." Abbie looked around the room. Most of the people in the chairs were men, some of them drinking and smoking cigars. A few were accompanied by women, well-dressed but not excessively rouged. She felt plain in comparison, but at least she was in respectable company. And the chair was deep and soft.

"How can I help you, Mrs. Bergholtz?"

"I just . . . I thought you might have had heard from Miss Kelley and learned something about . . . her circumstances. And young Miss Fulton's. Her mother is here with me."

"Louise wrote me the day before she expected to be arrested. She had been avoiding it for weeks, on account of Miss Fulton, but at last, she gave in, at Miss Fulton's insistence."

"Did she ask you to come to Washington?"

"No, I came on my own. I hired a lawyer to try to get both of them released, and he was able to visit them yesterday at the workhouse. But they don't want to be released. Louise wants . . . may I confide frankly in you? It might be best not to tell Miss Fulton's mother the details."

"Of course."

The waiter brought their tea. Abbie added milk, and Mr. Harris stirred two sugar cubes into his cup. "Louise wants the prison superintendent prosecuted for cruelty and abuse. She says he ordered the guards to rough the women up when they first arrived. But the suffs' lawyers brought a suit against him two months ago, and the prison committee blamed his behavior on the suffs, as if they drove him to it by being so contrary."

"Why, that's ridiculous!"

"I agree. The lawyer explained to Louise that the man can't be tried again for the same offense, and she broke down in tears, raving that he's an evil man. I'm worried about her."

"She's not one to cry easily," Abbie agreed. "Did he say anything about their health or how they looked?"

"He said Miss Fulton was pale but seemed otherwise robust. Louise was weak and exhausted. They're both on hunger strike."

"Did you hear about the new lawsuit?"

"Yes, the hearing is the day after tomorrow. I spoke to O'Brien, and apparently there's precedent for the case. A man was remanded back to the District jail from Occoquan a year ago. O'Brien's also going to ask for testimony on conditions at the workhouse, to justify the transfer, so he's called for the prisoners to be sent, although he's not sure if the judge will accept their testimony."

"Then we'll see them."

"It's in Alexandria, Virginia, eight miles from the city. I came down from New York in my motorcar. I would be pleased to drive you and Mrs. Fulton to the courthouse, if you like."

"All right. Thank you."

"My pleasure."

Abbie studied his brown eyes, finding in them sincerity and purpose, as well as the shadow of his concern for Louise. Perhaps he drank a little, but he was affluent enough to stay at the Metropolitan, and he had been courteous so far. Given the unusual situation and her own worries, she found the courage to say, "May I ask you a personal question?" He nodded. "Are you in love with Louise?"

He took a swallow of tea and replaced the cup with deliberation. "I'm trying not to be."

"What do you mean?"

"She's so restless, always moving around. I'm in real estate, dealing in homes for people to live in, to stay one place. I don't dare fall in love with her."

"But you came all the way here and hired a lawyer to help her."

"I know." He fiddled with the two gold rings on his right hand.

"Have you ever asked her to stay in one place?"

"No. I don't think she'd want that."

"Maybe she thinks *you* don't want it."

He looked at Abbie doubtfully, then shook his head. "She's too . . . free for that."

"Prison may have changed her. You never know."

The tiny courtroom was jammed with people. Miss Miller, the young woman Abbie had met at Cameron House, sat on one side of her, Mrs. Fulton on the other, and Mr. Harris just behind them. Disoriented by the breathtaking speed of the automobile ride, Mrs. Fulton was expressing less belligerence than she had of late, as they waited for the proceedings to begin.

The bailiff instructed everyone to rise for the entrance of Judge Edmund Waddill, a white-haired, bewhiskered man with a nose like a wad of dough. As they regained their seats, he convened the court, speaking with a mild Virginia drawl. Miss Miller pointed to a pot-bellied man with pasty skin and small, hard eyes. "That's Raymond Whittaker. He's the Occoquan superintendent."

"He looks frightening," Abbie said.

"He is. And next to him, that's Louis Zinkhan, warden of the District jail. He doesn't want more suffs in his jail. They're too much trouble."

The attorneys for the Woman's Party, Matthew O'Brien and Dudley Field Malone, reminded Abbie of a pair of racehorses, straining at the bit in their eagerness to be off. The two government lawyers, while keeping poker faces, nevertheless kept fidgeting in their seats.

When the prisoners filed in, a collective gasp passed through the room. The prison dresses hung on the women's bodies like billowing bags but could not cover the thinness of wrists and necks, the drawn, ghostly faces, or the exhaustion that showed in their plodding steps. One woman fainted and was carried into the next room. "They do go in for theatrics," said Mrs. Fulton.

"It looked real to me," Abbie replied.

"And their hair is all knotted and filthy. That adds to the show, I'm sure."

"They're not allowed combs in prison," Miss Miller said tartly.

"Really?" Mrs. Fulton looked appalled.

"Oh, there she is," Abbie said. Jessie was walking with slow dignity to her seat.

"Jessie," her mother called out in a stage whisper, and she looked over. Surprise registered, and she smiled faintly, then shifted her attention back to the judge. "She's forgotten me," said Mrs. Fulton.

"No, she hasn't, she's under a tremendous strain. I'm sure she can't even think straight. It looks like she's all right, though."

"Thank the Lord," Mrs. Fulton whispered, and Abbie saw a tear squeeze from the corner of her eye. As the prisoners continued to file in, Mrs. Fulton added, "Why, there are dozens of them!"

Mr. Harris leaned forward. "Do you see Louise?"

"No, I . . . wait, is that Louise?" Abbie indicated the last pair of women to enter. The taller one, who was leaning on the other's arm, sat down abruptly, her hollow cheeks and dull eyes barely suggesting Louise's features. She tilted sideways, crumpling down to lie on the bench. The other woman removed her own coat and folded it for a pillow, which she tenderly placed under Louise's head. Abbie's eyes filled.

Malone, the lawyer, was asking why Lucy Burns and Dora Lewis had not been brought to court. Whittaker said they were too ill to appear. Miss Miller muttered, "I hear Lucy's got marks on her wrists from being handcuffed to the bars. They don't want us to see."

"Handcuffed?" asked Mrs. Fulton. "Are you sure?"

The two women had been transferred a few days earlier from Occoquan to the District jail, so Malone asked the warden to take the stand. "Dr. Zinkhan, is it true that Miss Burns and Mrs. Lewis are being forcibly fed?"

"Yes," said Zinkhan. "They were in serious danger from their refusal to eat. We are keeping them alive."

"For the feeding, how many men does it take to hold Miss Burns?"

"Four."

"Then, your Honor, if it takes four men to hold Miss Burns to give her forcible feeding, don't you think she is strong enough to appear in court?"

"My goodness," Mrs. Fulton said. "Four men?"

"Miss Burns is ferocious," Miss Miller replied. Mrs. Fulton nodded approvingly.

The judge ordered Miss Burns and Mrs. Lewis to be brought to court the following day. Malone proceeded to question Zinkhan about his reasons for placing the rest of the prisoners at the workhouse when the sentencing papers specified they were to be incarcerated at the District jail. Zinkhan said the opportunity to perform useful work at Occoquan justified the transfer of able-bodied prisoners for what he called "humanitarian" reasons.

"Humanitarian?" muttered Mrs. Fulton. "How is enforced labor humanitarian?"

"The monotony at the jail is killing," explained Miss Miller. "They're not allowed to read or write, and they get almost no exercise."

"Were you actuated by humanitarian motives," demanded Malone, "when you sent Mrs. Nolan, a woman of seventy-three years, to the workhouse? Did you think that she could perform some service at Occoquan that it was necessary to get her out of the District jail and down there?"

Zinkhan cleared his throat and shifted his seatbones side to side. When the question was repeated, he answered thinly, "Yes."

"Mrs. Nolan, would you please stand up?" Everyone in the courtroom turned to look at a little woman with white hair and a white face. She rose to her feet, looking frail enough to be swept off by a brisk wind.

"That woman was in jail?" Mrs. Fulton leaned forward to seek confirmation from Miss Miller.

"Sentenced to six days."

"For carrying signs? These men are beasts!"

The judge ruled that the prisoners belonged in the District jail. The government lawyers declared their intention to appeal the decision. Therefore the women were paroled in the custody of counsel until a judge ruled on the appeal. However, the decision meant that testimony regarding their experience at Occoquan would not be heard, so the session was adjourned. Some of the women were smiling as they left the courtroom, Louise again leaning on a companion. She hadn't looked once in the direction of the spectators.

Malone came over to Miss Miller for a brief discussion, and it was decided the women would be taken to Cameron House. Mrs. Fulton nearly broke into a run on the way to Mr. Harris's automobile.

They arrived at Cameron House ahead of the vans transporting the suffs. Mrs. Fulton marched straight through the door and informed the woman at the desk, "They're coming, any minute now."

"Yes, I know. Miss Miller telephoned. Who are you?"

"I'm Jessie Fulton's mother. How are we welcoming these poor, maltreated women back? What are we going to feed them?"

"Don't worry, we planned for this contingency." She recruited Mrs. Fulton to arrange pots of tea and plates of soda crackers with pear slices for the breaking of the hunger strikers' fast. Abbie was set to lighting the fireplace. As the vans pulled up, the handful of staff remaining in the office brought out tricolor banners. Prisoners' relatives, who had followed the vans, crowded around to help the women down and into the house. The cheering was warm but muted, as the prisoners gathered in a reception room, the motley group holding each other up. They had hastily thrown on their own clothes, which were now baggy and loose, with collars askew and hems drooping.

In the chaos of greetings, Abbie couldn't find Louise or Jessie until a hand touched her sleeve. Jessie hugged her and asked, "What are you doing here?" Mrs. Fulton stepped forward. Jessie flung her arms around the bulky figure and sobbed.

"My dear girl, I am sorry for what those barbarians have put you through." She stroked her daughter's bony back.

"I couldn't do it," sobbed Jessie. "I tried not to eat, but when they put a warm baked apple with cream right in front of me and said I couldn't testify unless I ate, I believed them, and it . . . it smelled so good."

"My goodness, child, that's nothing to be ashamed of." Mrs. Fulton held her close. Other women reassured Jessie they didn't think badly of her. Abbie stepped away, looking for Louise. There she sat, propped up by Mr. Harris's encircling arm, a contented smile on her worn face, much to Abbie's relief.

When the welcome had been celebrated, the hunger strikers reintroduced their bodies to nourishment. They performed this ceremony with profound solemnity, savoring every crumb as if it changed their very identity by becoming part of them.

As they were finishing the food, Malone stood up on a chair against the wall and explained the dilemma they now faced. "Some of you, the repeat offenders, were sentenced to several months. If the government's appeal fails, as we expect it will, you won't have to go back to prison. But those of you from out of town, who earned only a short sentence, are more than halfway through your time. If by some chance the appeal succeeds, you'll have to return to Washington at some future date to finish your sentence. You might want to consider going back tomorrow to serve the last few days. It will be less severe at the District jail, with no Whittaker, and the warden should be on good behavior after today's hearing."

A middle-aged woman stood up. "I was sentenced to thirty days, of which I have served ten so far. I will go back to jail."

"It's for the suffrage cause," said another, "and for sisterhood. I'm going back too."

One by one, they all agreed, regardless of their sentence, except for three women who felt too ill to return. Jessie ignored her mother's imploring looks and cast her lot with the larger group. Louise hesitated before saying, "As long as we're nowhere near that sadist Whittaker, I can keep going."

"Are you sure?" asked Mr. Harris.

"Yes. We'll be in with Miss Paul, and it'll be an honor."

"With this trial and the publicity, the situation is changing," Malone said, "and I hear Congress is also shifting on suffrage. We'll keep up the pressure over the next few days and see if anything gives way. You may not be in for long."

Abbie had to admire their valor, but it was disappointing she and Mrs. Fulton wouldn't be leaving for a while yet.

The women sipped hot milk around the fire and talked about their imprisonment. An almost psychic intimacy seemed to prevail among the prisoners, women completing each other's sentences and communicating as much through glances as through words. Young Dorothy Day, sitting next to Jessie, admitted she had also eaten during the hunger strike, consuming a crust with desperate pleasure during the first week. Kathryn Lincoln confessed she had succumbed to the baked apple ruse before the court appearance.

Then Mr. O'Brien, the other lawyer, burst through the door. "They're all being released!" he shouted. "Even Miss Paul and Miss Burns. It's just what Miss Paul was trying to do. We've overtaxed the system, and they can't handle all the prisoners."

The uproar of joy made Abbie feel giddy. When the van arrived with the prisoners from the District jail, Alice Paul was the first to step down. Steel and fire glinted through her gaunt, gossamer form.

Once all the women were seated inside, their leader addressed them briefly. "I am not known as someone who gives appreciation easily. I have been taught to do it, just to keep peace, but my native understanding is that we are performing these efforts on behalf of all women, and I am not in a position to give thanks. Today, however, my heart is full of gratitude for all the strong women here, some who have picketed, some served sentences, some kept the work going while we were in prison. And I am sure the women of this great country, someday, will be grateful for what we have done together."

"I hope they're not going back out to picket," Mrs. Fulton murmured to Abbie. They were learning to be cautious in their hopefulness.

Perhaps Miss Paul overheard, for she announced, "We're calling off the picketing, at least for now. Mr. O'Brien informs me that the House is moving toward approving a suffrage committee for the first time, and that's a big step towards passing the amendment. It'll take work, but we're going to throw all our energy into getting the votes."

"Oh, thank God," Mrs. Fulton said. Her comment was drowned out by cheering.

Tables were brought in and set for a meal. Midway through the vegetable soup, Louise doubled over with a cry of pain. "What's wrong?" asked Mr. Harris.

"Cramps. I ate on the first day, and I think the meat in the soup was tainted. Excuse me."

Louise rose from the table, but halfway across the room, she sank to the floor. Mr. Harris raced over and lifted her onto a settee. Her head lolled back against the carved wooden arm. "She's unconscious," he said.

Miss Miller brought smelling salts, and Abbie passed them under Louise's nose. She revived with a start. "What happened?" she mumbled.

"We should take you to a hospital," Abbie said. "You are very ill."

"I don't want to go to a hospital," Louise moaned. "I'll be all alone. I don't want to take my friends from their work, and—"

"I'm taking you home," Mr. Harris declared.

"But I haven't a home. I haven't had a home of my own for years. I have nowhere to go." Louise began to cry.

"No, I meant I'm taking you to *my* home." Mr. Harris's fingertips touched her cheek, wiping away tears. "I want you to live with me, and . . . and if you like living there . . . then I want you to be my wife."

Abbie held her breath, watching Louise's face, which registered first bewilderment, then a fresh burst of tears. "Do you really mean it?" she asked him.

"Do you think I came all the way here on a whim?" She grabbed his hand, and he stroked her hair. "You don't have to answer me now. You're not ready to make decisions. But I can drive you to New York. The automobile has a wide back seat for you to lie on. Then you can stay at my house and get your strength back."

"I'd like that," Louise mumbled into his chest. Mrs. Fulton looked scandalized at the thought of an unmarried couple living together, but she had too much on her mind to comment. Abbie, who was getting used to the idea, felt happy thinking of Louise's happiness.

"I wonder if you would come with us, Mrs. Bergholtz," Mr. Harris said. "To look after Louise on the trip. With the rigors of driving, I could use assistance."

"I'd be glad to," Abbie replied.

Mrs. Fulton cleared her throat, throwing a glance at her daughter. Instead of the command Abbie expected to hear, the woman asked, in a timid voice, "Jessie, my dear, would you ride up on the train with me?"

Jessie smiled. She had tamed her mother at last. "I would like a rest. Yes, I will ride with you. But I might come back in a few weeks to lobby Congress for the amendment."

"Of course, dear. It's your decision."

Abbie had ridden in automobiles several times before, but not for eight hours at a stretch. After the first flurry of getting acquainted, while Louise slept, Abbie reached a first-name basis with Jonathan Harris. She talked about her children. He told her about the Harlem apartment he had just renovated for himself, with the hope that some day Louise would join him there. The day was sunny, and although the calendar had rolled well into autumn, weather at the southern latitude was still temperate. Louise was well-bundled in blankets in the back seat, with the side curtains pulled down over the back windows. Jonathan had provided shawls and lap robes to protect Abbie from the breeze through the front passenger window. He explained he couldn't yet afford the price of a California top, with enclosing glass along the sides.

She watched the broad, brown fields of Maryland whiz past, sometimes as fast as forty miles an hour. They made a brief stop in Baltimore, then continued north, Louise immediately falling back to sleep. At points, the asphalt petered out, and they bounced along dusty, rutted stretches until Abbie thought her teeth would crack from the jolts.

Approaching New York, they stopped in a small New Jersey town to buy sandwiches. Abbie tried to wake Louise, but she made no response. The skin on her sunken cheeks was dry and pallid. "Have you a watch with a minute hand?" Abbie asked Jonathan. He pulled out a gold watch from a vest pocket and detached it from its chain. She took Louise's pulse. "It's under sixty. And I can't wake her."

"That's bad."

"Maybe we should take her to a hospital."

"My experience of hospitals . . . I don't know that the care is so very good, unless it's a matter of a broken limb. Do you know a doctor who could attend her at home?"

"Yes, my neighbor Dr. Shirmer is excellent. But he can't go all the way to Harlem."

"I don't know how . . . that is, I've been away and have to take care of my business. She'll need someone familiar around when she wakes up. Do you think—"

"Of course, we can take her to my house."

"I'm sorry to suggest it," said Dr. Shirmer, folding his stethoscope. "I know it's ironic and troubling, after what she's been through. But we have to get nourishment into her. I believe her condition is due to a combination of emotional trauma and fasting."

Louise looked more like a marble statue than a living person as she lay under the pile of blankets. The doctor opened a black case and withdrew a red rubber tube with a funnel attached to one end. Abbie's throat contracted. "What if she wakes up during the feeding? She'll be even more traumatized."

"Better that it wakes her than that she sleeps forever."

"It'll go through her mouth, won't it?" Jonathan asked. "Not her nose?"

"The mouth, yes."

Jonathan covered his face with his hands, then let them fall. "It's awful, but it has to be done."

"Mrs. Bergholtz, kindly warm up some milk."

Walter sat with them in the parlor, holding Abbie's hand and giving her news of the children. Nell had agreed to bring them home the next day. Abbie was thinking of the first time she had been separated from Walter, when she had been trying to fatten up Ivy. Thank goodness her baby had not had to be forcibly fed. How had she come to this role once again, desperately trying to nourish the undernourished? Jonathan leaned his head back on the sofa and closed his eyes.

Dr. Shirmer came down the hall. "She didn't waken."

"How often must she be fed?" Jonathan asked.

"At least twice a day. I won't be able—"

"I'll hire a nurse. Perhaps you can recommend one."

"Certainly. We'll just hope that rest and nourishment will rejuvenate her system. I'll be back tomorrow."

The cries of "Mama" resounded sweetly as Abbie gathered her three little chicks in her arms. Ivy showed off the red velveteen bow Aunt Nell had bought for her hair. Sam and Ben each clutched a handful of toy soldiers from their cousin Charlie, who was just outgrowing his army. None of them seemed any the worse for having been away from their mother for a week, although they clung to her for the next day or so, even as she clung to them.

The children distracted her from worry about Louise. She also had house-cleaning to catch up on and a club meeting to attend. Each time Jessie and her mother stopped in, Abbie was surprised at how stimulated she felt by the memories of Washington they brought along. Despite the tension of the trip, she had been enlivened by the atmosphere of drama and the association with women of grit and integrity. Still, she was relieved to return to the security of her family. If only Louise wasn't lying there in the back room, in a state between life and death, her fate unknowable.

Jonathan visited every evening to sit at Louise's side and consult with the nurse. He looked increasingly haggard. When he conversed with Abbie, he spoke more about his business than about Louise. Abbie had the impression he was withdrawing his emotions to cope with the possibility of his lover's death. Perhaps Abbie was doing the same.

A week went by, and Louise still had not stirred. One afternoon, the nurse called out, and Abbie rushed to the room, hoping for good news. The nurse was standing with the rubber tube in her hand, and Louise's body was convulsing, abdomen arching, arms and legs flopping. The seizure stopped abruptly, and Louise lay still, bedclothes cast to the floor. The nurse tried to rouse her, with no success. Abbie sent for Dr. Shirmer.

"I can give her an anti-seizure medication," he said. "But this development is quite serious. Convulsions can lead to brain damage."

That night, as Abbie lay crying on the bed, Walter made a radical suggestion. "You know that my brother has become a Christian Scientist. He must know spiritual healers."

Surprised, she sat up and reached for a hankie. "I know the Christian Scientists don't use doctors. But do you think their method really works?"

"When you were in Albany, Joe and I had a long talk about it. And then the woman minding the children cut her finger rather badly while she was chopping vegetables. She and Joe prayed together, and the finger stopped bleeding immediately. Two hours later, you could hardly see it had been cut."

"Is she a Christian Scientist too?"

"Oh, yes."

"But can he heal a non-believer?"

"Certainly at the start, there weren't any believers except Mrs. Eddy, the founder. She went about healing all kinds of people. But nowadays, I'm not sure. I'll write to him and ask."

"I suppose it couldn't hurt to try." She'd learned to accept so many modern ideas that had seemed unappealing or impractical at first. Perhaps she should give this one a chance.

Two days later, a stout woman with round, red cheeks appeared at the door and introduced herself as Emma Earnshaw, a Christian Science practitioner. Abbie brought her to Louise's room, explaining, "We don't really know what's wrong with her. She's been unconscious for ten days. Then she had convulsions, and of course it all started when—"

"It doesn't matter," said Mrs. Earnshaw, holding up her hand. "Mortal mind's tales are of no account to divine spirit." Without even removing her coat, she took a chair at the bedside and closed her eyes.

Abbie hovered in the doorway, waiting for the woman to speak prayers or place her hands on Louise's motionless form. Five minutes went by in silence. Abbie grew restless. "Do you need any—"

"No, thank you."

"Should I—"

"Whatever you like, stay or go. Just be quiet."

Abbie sat on a chair near the door. Ten more minutes passed. She marveled at the woman's profound stillness. It finally mastered her own disquiet, and a sense of peace crept over her for the first time in weeks. She thought of how she had initially disliked Louise but had come to love her so deeply. That love had never died away, although they had been at odds many times. Through the years, Louise had introduced her to new ideas and forced her to grow. Gratitude swelled, and Abbie had an urge to go and embrace her friend, but she sat still, letting the practitioner do her work, whatever it might be. An odd thought came to her, that all was well, no matter what happened.

"Thank you." The words were faint and came, not from Mrs. Earnshaw, but from the bed. Louise's eyes fluttered open.

Abbie rushed to the bed and knelt. "You're awake."

"My dear Abbie." A beatific smile lit the pale face.

Mrs. Earnshaw stood up. "She is well. There should be no relapse, but if you have any concerns, I can visit again. I will mail you my invoice at the end of the month." She took a card from her purse and handed it to Abbie, who stood up.

"But how did you do it?"

"I didn't. God did it. I simply argued the truth of being, which is entirely good. The lie of illness yields before divine love. But you must attend to your friend. I can let myself out." And she disappeared, leaving behind a faint odor of violet cologne.

"Who was that?" Louise asked, and Abbie was surprised by the strength of her voice.

"A healer my brother-in-law sent. We've all been so worried about you."

"I'm terribly hungry."

"That's wonderful! I'll go make you something."

"Wait!" Louise struggled up against the pillows. "This is your house. Why am I here?"

Abbie sat down on the bed. "You've been very sick. Jonathan felt I could take better care of you than he could, and my doctor is nearby. You were unconscious for over a week." She chose not to mention the feeding tube just yet.

"A week? And you've been . . .Oh, Abbie . . ."

"Hush, you need to get your strength back. I'll go heat up some milk for you."

Louise grabbed her hand. "I don't deserve you. After all I've done, criticizing you, bringing Jessie to Washington, making you go down there. And yet you've taken me in and looked after me."

"Don't be silly. I would do it for anyone I love." But in truth, she savored Louise's words, both on her way to the kitchen and at many moments thereafter.

Chapter 27

TO VOTE

"A reception? For you, me, and Jessie? From a club that's not allowed to talk about suffrage?" Louise shook her head. "That's bizarre."

"Mrs. Fulton's conversion had a big effect," Abbie said. "Frankly, even though Mrs. Hoag proposed it at the meeting, I suspect the reception was Mrs. Fulton's idea, to make up for oppressing Jessie all these years."

"Do you think that woman will ever let you call her by her first name?"

Abbie laughed. "I can't imagine calling her Lola. It just wouldn't fit." She looked around the kitchen at the shiny black gas range and the snow-white porcelain sink. A wood cabinet with twelve doors faced a capacious icebox, enviably up-to-date. "Jonathan did a good job setting up this kitchen, didn't he?"

"Yes. If only I liked to cook. Thank God he can afford to hire someone."

"That reminds me. I brought you some apple tarts."

"Thanks. Jonathan's cook is fine, but I miss your food." After Louise had regained consciousness, she'd stayed with Abbie for two more weeks, filling out on her cooking, before moving to Harlem. She was still underweight but had pink cheeks and the glow of a woman in love. "How do you feel about this reception?" she asked.

"A bit silly. You and Jessie are the real heroines. I just gave you a place to lie still and recover."

"We're not heroines. We just did what was needed. And you went to Washington with Mrs. Fulton. That was pretty heroic."

"It wasn't easy," Abbie admitted.

"And Jessie? Is she excited about the reception?"

"She's looking forward to it. After all these years in her mother's shadow, she's finally getting recognition."

"Do we have to make speeches?"

"I expect so. Short ones."

"All right. I like making speeches. And Abbie . . ." Louise touched her friend's hand. "Jonathan told me the advice you gave him in Washington. Without it, I wouldn't be here in his house. I have to thank you again."

Abbie gave the still bony hand a squeeze. "I couldn't help it. I'm just so old-fashioned."

The date chosen for the reception, January 11, turned out to be fortuitous. Two days earlier, President Wilson had made a statement to the press, definitively endorsing a suffrage amendment for the first time. The next day, the House of Representatives voted in favor of holding a referendum. The Senate vote was still to come, and the amendment would ultimately need approval by two-thirds of the state legislatures, but this giant step toward full suffrage was galvanizing the movement.

Louise was euphoric, and Abbie's gladness was proof of how thoroughly she had come to believe in the right of women to vote. She wondered how the rest of the club members felt, especially given Mrs. Fulton's change of heart.

In the week leading up to the reception, Abbie sewed every afternoon on a moss-green organdy dress, mending the waist, widening the collar, and adding lace to the cuffs. When she walked into the reception room in her updated frock, she felt appropriately elegant. She didn't even mind that Louise showed her up by appearing in a wine-colored suit with loose trousers. Although the trousers raised eyebrows, it was generally admitted that the tailoring gave her a sophisticated air. Jessie wore a simple dress of indigo broadcloth that made her blue eyes electric.

The club members applauded the three of them, standing together at the front of the room, which was decorated in suffrage yellow. A sense of vertigo overcame Abbie as she recalled the gathering at Cameron House, less than two months ago, when she had celebrated with a group of women who were fresh out of prison and weak from fasting. That meeting had changed her.

After Mrs. Hoag's words of praise, Louise thanked the club for introducing her to Abbie and Jessie and giving her practice at presenting papers, which had helped prepare her for suffrage work. She understood not all the clubwomen were suffragists, but she still felt they played an important role in teaching women to stand up for their rights and make society better. "Not everyone can be an Alice Paul, which I'm sure is good. Each person makes a contribution."

Abbie started her speech by acknowledging her shift from skepticism about suffrage to a gradual embrace of its usefulness. "Now that I have been witness to the dedication of Miss Kelley, Miss Fulton, and their compatriots in Washington, I am convinced that we can and will win the vote for all American women. I have joined the National Woman's Party and will be organizing letter-writing campaigns from residents of our state to our representatives in Congress, urging support of a national amendment." Murmurs of surprise rippled across her audience. "Now that we New Yorkers can vote, I'd like to know where our clubwomen stand on national suffrage."

The awkward silence that would have reigned a few months ago did not manifest. Mrs. Hoag jumped right in. "When the national amendment passes, I'll be proud some of our club members helped make it happen."

"I'm glad to hear you say that," said Louise. "Carrie Catt and the National women are trying to take the credit for getting the House bill passed, as if picketing did nothing to keep the issue in people's thought."

"I think it passed because of the war," said Mrs. Flint. "As the president said, women have taken over the jobs of the men who've gone to fight, and we're proving we can do the work just as well as the men did."

"Oh, he has to say that," said Jessie. "He can't admit protesting has any effect because he doesn't want to encourage it. But I think he was worried about looking like a villain for tormenting women just because he was afraid of us."

"It's all about the votes," Mrs. Lowitz declared. "New York women got the vote, and that makes enough women to vote the Democrats out of office if they don't pass the amendment. But I do think the disgraceful treatment of the pickets has turned people against do-nothing politicians."

Abbie noticed no one had come right out in favor of suffrage, but those who had spoken seemed both open and knowledgeable. Their willingness to discuss the subject at all was encouraging.

"Enough of this suffrage talk," said Mrs. Varian. "I have a question for Miss Kelley. What's that on your finger?"

Louise extended her left hand to show off a ring with a diamond the size of a pea, "As a matter of fact, I am engaged to Jonathan Harris. But I'm going back to Washington next week. We don't have enough votes yet in the Senate to pass the amendment. It's going to be quite a battle."

"What about college?" asked Jessie.

"Mr. Harris has enough money to hire a housekeeper and send me back to Barnard. He's completely in favor of it because it'll make me stay in one place, once we're married."

"And when is the wedding?" inquired Mrs. Hoag.

"Not until we all have the vote."

"That's one way to get a man to work for suffrage."

"Exactly."

Jessie held up a newspaper. "Now it's my turn. I have two pieces of news. Mrs. Sanger's case, about her clinic, was appealed, and the court just gave its verdict. The judge said she was guilty, since she's not a doctor, but he ruled that birth control itself is legal. Birth control advice is allowed if it's needed to prevent disease, which is defined as . . ." She read from the newspaper, ". . . 'an alteration in the state of the body . . . causing or threatening pain or sickness.'"

"I wouldn't call childbirth a disease, but it's certainly a cause of pain," said Mrs. Lowitz. "Don't we know that all too well?"

"The judgment doesn't limit the application to any specific disease, and so it means birth control clinics are permitted."

"What a blessing!" said Mrs. Everett, and others chimed in.

Abbie was surprised by the women's enthusiasm. They had been ambivalent about her paper on birth control, but obviously their true feelings ran deep.

"And my other news," said Jessie, "is that I've made a decision. I'm going to train as a nurse."

"Oh, how wonderful!" the women chorused. Even Mrs. Fulton's smile was radiant.

"I want to start a birth control clinic, so women can learn how to have smaller families, if they want. I'm hoping the club will help me raise money for the training, and when the time comes, help me set up a clinic."

Yeses and nods went all around the room. Abbie, pleased for Jessie, also thought of the pessary she would get at last.

"But only doctors can give birth control advice," Louise said. "That's what the judge decided."

Jessie gave her a defiant look. "I can hire a doctor, and he'll need a nurse. I can still run the clinic."

Abbie glared at Louise. Why wasn't she supporting this fledgling idea? It needed encouragement and tending.

Louise caught Abbie's eye and pursed her lips, then turned back to take Jessie's hand. "You can go to medical school, you know. You can become a doctor."

The light dawning on Jessie's face was pure pleasure to behold.

Finally, Facts

Following President Wilson's first endorsement of woman suffrage and the House passage of the amendment, the Senate voted it down. Alice Paul and the National Woman's Party eventually returned to picketing and hunger striking because they felt Wilson was not sufficiently speaking out in support of the measure. On June 4, 1919, Congress finally passed the 19th Amendment, which would grant women nationwide the right to vote. Then two-thirds of the state legislatures had to ratify the amendment before it could go into effect. Miss Paul rallied her troops to go to the states and campaign for approval.

On August 18, 1920, the Tennessee legislature was poised to become the last of the thirty-six states required for ratification. The House passed the amendment by one vote when twenty-four-year-old legislator Harry Burn, who was ambivalent about suffrage, followed his mother's advice and cast the final vote in favor. At last, women had the right to join the other half of the U.S. population in electing government representatives.

Alice Paul went straight back to work, earning three law degrees and crafting a national Equal Rights Amendment as a means of codifying further rights for women. As of 2021, that amendment still has not become part of the U.S. Constitution. However, women continue to fight and win battles for expansion of their rights. Margaret Sanger's efforts led to the establishment of Planned Parenthood, although her later interest in eugenics has made her a controversial figure to the modern world. Dorothy Day, the young hunger-striker, went on to found the Catholic Worker, a prominent social service organization.

Techniques of nonviolent civil disobedience, as developed by Alice Paul and other suffragettes, have been used in such crusades as the civil rights movement.

Author's Note

I made a concerted effort to present every historical event and every historical personage with as much accuracy as I could glean from my research, determining not only the year but the actual date of most events. The interactions of my fictional characters with real people such as Alice Paul and Harriot Stanton Blatch are, I believe, consonant with the qualities contemporary writers have reported of those illustrious women. The only error I have knowingly committed, for dramatic effect, is the placing of Louise's "silent speech" prior to the 1912 parade. The stunt was actually pioneered the following year. I also compressed the events surrounding both the sentencing and the release of the pickets arrested in November 1917, but the essence of those events remains intact.

Abbie and Walter are loosely based on my great-grandparents, Mary and August Wingebach, although their timeframe has been shifted. Their daughter, my grandmother, was born in 1904, not 1912, and her twin brothers came along in 1906, not 1914. However, many details of their lives have made it into the novel, thanks to letters Mary preserved. I do not have letters from the period after the twins were born, and most of the events of Abbie's life in that section of the book are pure fabrication, including her third pregnancy, her encounter with Margaret Sanger, and her trip to Washington. However, Mary eventually became president of the Athenaeum Club and the Bronx Borough representative to the General Federation of Women's Clubs of New York City, so she did move into deeper community involvement. I wish I had copies of papers she wrote for the club. (She mentions writing a paper on Napoleon III.) I kept the first name of Mary's sister-in-law, Nell, a dynamic woman who joined both the Winter Club and the Froebel Club. Her husband, Joseph, was an educator and served as a reader in a Christian Scientist church.

Louise, Damaris, and Jonathan are invented characters. So are the Fultons, although I was inspired by two photographs of the Athenaeum members, which include what appear to be a formidable mother and clinging, twentyish daughter. I kept the actual names of most of the clubwomen, despite knowing little about them, wishing to acknowledge their ventures into early 20th century feminism.

The photo on the book cover shows the Athenaeum Club in 1914. A family member marked Mary with an "X" so future generations could identify her.

Acknowledgements

Many thanks to:

Crossing the Stream Writers Circle for first reading and feedback by Ann McGillicuddy, Carol Bean, Valerie Linet, Linda Pattie, and especially Lori Handelman, who whipped the entire manuscript into shape;

Gerry Griffin, Deb Brindis, Ivonne Lamazares, and Michelle Spark for reading and encouragement;

Bob Wyatt for brilliant advice on title and pitching;

Susan Lipkins for her intimate knowledge of string instruments;

Sparrow and Sylvia for suggestions and support.

CPSIA information can be obtained
at www.ICGtesting.com
Printed in the USA
BVHW082358210721
611988BV00004B/13